SECOND EDITION

Research Handbook for

HOME ECONOMICS EDUCATION

by

Olive A. Hall

Counselor
El Camino College
Torrance, California

Burgess Publishing Company

426 South Sixth Street • Minneapolis, Minn. 55415

PREFACE TO THE SECOND EDITION

Although the brief span of five years has brought profound changes in the nature and volume of research in the United States, we are still seeking answers to these fundamental questions in home economics education: what to teach, how much to teach, to whom should it be taught, when to teach, and how to teach most effectively. There is growing emphasis on designing research that is grounded in the findings of a basic science of human behavior. Experimental research is being directed toward valid inferences about causal relationships between teaching and desired outcomes of instructions. The process of teaching is viewed as an act of communication which is amenable to improvement and which can be studied scientifically.

Emphasis in this edition continues to be on the planning that goes into research design and analysis of research evidence. Toward this end, I have included in Appendix A three models to clarify the meaning of a theory, hypothesis, and assumption. These models are not intended to be followed literally, but they are merely illustrative of how some research theory might be applied to problems of historical, survey, and experimental design.

Several sections of the book have been expanded in this edition. The importance of theory is recognized by devoting a separate section to it in the chapter on selecting a research problem. More emphasis is given to methods of electronic data processing, which are making knowledge more readily available and challenging researchers to work on problems of a more complex nature than would have been tackled a few years ago. Since the kind of judgment a person wishes to make when using a particular instrument might require any of four types of validity, I have discussed differences between content, predictive, concurrent, and construct validity. Two scaling techniques, which are being used in social science research, should be considered in home economics education research: Q Sort and Semantic Differential. Furthermore, this revision contains information on nonparametric statistics that can be used whether or not the population variance is normally distributed.

Your response to the first edition has been most gratifying. It is my sincere hope that this second edition will clarify many aspects of research design and stimulate you to make substantial progress toward expanding our knowledge and improving the effectiveness of home economics education.

March, 1967   Olive A. Hall

PREFACE

Research in all areas of home economics and in all phases of education has implications for home economics teachers. Yet, too often young teachers struggle along trying to find answers to the questions raised by their students, without knowing efficient and accurate methods for obtaining the necessary information. More mature teachers, who should be contributing to an ever-expanding body of facts on which to improve home economics teaching, often think of research as something far beyond their interests and abilities.

The view of this book is that home economics teachers can enrich their teaching by being intelligent consumers and producers of research. Four beliefs have guided me in writing the book: (1) home economics teachers who understand the meaning and values of research will become interested in improving their teaching in directions that research indicates will be fruitful; (2) persons who have direct contact with students are in a position to contribute new ideas or to test a variety of procedures, but if they are to make an effective contribution, they need to understand research design and interpretation; (3) basic to an understanding of the research approach is the ability to locate materials which are related to the problem under consideration and which will be helpful in its solution; and (4) the ability to read and interpret research reports gives a teacher insight into sound facts and motivational techniques from which she may draw in planning timely, challenging courses.

This book does not offer a summary of research findings with specific applications for home economics education. Neither does it provide answers to the many problems confronting home economics teachers. I believe the major purpose of a research handbook is not to give students the answers to a great variety of questions but rather to help them ask important questions and to find satisfactory ways of solving vital problems. It is my hope that this book will contribute to an understanding of research methods. It gives consideration to various approaches that may be helpful in solving problems, and it offers help in arriving at conclusions that are justifiable within the limitations of a study. I have drawn upon a wealth of illustrations from home economics and other fields of study, hoping they will help home economics teachers to find ways of solving certain educational problems. The presentation of research findings and their applications is only of incidental value. Within the framework of the research point of view that is developed throughout this book, the reader is guided in recognizing and solving his own problems as well as evaluating the work of others. Further assistance can be obtained from the extensive references that are included in each section of the book.

A research approach to home economics education should be of interest and value to several groups of home economists. First, advanced undergraduate students are learning to be good consumers of research as they gain ability to locate and interpret materials related to home economics education. Undergraduate or graduate students who are taking a proseminar or seminar in which they are required to write a term paper will find that this book offers them both guidance and reference materials. I hope that graduate students will gain an interest in experimenting with new ideas and accept the challenge to become producers of high-quality research. Teachers who are currently in service, and those who are planning to return to teaching after a period of absence from active service, will find that a research approach can vitalize their teaching and stimulate them and their students to higher goals and more rewarding achievement. Administrators and supervisors who are called upon to provide research evidence on the contributions of home economics education should find the footnotes and selected references of particular value, and they may benefit also from trying some of the techniques that are discussed.

No field of human endeavor offers greater satisfaction than that of helping young people to develop into good citizens and family members. No greater challenge is afforded the home economics teacher than that of learning how to work more effectively with her students and community. Research must play an important part in this process if home economics is to solve its educational problems and promote good teaching at all levels.

This handbook has developed from several years of work in organizing material with which to assist graduate students in their introduction to home economics education research. I am deeply grateful to many of my former students for giving me a chance to try these approaches and for their frank criticisms of the manuscript. Also, I want to acknowledge and thank the many persons in home economics and in other branches of education who granted me permission to refer to and quote from their writings. Specific references to these works are given in the footnotes throughout this handbook. Further, I wish to express my sincere appreciation to Virginia Richard for her contributions in editing the manuscript and to William Brock for preparing the graphic illustrations.

March 1962   Olive A. Hall

TABLE OF CONTENTS

LIST OF TABLES

LIST OF FIGURES

Chapter 1

ORIENTATION TO RESEARCH

*Prejudice is a great time saver; it enables one
to form opinions without bothering to get facts.*
-- Teacher Tipper

Creative thought is of great significance in today's society. Many advances which
we accept as commonplace without thinking of their origin, arose from the ability of an
individual to perceive a problem and think of an original solution to it. Homes and families
today enjoy many physical conveniences and health safeguards that are practical applications of someone's search for a better way of living. In our world of today individuals
and groups have access to a great body of scientific facts on which to base their decisions,
but one of its greatest needs is to develop individuals with the imagination and ability to
think creatively.

IMPORTANCE OF HOME ECONOMICS RESEARCH

A fundamental characteristic of a democratic society is the freedom accorded to each
individual. This freedom is based upon a belief in the ability of a majority of the people to
think independently and arrive at their own conclusions. Inherent in the individual's right
to reach his own conclusions is the privilege of exploring various ways of solving his problems. Freedom to experiment underlies progress in all professions, including home economics education.

The extent to which new knowledge is freely developed in a nation is a determining
factor in the prosperity and security it enjoys. The important role of the home economist
in the development and interpretation of research was pointed out by Elvehjem:

> *The home economist stands between the producer and the consumer, between
> educational institutions and industrial organizations, between the individual and
> social groups. For example, great advances have been made in building materials,
> in home furnishing, in textiles, in clothing, and so on, as a result of basic research
> carried out in academic institutions and by industry; but the introduction and use of
> these in the home has been left to the home economist .... The home economist
> reaches into some of the basic concepts of education, such as the child development
> programs and the so-called preschool laboratories. Because home economists have
> bridged these different disciplines, new techniques have been developed and new
> principles have been established and verified.*[1]

Home economics teachers are in a key position to interpret research findings pertaining to scientific developments as they relate to nutrition and textiles. They also interpret research in the social sciences where family relationships and child development
are concerned or economic changes affecting standards of living. Moreover, teachers are
responsible for helping others find answers to their problems, for they know where to obtain sound information on any phase of home economics. And finally, home economics

---

[1]C. A. Elvehjem, "From the Minds of Men to the Lives of People." <u>Journal of Home Economics</u> 49: 506; September, 1957.

teachers have the opportunity to share in expanding knowledge on the effectiveness of various methods of teaching, desirable curriculum content, and other educational problems.

SELECTED REFERENCES

Adams, Georgian. "Fifty Years of Home Economics Research." *Journal of Home Economics* 51: 12-18; January, 1959.
Elvehjem, C. A. "From the Minds of Men to the Lives of People." *Journal of Home Economics* 49: 503-507; September, 1957.
Lehman, Ruth T. "The Next Fifty Years in Home Economics Education Research." *Journal of Home Economics* 52: 23-26; January, 1960.

MEANING OF RESEARCH

Every day people face situations in which they must chose between several ways of accomplishing a specific task. Many of these decisions are relatively minor and become rather automatic after a period of time. Others, such as deciding what to prepare for dinner, can be resolved quite logically and with little effort. There are some, however, which demand a more thorough analysis of the problem situation and a careful plan to insure the solution of more important aspects of the problem.

Webster's dictionary gives the following entry for "research".: [2]

2 a : studious inquiry or examination; *esp* : critical and exhaustive investigation or experimentation having for its aim the discovery of new facts and their correct interpretation, the revision of accepted conclusions, theories, or laws in the light of newly discovered facts, or the practical applications of such new or revised conclusions, theories, or laws ⟨gave his time to ∼⟩ **b** (1) **:** a particular investigation of such a character **:** a piece of research (2) **:** a presentation (as an article or book) incorporating the findings of a particular research **3 :** capacity for or inclination to research ⟨a scholar of great ∼⟩ **syn** see INQUIRY
²**research** \"\ *vb* [MF *recercher* to research, seek out, fr. OF, fr. *re-* + *cercher* to search — more at SEARCH] *vt* **:** to search or investigate exhaustively **:** make researches into ∼ *vi* **:** to make researches or investigations
re-search \(')rē¦sərch, -sȯch,-sȯich\ *vt* [*re-* + *search*] **:** to search again or anew ⟨decided to *re-search* the chest for the lost letters⟩

Research is more than a search, even a diligent search. Research is a means of seeking out answers, but the investigation must be purposeful, systematic, adapted to scientific ways of problem solving, and carried out with a genuine desire to know the truth rather than to prove a point.

Although a person is inclined to be disappointed if his research results appear to be unsuccessful, results are by no means an adequate measure of the value of research. If a study has been made systematically and thoroughly, and with sound methods, a contribution has been made toward expanding knowledge even though findings from the study are inconclusive. Studies that are apparently unsuccessful sometimes form the basis for further investigations on a larger scale or with more highly refined techniques. As Rummel stated, *"Research is a careful inquiry or examination to discover new information or relationships and to expand and to verify existing knowledge."* [3]

[2] By permission. From Webster's Third New International Dictionary, copyright 1961 by G. & G. Merriam Co., publishers of the Merriam-Webster Dictionaries.

[3] J. Francis Rummel, An Introduction to Research Procedures in Education. Second edition. New York: Harper & Row Publishers, Inc, 1964. Page 2.

Kettering, who viewed research from the standpoint of a large business firm, pointed out that research is a way of living and has practical application in one's personal life as well as in his professional field:

> *Research is a high-hat word that scares a lot of people. It needn't. It is rather simple. Essentially, it is nothing but a state of mind--a friendly, welcoming attitude toward change. Going out to look for change, instead of waiting for it to come. Research, for practical men, is an effort to do things better and not to be caught asleep at the switch. The research state of mind can apply to anything. Personal affairs or any kind of business, big or little. It is the problem-solving mind as contrasted with the let-well-enough-alone mind. It is the composer mind, instead of the fiddler mind; it is the "tomorrow" mind, instead of the "yesterday" mind.*[4]

SELECTED REFERENCES

Barnes, John B. *Educational Research for Classroom Teachers*. New York: G. P. Putnam's Sons, 1960. Pages 15-22.
Best, John W. *Research in Education*. Englewood Cliffs, New Jersey: Prentice-Hall, Inc., 1959. Pages 6-8.
Rummel, J. Francis. *An Introduction to Research Procedures in Education*. Second edition. New York: Harper & Row Publishers, Inc., 1964. Pages 1-5.
Whitney, Frederick L. *The Elements of Research*. Third edition. Englewood Cliffs, New Jersey: Prentice-Hall, Inc., 1950. Pages 19-29.

THE RESEARCH WORKER

Home economics education is a field of opportunity for qualified, interested persons to engage in research. Although many home economists have no desire to become research specialists, we can all contribute more effectively to our profession as we grow in our understanding of scientific procedures and in our ability to interpret research findings. Consumers of research can increase their ability to appreciate and evaluate research information as they cultivate the abilities that characterize research workers.

Foremost among these abilities are intellectual honesty and open-mindedness. A research worker, or a person who is interested in obtaining sound facts, must view his problem objectively and be willing to discover the truth. Preconceived notions and personal bias have no place in the thinking of a research investigator whose aim is to <u>know</u> rather than to <u>prove</u>. Both the producer and consumer of research must guard constantly against making premature assumptions. Sound decisions are based upon familiarity with <u>all</u> available evidence. Adverse evidence cannot be ignored; it should be explained or refuted.

Another aid in conducting and interpreting research is a compelling drive to satisfy one's curiosity, to find pleasure in self-expression, or to make a discovery of value to others. Courage, faith, persistence, humility, and self-direction are among the desirable traits that develop a strong motivation or interest in research. Emotional factors, as well as the practical and scientific requirements of research, are important to the success of a research study.

---

[4]C. F. Kettering, "More Music Please, Composers!" <u>Saturday Evening Post</u> 211: 32; 1938.

Since research demands careful and thorough study, a person must possess certain qualities of scholarship and accuracy. Exactness in observation, system in recording evidence, and discrimination in handling data contribute to high quality research information. An individual must develop the ability to discipline his imagination and criticize his own approach. As Faraday said:

> *The world little knows how many of the thoughts and theories which have passed through the mind of a scientific investigator have been crushed in silence and secrecy by his own severe criticism and adverse examination; that in the most successful instances not a tenth of the suggestions, the hopes, the wishes, the preliminary conclusions have been realized.*[5]

As home economics educators become familiar with research procedures and results, they develop insight and understanding which enable them to foresee the results of projected ideas and actions. A research approach helps home economics teachers to seek responsible leadership, and it encourages those who are capable to take part in this leadership.

SELECTED REFERENCES

Good, Carter V. *Essentials of Educational Research.* New York: Appleton-Century-Crofts, Inc., 1966. Pages 22-30.

Hillway, Tyrus. *Introduction to Research.* Second edition. Boston: Houghton Mifflin Co., 1964. Pages 29-31.

---

[5]Karl Pearson, The Grammar of Science. Part I: Physical. London: Adam and Charles Black, 1911. Page 32.

Chapter 2
DEFINITION OF A RESEARCH PROBLEM

Going 'round a problem
Doesn't help a bit --
That is, if it's our object
To reach the roots of it.
-- Alec the Great

The selection of a research problem is of vital importance, although it is but a small part of the work that should precede the gathering of data. The kinds of data you gather depend upon the manner in which your problem is defined. The formulation of a problem not only helps to direct your thinking, but it may even restrict your results, since you are most likely to see those things for which you are looking. Consequently, the selection of a research problem might be considered incomplete unless and until the problem has been delimited to manageable size and outlined clearly to show the steps that must be taken to fulfill the purposes of the study.

SELECTION OF A PROBLEM

Meyer said that describing the purpose of your research *"is like taking a trip. You have reasons for going, a point of departure, a means of conveyance, a route to follow, interim stops along the way, and a final destination."*[1]

When you are selecting a problem area and clarifying a problem within that area, you should consider three basic questions:

1. Is the problem important?

    Will the problem that you have selected advance the knowledge of home economics education appreciably? Will the findings be of practical value to teachers, students, parents, or administrators? Is it a new topic, or does it represent an original, timely approach in an area that has been studied previously? Is it a conscious repetition of previous studies to verify their accuracy or to extend our generalizations? Is the field sufficiently limited to permit thorough treatment of the problem? Will the study require your best thinking and intellectual performance? Is the project likely to stimulate the development of other investigations?

2. Is the investigator qualified?

    Are you, as the investigator, sincerely interested in the general field and in the specific problem? Do you have adequate background in the field you have chosen, as well as in related fields, and in research methods which are appropriate for your problem? Do you possess the necessary skills to carry out

---

[1]Burton Meyer and Loretta E. Heidgerken, Introduction to Research in Nursing. Philadelphia: J. B. Lippincott Co., 1962. Page 81.

the study, or can you equip yourself with the skills which you lack? Are you free from strong biases?

3.   Is the study feasible?

Are the time, energy, and money requirements compatible with your resources? Will the cost of the study be justified on the basis of its returns? Can the study be completed within a reasonable length of time and yet provide sufficient understanding of long range value? Can you obtain adequate and accurate data? Are the available techniques adequately refined and sufficiently reliable? Are the necessary library facilities, calculating equipment, data-processing machines, or other equipment available? What possible hazards or handicaps must be overcome before the research plan can be carried out? Can you obtain the necessary administrative support and cooperation to conduct the study?

As a beginner in research, you will probably need help in locating a suitable problem area. However, you should realize that the actual selection of a problem begins long before you are aware that it might be the basis for a suitable research study. If you look upon your job as a creative, challenging experience, you will be conscious of many problems or obstacles which provide opportunity for research. If you learn to listen carefully and read critically, you will become aware of areas in which there are many problems awaiting solution. If you enjoy trying different ways of doing a task, you will be opening the way for experimentation with, and evaluation of, various approaches.

Professional literature can help you select a problem and gain assurance that you have chosen a worthwhile area for study. Wide reading will enable you to keep up-to-date on completed research studies, the analysis of trends as viewed by experts in various fields, statements of needed research, and titles of research which is currently underway.

Although the list is by no means complete, the following summary shows the breadth of topics on which research can help improve the teaching of home economics:

GUIDANCE--to discover the interest and abilities of students who take home economics, to determine the problems and needs of home economics students, to learn reasons why other students do not take home economics, to acquaint students with vocational opportunities related to home economics, and to find out how home economics helps students who have taken it.

ADMINISTRATION--to determine criteria for judging the adequacy of space and equipment for teaching home economics, to resolve problems of scheduling classes and determining teacher load and other problems concerned with the organization of the home economics program.

TEACHER EDUCATION--to identify the competencies needed by home economics teachers, to develop programs for preparing students to teach, to provide teachers with in-service training, and to describe the characteristics of superior and ineffective teachers.

EVALUATION--to measure the effectiveness of home economics in developing knowledge, attitudes, and skills that are fundamental for home and family living.

METHODS AND MATERIALS--to discover what teaching materials are available, how they are being used, what further aids teachers would like to have, and to compare the effectiveness of various procedures that are being used in teaching home economics.

CURRICULUM AND COURSE CONTENT--to determine what should be taught in home economics classes and to establish a desirable sequence for including the experiences.[2]

SELECTED REFERENCES

Association for Supervision and Curriculum Development. *Research for Curriculum Improvement.* Washington, D.C.: The Association, a Department of the National Education Association, 1957. Pages 182-185.

Hillway, Tyrus. *Introduction to Research.* Second edition. Boston: Houghton Mifflin Co., 1964. Pages 113-115.

Rummel, J. Francis. *An Introduction to Research Procedures in Education.* Second edition. New York: Harper & Row Publishers, Inc., 1964. Pages 28-34.

THEORY

A person who is interested in doing research needs to be concerned not only with WHAT relationships exist between various data but also WHY these relationships occur. A theory is a statement which attempts to relate facts meaningfully. It involves sketching out facts and relationships that are not observable directly but which underlie the phenomena observed. A theory is more than a generalization about what might happen. It is a set of propositions that generate predictions and guide a person to look for certain things. By means of a theory or a related body of concepts, a person can bring a great many things into focus at one time.

Theories abound in daily life, but many of them are of dubious value. A good theory is useful in helping to explain what is observed and in adding to the body of knowledge pertinent to home economics education. The research process starts with ideas about the nature of the phenomena observed. Theory permits a deeper understanding of these phenomena--their significance, relationships, and potential for meaningful research.

Mouly stated several characteristics of a good theory:

1. A good theoretical system permits interpretations and deductions that can be tested empirically. It provides the means for its own verification.

2. A good theory is compatible with observation and with theories that have been validated previously.

3. A theory must be based on empirical facts and relationships. Hypothetical constructs aid explanations but they must not be used as though they existed in reality.

4. The best theory is stated in the simplest terms. This is the <u>law of parsimony</u>. It explains the data adequately, but is not so comprehensive and detailed as to be unwieldy.[3]

---

[2]Olive A. Hall, <u>Home Economics--Careers and Homemaking.</u> New York: John Wiley & Sons, Inc., 1958. Pages 245-246.

[3]George J. Mouly, <u>The Science of Educational Research.</u> New York: American Book Company, 1963. Page 58.

The need for applying the law of parsimony was aptly illustrated by Galfo and Miller:

> *If a child is observed falling from a ladder, one might conclude that the child was driven by Thanatos, Freud's death wish. A more parsimonious explanation would be that the child's foot slipped because the rungs of the ladder were wet. Further investigation, which could be used to confirm the second explanation, might confirm the presence of water, oil or some slippery substance on the rungs of the ladder. Or some psychological problem could be identified through careful analysis of the child's background that would lead us to partially reject the rational aspects of behavior.*[4]

Van Dalen pointed out that *"isolated facts are useless unless someone structures a theory that will make them fall into a meaningful pattern. Theories provide logical explanations for facts."*[5] Among the ways in which theory contributes to the advancement of knowledge, Van Dalen mentioned the following:

1. Defining the relevancy of facts.

    As a home economist doing research, you will find that you cannot gather facts about everything. When you theorize that there is a relationship between two things, you know which specific facts will be necessary to provide the evidence that will confirm or reject your theory.

2. Classifying phenomena and structuring concepts.

    Major advances in classifying educational objectives are illustrated in the Taxonomy of Educational Objectives. In one section the theorists developed the following system for classifying educational objectives about interests, attitudes, and appreciation of esthetic and moral values:

    a. *Receiving (or attending to) affective stimuli*
    b. *Responding to affective aspects of the situation*
    c. *Valuing the affective components for their own sake*
    d. *Organizing multiple and simultaneously-perceived values into larger sets*
    e. *Characterizing new experiences in terms of a larger set of values.*[6]

3. Summarizing facts.

    Theory synthesizes isolated data into a conceptual scheme of wider applicability and predictability. Van Dalen gave an example that could apply to home economics education. After observing such phenomena as honor societies and certificates of achievement, you might notice a relationship between them and draw the generalization that public recognition rewards are a means of motivating students. Your theory describes a relationship between phenomena, provides facts with meaning, and places facts in perspective.

4. Predicting facts.

    When you have stated a generalization that is supported by your data, you are in a position to predict the existence of unobserved instances that conform to

---

[4]Armand J. Galfo and Earl Miller, Interpreting Education Research. Dubuque, Iowa: Wm. C. Brown Co., 1965. Page 81.
[5]Deobold B. Van Dalen and William J. Meyer, Understanding Educational Research. New York: McGraw-Hill Book Co., Inc., 1962. Page 58.
[6]David Krathwohl; Benjamin Bloom; and Bertram B. Masia, Taxonomy of Educational Objectives: The Classification of Educational Goals. Handbook II: Affective Domain. New York: David McKay Co., Inc., 1964. 196 pages.

it. Van Dalen illustrated this by saying that, if you have confirmed your generalization that a high rate of truancy is associated with slum areas, you can expect to find this pattern in a slum area where statistics on truancy have not been compiled.

5. Pointing out the need for further research.

A theory is not an end in itself; it is a tool for obtaining further supporting evidence. If you find that public recognition rewards motivate high school students, you might ask whether or not this would hold true for elementary school students and in adult education classes. Would it be true of adolescents in other cultures? Would the intellectual ability of the students make any difference? Are the rewards equally effective in motivating boys and girls?[7]

SELECTED REFERENCES

Hillway, Tyrus. *Introduction to Research.* Second edition. Boston: Houghton Mifflin Co., 1964.
   Pages 120-129.
Mouly, George J. *The Science of Educational Research.* New York: American Book Company, 1963.
   Pages 49-60.
Van Dalen, Deobold B. and William J. Meyer. *Understanding Educational Research.* New York:
   McGraw-Hill Book Co., Inc., 1962. Pages 57-63.

HYPOTHESES

Hypotheses have their roots in theories. Usually when you think about a problem area in which research is needed, you begin to speculate about what has caused the problem and what might happen if you tried various ways of solving the problem. Ultimately you reach a conclusion or a generalization, which is sometimes referred to as a theory. In the meantime, the term "hypothesis" is used to refer to a temporary theory which is a reasonable guess based upon the evidence available. It is held on a provisional basis until new evidence has been collected and a possible solution is decided upon as the correct one.

Good defined a hypothesis as *"an informed or shrewd guess or inference, with a reasonable chance of being right, formulated and tentatively adopted to explain observed facts or conditions and to guide in further investigation, in other words, to serve as the investigator's 'eyes' in seeking answers to questions. The scientist's hypothesis parallels the common man's personal opinion or hunch.*[8]

Travers gave the following illustration of a theory and a hypothesis:

THEORY: If a young child is given freedom, he tends to develop greater motivation to achieve and to succeed than if he is raised in an environment that places many restrictions upon him.

HYPOTHESIS: Children whose parents greatly restrict their freedom to visit places outside of the home tend to obtain lower school grades than children of comparable ability as measured by an intelligence test who enjoy greater freedom of movement.[9]

---

[7]Van Dalen, op. cit., pages 58-61.
[8]Carter V. Good, Essentials of Educational Research. New York: Appleton-Century-Crofts, Inc., 1966. Page 112.
[9]Robert M. W. Travers, An Introduction to Educational Research. Second edition. New York: Macmillan Co., 1964. Page 16.

Hypotheses set a clear goal before the research worker and provide a way of thinking about the phenomena or behavior that he is studying. More than one hypothesis can be tested in a single study. When the results of several studies give consistent support to a theory, we can formulate a generalization or principle on this basis.

A properly structured hypothesis is logically consistent and pertinent to your study. It is not contradictory to the laws of nature. Its consequences can be tested empirically. The hypothesis that *"home economics students show greater moral growth than students who do not study home economics"* is not testable. Moral growth is not measurable. An example of a testable hypothesis is: *"There is no difference in the achievement of students whose teachers have a positive attitude toward children and those whose teachers have a negative attitude toward children."*

According to Barnes, a good hypothesis must:

1. *be clear and unequivocal. It must be worded in operational terms; what action, who is involved, what is the prediction, in what quantity or to what degree?*

2. *be specific. Is it testable? Are the predictions and operations of the test spelled out? If sub-hypotheses are needed to detail the test, are they provided?*

3. *be directly related to empirical phenomena. Are the words "ought," "should," "bad," and other normative or moral judgments avoided? These concepts can't be tested.*

4. *be related to available techniques. If the hypothesis satisfies all other tests, it is still worthless if procedures for testing it are not known.*

5. *be related to knowledge or theoretical constructs concerning the original problem area. Professional knowledge or acquaintance with other relevant research studies can help sharpen a hypothesis.* [10]

Barnes pointed out that:

Hypotheses frequently are worded in "if-then" phraseology: "If students choose the desks at which they wish to sit in the classroom, then they will have feelings of being accepted by the group." But this style of wording is not the only way to phrase a hypothesis. Any other wording is acceptable, provided the hypothesis makes a clear prediction that a specific action will produce a specific result.

The hypothesis forms an intellectual bridge between the problem and the test of the problem. The hypothesis conditions the design of the test, the obtaining of data, and the generalizations that may be drawn. It is, indeed, the pivotal point on which the whole research project turns. [11]

When writing down a hypothesis, you must be careful not to express your own personal bias or the outcome you would expect from your study. One approach is to enumerate specific characteristics that might be associated with the factor being studied. For example, Bateman studied the use of the home as a community resource in home economics programs. She hypothesized that the extent to which a home economics teacher uses the homes of students as a community resource varies with the following factors: *the amount of teaching experience, the number of years in her present position, her training*

---

[10]Fred P. Barnes, "A Guidebook in Research Methods for Practitioners in Education." Illinois Curriculum Program. Springfield, Illinois: Office of the Superintendent of Public Instruction, 1956. Page 6.
[11]Ibid., page 6.

in the use of community resources, the time allotted to her for home visits, the size of her classes, and the size of the community in which she teaches. She stated further the hypothesis that extensive use of the home enriches the home economics education program in the following ways: *guiding the home economics students in their classwork, bringing girls and boys into closer contact with their parents, and making school work more significant.*[12]

Another procedure is to state a <u>null</u> <u>hypothesis</u>--that any difference found between the groups on the factors being considered is due to chance. Two advantages of this approach are that the statements are not likely to express personal bias, and they are in a form that can be tested and interpreted with a high level of confidence. Slight differences may occur as a result of chance errors in sampling or measurement, but the null hypothesis denies the existence of a real difference until chance has been eliminated as a possible cause. When the statistical treatment of data indicates a significance difference, the null hypothesis is rejected on the grounds that the difference is nonchance or real. When the difference is large, you can have a high degree of confidence that it is not merely a chance occurrence and that the factors under consideration probably did have a measurable effect in bringing about the differences between the groups. The use of a null hypothesis may be illustrated by Porter's study in which his aim was: *"to study the relationship, if any, that exists between marital adjustment and parental acceptance of children."*[13] His procedure involved determining the marital adjustment scores of 100 subjects and relating these to their parental acceptance scores. He tested the significance of the differences in mean scores to determine whether they were indicative of real differences or whether they were likely to be the result of sampling variation.

Experimental studies lend themselves readily to the stating of hypotheses, but not all types of research can be treated in the same manner. Even though your study may not be suited to the stating of formal hypotheses, you must state your problem very carefully --that is, <u>what</u> you are studying. A good way to evaluate your statement of the problem is to put it in the form of a question that is to be answered. Each question should be important in itself and should be essential to fulfilling the purposes of the study. The California Co-operative Study of Attitudes illustrates the use of questions in outlining a problem:

> *In making the study, answers were sought to the questions: (1) Why do, or do not, students enroll in homemaking classes? (2) How does homemaking help students, schools, and communities? (3) What can be done to strengthen the homemaking program offered in California public schools?*[14]

The development of a list of questions or hypotheses is perhaps the most important single step in a research study. Hypotheses serve as the framework around which all of the other steps must fit in order to have a sound project. They give shape to the study and suggest the methods and techniques which should be followed. If the basic framework is weak, no amount of building upon it can produce a strong structure. Insofar as the framework is inadequate, the building may be restricted and important hypotheses may be overlooked.

---

[12]Jessie W. Bateman, "The Enrichment of Homemaking Programs through the Use of the Home as a Community Resource." Unpublished Doctor's dissertation, Cornell University, 1953. Page 3.

[13]Blaine M. Porter, "The Relationship between Marital Adjustment and Parental Acceptance of Children." <u>Journal of Home Economics</u> 47: 157-164; <u>March, 1955.</u>

[14]Olive A. Hall, <u>What's the Next Move in Homemaking Education?</u> Bulletin 24, Number 2. Sacramento: California State Department of Education, 1955. Page 1.

SELECTED REFERENCES

Barnes, Fred P. "Practical Research Processes." Illinois Curriculum Program. Springfield, Illinois: Office of the Superintendent of Public Instruction, 1956. Pages 4-7.
Good, Carter V. *Essentials of Educational Research.* New York: Appleton-Century-Crofts, Inc., 1966. Pages 112-118.
Hillway, Tyrus. *Introduction to Research.* Second edition. Boston: Houghton Mifflin Co., 1964. Pages 129-131.
Rummel, J. Francis. *An Introduction to Research Procedures in Education.* Second edition. New York: Harper & Row Publishers, Inc., 1964. Pages 60-61.
Travers, Robert M. W. *An Introduction to Educational Research.* Second edition. New York: Macmillan Co., 1964. Pages 89-94.

BASIC ASSUMPTIONS

As an aid in setting up the hypotheses to be tested in your study, you might profit from listing the things that are already known and widely accepted--these statements are called underlinedassumptions. According to Hillway, *"A basic assumption is any presumed fact so commonly known and accepted that it needs no proof."* [15] Facts or attitudes that are commonly accepted as being true are like a springboard when planning a study; they serve as a point of departure for outlining new hypotheses. Although not every reader will be willing to accept the assumptions that you propose, your responsibility is to be sure that your assumptions are in agreement with generally accepted concepts, and then state that your hypotheses rest upon the acceptance of these assumptions.

Underwood has indicated two fundamental assumptions that underlie all research efforts:

1. A given event has a limited number of possible causes. This assumption is referred to as underlinedlimited or finite causality.

2. Every natural event has a cause which can be discovered if we look diligently for it. This is the principle of determinism. [16]

A common assumption is that the characteristic being studied can be measured, or that a certain technique is a satisfactory way of measuring a given characteristic. For example, in studying vocational interests of college home economics students, you might try to identify interest patterns that are characteristic of students in the various major curriculums. One of your fundamental assumptions would be that interests can be measured. A second assumption might be that a specific instrument and method are valid means of measuring interests of college home economics students.

Another type of assumption that is fundamental to many studies in home economics deals with the basis for selecting certain types of participants. As an example, a study of the reasons why high school students do or do not take home economics courses is likely to be influenced by the prevailing philosophy of home economics education. When this philosophy expresses the belief that boys as well as girls are homemakers and should be given preparation for their home life, a research study would include opinions of boys as well as those of girls. In addition, the investigator would assume that the data from a sample would be representative of the total population.

[15] Tyrus Hillway, Introduction to Research. Boston: Houghton Mifflin Co., 1956. Page 133.

[16] Benton J. Underwood, Experimental Psychology. Second edition. New York: Appleton-Century-Crofts, Inc., 1966. Pages 5-7.

A third type of assumption is basic to the choice of procedures. For example, you might be interested in finding out what your students should be achieving in high school home economics courses. If you believe that curriculum planning should be a cooperative function of teachers, parents, and students, your study might employ some technique of discovering what parents, teachers, and students think should be accomplished. You would be assuming that each group whom you select to study would be in a position to supply information pertaining to your problem.

An illustration from the Central Regional Co-operative Research project clarifies the difference between an assumption and hypothesis. In reporting her study of "College Students' Attitudes Toward Families, Lehman said the study was based on three assumptions:

   1. Teachers who accept persons different from themselves are more effective teachers than they might otherwise be.

   2. The college has a responsibility for helping students to assess their own attitudes and broaden their experience with other groups, particularly with those of whom they have little firsthand knowledge and toward whom they have strong prejudice.

   3. Understanding comes with experience, and, with understanding, acceptance.

Lehman developed an instrument consisting of twelve problems related to acceptance of farm families, broken families, parents with young children, families from different socioeconomic and religious groups, and families in industrial areas. In testing three major hypotheses, she stated them in the form of null hypotheses:

   A. Attitude scores on the inventory are not related to certain socioeconomic factors: (1) the size of community in which the students lived, (2) educational level of their parents, and (3) father's occupation.

   B. Attitude scores on the total inventory are not related to certain aspects of past experience: (1) the pleasantness or unpleasantness of experience with a given group, (2) the number or types of experiences one has had with groups unlike his own, and (3) the specific experience.

   C. Scores are not related to students' stated attitudes toward groups whether their statements are the result of forced choice or are given in interviews or in free writing.[17]

SELECTED REFERENCES

Good, Carter V. *Essentials of Educational Research.* New York: Appleton-Century-Crofts, Inc., 1966. Pages 111-112.
Hillway, Tyrus. *Introduction to Research.* Second edition. Boston: Houghton Mifflin Co., 1964. Pages 264-267.
Rummel, J. Francis. *An Introduction to Research Procedures in Education.* Second edition. New York: Harper & Row Publishers, Inc., 1964. Page 60.

[17]Ruth T. Lehman, "College Students' Attitudes Toward Families." Journal of Home Economics, 54:470-473; June, 1962.

DELIMITATION OF A PROBLEM

When you are having your first experiences with a research problem, you are likely to experience one of two common difficulties--either the topic represents a very broad field that should not be undertaken in a single research study, or the topic is so narrow that its findings would be of little value to you and would make no contribution to the advancement of home economics education. Regardless of whether the problem as stated at first is rather broad, or whether it is very restricted, you need to focus or delimit it. Each part of the study needs to be defined and its boundaries determined. If your topic is too broad, your next step is to limit it so that it will be practical for you to handle and still yield important results. When your chosen topic is too narrow, delimitation may help you to extend its boundaries, making it into a more worthwhile problem.

As an example of how you might proceed in delimiting a problem, assume that you are a home economics teacher of adult classes. You are interested in finding out what kind of person enrolls in adult education, and specifically, in home economics courses. Does this interest express a problem? Immediately several questions might be raised, such as: What home economics students should you study? What characteristics of the students should you consider? Of what value would such a study be?

Your _purpose_ in doing a study should make clear _why_ you are carrying out this particular study, or define its possible benefits. If you are in charge of planning the adult education courses for a school system, a study of the adults who participate, or who might become interested in participating, in such a program could help to increase the enrollment in home economics courses. If you are a new teacher in the community, this type of study might help you to plan a home economics program in accordance with the needs and interests of adults in the community. These are but a few of many possible motives for wanting to know about the backgrounds and needs of persons who enroll in adult home economics classes. You may have several purposes as you carry out a single study, but you do need to focus your problem.

How you delimit your problem depends upon what results would be of greatest value in a specific situation. As a teacher of adult classes, you could learn much about your students by studying the characteristics of students who have enrolled in adult home economics courses during the past few years. From the records in your school or school system, you might discover such factors as the age groups represented most frequently, the educational levels attained, and the courses in which enrollment was heaviest. Another approach would be for you to learn about the students who are enrolled at the present time. You might ask them to supply such information as how they learned about the program, why they were interested in the home economics courses, and what types of courses they would like to have available in their community. A third approach would be to investigate the types of home economics programs being made available for adults by other organizations in the community. From your analysis you might discover what types of people in the community are not being reached by any other organized program and plan ways in which your adult education program might reach these persons and thus supplement the work of other organizations.

All three of the above approaches involve a _survey_ of students who have enrolled, who are enrolled currently, or who might become interested in the adult home economics program. Another research method involves a plan for action, or _experimentation_ with a specific procedure that you hypothesize would improve your program. Lippeatt illustrated with six steps how research could be used in strengthening home economics program for adults. For example:

> _Step 1._ _Identify problem area:_
>   _Adult homemaking classes._

Step 2.   Clarify problem:
How can we increase and maintain attendance at adult homemaking
classes?
Step 3.   Decide on a possible solution and state hypothesis:
If adults help to plan content around their problems, they will attend
more regularly.[18]

As you read later chapters in this book, you will learn about other possible approaches for this type of study. The specific design of a research study depends upon which approach would be most helpful in solving a given problem, as well as the time and resources available for the study. In general, the delimitation of a study should specify such factors as the nature of the problem to be studied, time and place of the study, type of sample to be used, and general procedures for obtaining the desired information.

SELECTED REFERENCES

Association for Supervision and Curriculum Development. *Research for Curriculum Improvement.*
   Washington, D.C.: The Association, a Department of the National Education Association, 1957.
   Pages 72-79, 125-127.
Hillway, Tyrus. *Introduction to Research.* Second edition. Boston: Houghton Mifflin Co. , 1964.
   Pages 115-119.
Rummel, J. Francis. *An Introduction to Research Procedures in Education.* Second edition. New
   York: Harper & Row Publishers, Inc. , 1964. Pages 40-57.
Whitney, Frederick L. *The Elements of Research.* Third edition. Englewood Cliffs, New Jersey:
   Prentice-Hall, Inc. , 1950. Pages 80-85.

DEFINITION OF TERMS

The delimitation of a study puts it into workable form, suggesting procedures that should be followed in gathering and interpreting the data. The definition of terms is a step that helps to give others a better understanding of your intent.

Definitions may be of two types: (1) conceptual or literary--relating the term to other concepts as in the form of dictionary definitions, in which the measuring procedures are not usually specified; or (2) operational--identifying a phenomenon by specifying the procedures or operations involved in measuring it. Underwood has clarified the difference in this way:

Literary definition of anxiety: *"painful uneasiness of mind."*

Operational definition of anxiety: *"Here is a questionnaire; here are the instructions to Ss; it was scored in this manner and this is the reliability. What we mean by anxiety is the score obtained on this questionnaire."*[19]

If it is possible to find a commonly accepted definition of a term or phrase that is adequate for your particular study, you may use that definition. Examples of definitions that are used widely in home economics education research follow:

---

[18]Selma Lippeatt, Adventuring in Research to Improve School Practices in Homemaking Programs: An Individual Approach. Misc.
   3512-I. Washington: U. S. Department of Health, Education, and Welfare, Office of Education, Vocational Division, 1956.
[19]Underwood, op. cit. , pages 300-301.

ATTITUDE: a readiness to react toward or against some situation, person, or thing, in a particular manner, for example, with love or hate or fear or resentment, to a particular degree of intensity. [20]

CHOICE MAKING: an area of consumer education aimed at the development of a sound sense of what is most worth the expenditure of income, time, and energy and what is least worth such expenditure, all in terms of needs, wants, and satisfactions; education toward discrimination in regard to the general classes of goods and services that are worth buying, as distinguished from the more specific skills of actually buying them. [21]

COURSE OF STUDY: an inclusive outline of the experience, skills, projects, demonstrations, related information, and methods involved in teaching a school subject, covering a specified period of time. [22]

CURRICULUM: a systematic group of courses or sequence of subjects required for graduation or certification in a major field of study. [23]

EVALUATION: the process of ascertaining or judging the value or amount of something by careful appraisal. [24]

FAMILY-LIFE EDUCATION: (1) in the broad sense, education that is designed to promote satisfying and successful family living, offered at any level from preschool to adult, in separated courses or integrated; (2) in a restricted sense, a special program or course of instruction, usually at secondary, college, or adult level, to prepare youth or adults for successful marriage and parenthood; focused upon (a) the understanding of human personality and behavior as related to the development of emotional maturity and satisfying family relationships as well as physical well-being, and (b) the development of skills essential to effective family participation. [25]

HOME ECONOMICS EDUCATION: a program of instruction which assists boys and girls, men and women, to understand and solve problems in personal, home, and family living. The subject matter areas comprising the field of home economics include: child development and family relationships; foods and nutrition; clothing and textiles; family economics and home management; housing, home furnishings, and home equipment; family health. The term home economics *is often used to designate this educational field at the junior college and university level, which prepares students for such professional services as homemaking teacher, dietitian, nutritionist, nursery school teacher, and institutional manager.* [26]

HOME EXPERIENCES: learning activities related to family problems which are planned, carried out, and evaluated by the pupils in their homes, under the guidance of the teacher and parents, for the purpose of personal development and improvement of home life. [27]

---

[20]Carter V. Good, Dictionary of Education. Second edition. New York: McGraw-Hill Book Co., Inc., 1959. Page 48.
[21]Ibid., page 91.
[22]American Vocational Association, Definitions of Terms in Vocational and Practical Arts Education. Washington, D.C.: American Vocational Association, 1954. Page 10.
[23]Carter V. Good, Dictionary of Education. Second edition. New York: McGraw-Hill Book Co., Inc., 1959. Page 149.
[24]Ibid., page 209.
[25]Ibid., page 224.
[26]American Vocational Association, op. cit., pages 14-15.
[27]Ibid., page 15.

HOMEMAKING EDUCATION: education which is centered on home activities and relationships, designed to enable girls and boys, men and women, to assume the responsibilities of making a home, or improve home and family living.[28]

HOME PROJECT: the application of principles and techniques of homemaking to the solution of a particular personal or family living problem. The project is planned, carried out, and evaluated by the pupil in the home, with the guidance of the teacher and parents.[29]

HOME VISIT: a home call, usually not so complete as a home investigation, for the purpose of improving parent-teacher-pupil relationships, checking on attendance, improving instruction, or other purposes.[30]

INSTRUCTIONAL MATERIAL: any device, method, or experience used for teaching purposes, including textbooks, supplementary reading materials, audio-visual and other sensory materials.[31]

STUDENT TEACHER: a college student who is acquiring practical teaching experience and skill under the guidance of a supervising teacher or other qualified person.[32]

Often it is preferable for you to write your own definitions in keeping with the meaning that you wish to express and the situation in which your problem is to be studied. These should be in harmony with other related concepts and should be stated in such a way as to give your reader a concise and complete understanding of the concepts. Definitions should serve two purposes: (1) they may explain the meaning of a term that might not be clearly understood otherwise; and (2) they may be used to restrict a word that has more than one meaning.

A good definition fulfills the following criteria:

1. It gives the essence of that which is being defined.

2. It refers to the attributes possessed by, rather than those lacking in, the object being defined.

3. It contains the elements that are essential characteristics of what is being defined, but eliminates superfluous factors.

4. It is expressed in clear and direct language rather than in obscure or figurative terms.

5. The subject of the definition and the defining clause are reversible.

6. The defining clause contains words whose meaning is clearer than the word that is being defined, and it does not, directly or indirectly, contain the word that is being defined.

---

[28]Ibid., page 15.
[29]Ibid., page 15.
[30]Carter V. Good, Dictionary of Education. Second edition. New York: McGraw-Hill Book Co., Inc., 1959. Page 272.
[31]Ibid., page 291.
[32]Ibid., page 530.

SELECTED REFERENCES

Association for Supervision and Curriculum Development. *Research for Curriculum Improvement.* Washington, D. C.: The Association, a Department of the National Education Association, 1957. Pages 122-124.

Bowers, Henry. *Thinking for Yourself.* Toronto: J. M. Dent & Sons, Ltd., 1946. Pages 112-115.

Drever, James. (Revised by Harvey Wallerstein.) *A Dictionary of Psychology.* Baltimore: Penguin Books, Inc., 1964. 320 pages.

English, Horace B. and Ava C. English. *Comprehensive Dictionary of Psychological and Psychoanalytical Terms.* New York: David McKay Company, Inc., 1958. 594 pages.

Fairchild, H. P., Editor. *Dictionary of Sociology.* New York: Philosophical Library, Inc., 1944. 342 pages.

Good, Carter V. *Dictionary of Education.* Second edition. New York: McGraw-Hill Book Co., Inc., 1959. 676 pages.

Gould, Julius and William L. Kolb (editors). *A Dictionary of the Social Sciences.* New York: The Free Press of Glencoe, Inc., 1964. 761 pages.

Harris, Chester W., Editor. *Encyclopedia of Educational Research.* New York: Macmillan Company and the American Educational Research Association, 1960. 1564 pages.

Winick, Charles. *Dictionary of Anthropology.* New York: Philosophical Library, Inc., 1956. 579 pages.

Chapter 3

LOCATION AND REVIEW OF RELATED MATERIALS

The lame in the path outstrip the swift
who wander from it. --Francis Bacon

Home economists frequently have occasion to look for research reports, either for their own background as consumers of research or in preparation for engaging in their own research studies. "How much material should I read on my topic?" is a perennial question when you are planning a research study. Research experts do not agree on the answer. Some believe that you should plan your study rather completely before reading extensively in order to promote original thinking on the problem. Others feel that you need to do wide reading first in order to evaluate the significance of a problem and to be sure that the problem has not already been solved satisfactorily.

When you are planning to carry out a research study, a survey of related literature is valuable for at least three reasons:

1. It reveals the importance of the problem.

    Only by making an intensive survey can you determine whether or not a problem has been solved satisfactorily in previous studies. The fact that a problem has been studied does not preclude another investigation. Valuable studies may result from deliberate repetition of a study. The conditions may be kept identical in order to verify the results, or they may be changed to provide for a comparison of two or more procedures. Repetition at regular time intervals enables you to observe trends and developments.

2. It guides in the formulation of the problem.

    Knowing what others have tried and how successful their efforts have been can stimulate ideas and enrich your study. You may find methods, techniques, or instruments that you can utilize. A combination of creative and informed thinking can lead to new approaches in problem solving without unnecessary waste of time or duplication of effort.

3. It aids in the interpretation of results.

    If your findings are in agreement with the results of other research studies, you have a more extended basis for confidence in your conclusions about that particular area. When your results differ from the comparative data, you will be stimulated to find out in what respects your data are different and explain possible reasons for these differences.

EFFICIENT USE OF THE LIBRARY

Each individual has certain study procedures that seem to be most suitable for him. For research purposes, a person must learn to be systematic, yet flexible, in taking notes. One of the most important steps is to form the habit of always making a complete bibliographical notation. Bibliographical styles are discussed more thoroughly in the latter part of this chapter, but a complete reference contains such information as the library call number, author's full name, title of the book or article, name and place of publication of a book, name and volume number of a journal, date of publication, and the total number of pages in a book, or the specific pages in a book or article to which you wish to direct attention. Whenever a quotation is included, its exact page reference should be noted.

An abstract is a good form in which to take notes when you are reading a research report. The essential parts of an abstract are: (1) purpose of the study; (2) method of procedure; (3) findings; (4) conclusions. A fifth step, which is a desirable part of an abstract, is an evaluation of the study. While the report is fresh in your mind, you might find it helpful to write brief comments on the quality or significance of the study, its pertinence to your problem, and the adequacy of the instruments or sampling procedures.

A flexible system of note-taking is desirable. File cards (preferably 5 x 8 inches) or a loose leaf notebook permit you to add materials, reorganize them, and assemble a bibliography quite easily. In addition to the content that was outlined in the preceding paragraph, a subject-heading at the top of each abstract enables you to organize materials readily.

Books and Reference Materials

The card catalog in a library lists each book by author, title, and subject. The main entry, containing the most complete information, is the author card.

Books may be catalogued according to the Library of Congress classification or the Dewey Decimal system. Browsing among the books in a classification that is closely related to your problem often helps you to locate materials that you might overlook otherwise. Among the classifications used in the Library of Congress cataloging are the following ones related to home economics:

GT Manners and Customs
> Houses and dwellings, dress and costume, customs relative to private life

HQ The Family. Marriage. Woman
> Sex relations, the family, marriage, home, woman, feminism

LA History of Education

LB Theory and Practice of Education
> Principles and practices of teaching, educational psychology, child study, preschool education, secondary education, education and training of teachers, higher education, school laws and legislation, school administration and organization, school architecture, school hygiene

LC Special Aspects of Education
> Community and the school, moral and religious education, vocational education, vocational education, education of special classes of persons, adult education

NA Architecture
   Domestic buildings

NK Art Applied to Industry--Decoration and Ornament
   Interior decoration, costume, furniture, textile arts and needlework

QP Physiology
   Nutrition

TH Building
   Building design and construction, heating, ventilating, lighting, decoration
   and decorative furnishings

TP Chemical Technology
   Food technology, pottery, glass, bleaching, dyeing

TS Manufactures
   Metal, woodwork, leather, textile industries

TT Mechanic Trades (Miscellaneous Arts and Crafts)
   Clothing manufacture, dressmaking and tailoring, home arts, decorative
   needlework, decorative hand-work

TX Home Economics
   History, study and teaching, the house, clothing, foods and food supply,
   cookery[1]

The Dewey Decimal Classification and Relative Index contains the following sections
that are helpful in home economics research:

130 Branches of psychology and pseudopsychology
      131 Physiological psychology
      132 Abnormal psychology
      136 Differential psychology
      137 Psychology of personality

360 Social welfare
      361 Social work and social agencies
      362 Welfare services

370 Education
      371 Teaching, school organization, administration
      372 Elementary education
      373 Secondary education
      374 Adult education
      375 Curriculum
      376 Education of women
      377 Religious and moral education
      378 Higher education
      379 Education and the state

---

[1]Classification. Washington, D. C.: Library of Congress, Processing Department, Subject Cataloging Division. (Editions from 1948-1955)

390 Customs and folklore
     391 Costume
     392 Customs of life cycle
     395 Etiquette
     396 Woman

610 Medical sciences
     612 Human anatomy
     613 Hygiene
     614 Public health and other public aspects of medicine

640 Home economics
     641 Food
     642 Dining and food service
     643 Home planning
     644 Heating, lighting, ventilation, water supply
     646 Management of clothing and personal appearance
     647 Household management
     648 Household sanitation
     649 Child care and home nursing

660 Chemical technology
     663 Beverages
     664 Food technology
     667 Cleaning, dyeing and related industries
     668 Other organic products

670-680 Manufactures and other manufactures
     677 Textile and fiber manufactures
     684 Manufacture of furnishings
     687 Apparel manufacture

720 Architecture
     728 Residential buildings
     729 Architectural design and decoration

740 Drawing and decorative arts
     744 Interior decoration
     745 Decorative art and design
     746 Textile handicrafts
     748 Glassware and stained glass
     749 Furniture and accessories [2]

    Although browsing may be enjoyable and fruitful, much time can be saved usually by going to the library card catalog or a reference book. The first step is to decide on possible subject headings that will lead to the desired material. Specific headings should be tried first, but if they are not fruitful, more general headings may be used. As examples of headings, the following are among those listed under home economics in the Library of Congress guide: consumer education, cookery, cost and standard of living, entertaining, food, furniture, house decoration, laundry, marketing, and sewing. Under such categories as family, children, and budget, other specific sub-headings are suggested. [3]

---

[2]Dewey Decimal Classification and Relative Index. Edition 16. New York: Forest Press, Inc., Lake Placid Club, 1958. 2439 pages. (Reprinted with permission of Forest Press, Inc., owners of D. C. copyright.)
[3]Subject Headings used in the Dictionary Catalogs of the Library of Congress. Washington, D. C.: Library of Congress, 1957.

Reference materials that might be helpful in locating books on home economics include the following:

1. The Encyclopedia of Educational Research, which is revised every ten years, is probably the home economics teacher's greatest asset. Its articles summarize significant research in all areas of education and contain selected bibliographies. Of special interest to home economists are the following sections: Adult Education, Childhood and Preadolescence, several on Colleges and Universities, Family Life Education, Home Economics, Parent-Teacher Relationships, Research Methods, several on Teacher Education and Teacher Effectiveness, Tests and Examinations and Vocational Education.[4]

2. The Cumulative Book Index lists all books published in English anywhere in the world with the exception of government documents, books of less than 100 pages and costing less than $1.00, material of purely local interest, propaganda and ephemera. It appears monthly except August, with cumulated bound volumes semi-annually and a two-year final cumulation. Author, title, publishing company, date, and price are given. It covers such topics as clothing and dress, fashion, food, home economics, house decoration, nutrition, textile fabrics and fibers.[5]

3. The Book Review Digest, arranged by author, gives monthly abstracts of reviews and references where the full reviews might be read. Reviews are classified as favorable, unfavorable, or both favorable and unfavorable. A subject index is included.[6]

Journals and Periodicals

Reference guides to articles in journals or periodicals are of two types--those whose sole function is as an index to articles, books, or bulletins on specific topics and those whose purpose includes both an index and an abstract or review of each publication. An index with which nearly every student is familiar is the Reader's Guide to Periodical Literature. Since its articles are of a popular, rather than technical or scientific nature, its usefulness is limited in home economics research.[7]

The most useful index for home economics teachers is the Education Index, which is published monthly. It covers more than 200 magazines and serial publications, including both popular and research articles in the field of education. Yearbooks and government publications are indexed. Among its subject headings are action research, administration of schools, adoption, adult education, community life, counseling, curriculum, family life, federal aid to education, evaluation, graduate work, home economics education, personality, student activities, teachers, tests and scales, vocational education, and vocational guidance.[8]

Among the indexes that are useful for specific areas related to home economics subject matter are the following:

---

[4]Chester W. Harris, Editor. Encyclopedia of Educational Research. New York: Macmillan Company and the American Educational Research Association, 1960. 1564 pages.
[5]The Cumulative Book Index. New York: H. W. Wilson Co., 1966.
[6]The Book Review Digest. New York: H. W. Wilson Co., 1966.
[7]Reader's Guide to Periodical Literature. New York: H. W. Wilson Co., 1961.
[8]Education Index. New York: H. W. Wilson Co., 1966.

1. Applied Science and Technology Index (formerly the Industrial Arts Index) deals with periodicals on engineering, trade, business, and related subjects. Among its subject headings are ability tests, accidents, agricultural chemicals, audio-visual instruction, buying motives, lunchrooms and catering, clothing and dress, consumers, family, food, home ownership, housing, nutrition, textile fabrics and fibers.[9]

2. Art Index is a cumulative listing based on periodicals dealing with such phases as architecture, fine arts, fabrics, and homes. Its subject headings include clothing and dress, household furnishings, interior decoration, textile design, textile fibers, textile finishing, and textile testing.[10]

3. Biological and Agricultural Index (formerly the Agricultural Index) covers governmental publications, publications of experiment stations, and journals dealing with agriculture, food technology, and nutrition. Among its subject headings are the following: adolescence, amino acids, apples, aptitude tests, ascorbic acid, attitudes, decision-making, meat, and wool.[11]

4. Bulletin of the Public Affairs Information Service is an annual culmination of weekly listings of books, pamphlets, periodicals, and government publications. It deals with economic and social problems such as adoption, advertising, agricultural products, automation, family budget, clothing and dress, communication, education, family life, home ownership, and investments.[12]

5. Index of Economic Journals, under the auspices of The American Economic Association, is a guide to articles on such topics as public finance, economic fluctuations, agriculture, population, consumer economics, health, education, welfare, regional planning and development, and housing.[13]

6. Social Sciences and Humanities Index (formerly the International Index) is a guide to scholarly American and foreign journals dealing with social sciences and humanities. Included among its subject headings are adolescence, advertising, child psychology, child welfare, clothing and dress, family life, food, health, housing, parent-child relationship, teachers, and vocational guidance.[14]

Abstract journals and annual reviews give the reader more information about the content of articles, but the additional time necessary to render this service often means that the references are not as current as those to be found in an index. References of particular usefulness in home economics education research include:

1. Abstracts for Social Workers, prepared by the National Association of Social Workers, covers these areas: field of service--aging and the aged, crime and delinquency, family and child welfare, housing and urban development, and schools; social policy and action; service methods--casework, community organization, knowledge of psychiatry and medicine, psychology and social psychology, sociology and anthropology.[15]

---

[9]Applied Science and Technology Index. New York: H. W. Wilson Co., 1966.

[10]Art Index. New York: H. W. Wilson Co., 1966.

[11]Biological and Agricultural Index. New York: H. W. Wilson Co., 1966.

[12]Bulletin of the Public Affairs Information Service. New York: Public Affairs Information Service, 1966.

[13]Index of Economic Journals. Homewood, Illinois: Richard D. Irwin, Inc., 1965.

[14]Social Sciences and Humanities Index. New York: W. W. Wilson Co., 1966.

[15]Abstracts for Social Workers. New York: National Association of Social Workers, 1965.

2. Biological Abstracts is valuable for specialized studies related to diet, nutrition, vitamins, food technology, genetics, gerontology, infancy and childhood.[16]

3. Chemical Abstracts, published biweekly, covers such topics as dyes and textile chemistry; foods; cosmetics; glass, clay products, enameled metals; building materials; fuels; waxes and detergents.[17]

4. Child Development Abstracts and Bibliography includes abstracts of articles and lists of books on such topics as physiology and biochemistry--growth, nutrition, vitamins; psychology--behavior, intelligence, learning, personality; psychiatry and clinical psychology--crime, delinquency; education--class curriculum, vocational guidance; and sociology and economics--laws, family, marriage and divorce; biology, clinical medicine and public health.[18]

5. Economics Abstracts is a semi-monthly review of abstracts on social and applied sciences, including a section on household management and economy.[19]

6. Journal of the Textile Institute Abstracts uses the following sections: fibres and their production, conversion of fibres into finished yarns and fabrics, chemical and finishing processes; analysis, testing, grading, and defects; laundering and dry-cleaning, mill engineering, sciences, and sociology.[20]

7. Nutrition Abstracts and Reviews includes chemical composition of foodstuffs, vitamins, physiology of nutrition, human diet in relation to health and disease, and other topics related to nutrition.[21]

8. Psychological Abstracts presents abstracts covering the child, community, education, evaluation, the family, the home, management, marriage, motivation, personality, psychology, social work, the teacher, tests and testing, and vocational guidance.[22]

9. Review of Educational Research is the most comprehensive summary and critical analysis of articles covering all phases of education. Most of the topics appear at intervals of three years. The list includes such topics as:[23]

Adult education
Curriculum planning and development
Education for socially disadvantaged children
Education of exceptional children
Educational and psychological testing
Educational organization, administration, and finance
Educational programs: adolescence; early and middle childhood; later adolescence
Educational research in countries other than the U.S.A.
Growth, development, and learning
Guidance, counseling, and personnel services

[16]Biological Abstracts. Philadelphia: University of Pennsylvania Press, 1960.

[17]Chemical Abstracts. Easton, Pennsylvania: American Chemical Society, 1966.

[18]Child Development Abstracts. Lafayette, Indiana: Child Development Publications, Purdue University, 1961.

[19]Economics Abstracts. The Hague, Netherlands, 1965.

[20]Journal of the Textile Institute Abstracts. Manchester, England: The Textile Institute, 1964.

[21]Nutrition Abstracts and Reviews. Aberdeen, Scotland: Aberdeen University Press, 1966.

[22]Psychological Abstracts. Washington: The American Psychological Association, 1966.

[23]Review of Educational Research. Washington, D.C.: American Educational Research Association, a Department of the National Education Association, 1966.

Higher education
Human relations in education
Instructional materials
Language arts and fine arts
Mental and physical health
Methodology of educational research
Natural sciences and mathematics
Philosophical and social framework of education
Statistical methodology
Teacher personnel
Twenty-five years of educational research
Vocational, technical, and practical arts education

10. Sociological Abstracts has sections on methodology and research technology; history, theory, and the sociology of knowledge; social psychology; group interactions, culture and social structure; complex organizations (management); social change and economic development; mass phenomena; political interactions; social differentiation; community development and rural sociology; urban structures and ecology; arts, education, religion, science; social control; demography and human biology; family and socialization; health and medicine; and social problems and social welfare.[24]

Educational Research Information Center

ERIC (Educational Research Information Center) is a national system for disseminating educational research results. ERIC acquires, abstracts, indexes, stores, retrieves, and disseminates significant research information. Several universities are participating in this project in cooperation with the United States Office of Education. Fields of vocational education, including home economics education, are handled by The Ohio State University.[25]

Each of the clearinghouses, or university centers, handles information on a specific area. Those that might be helpful to a home economics teacher or administrator include:

Preparation of Urban School Personnel City University of New York
Educational Administration University of Oregon
Small Schools and Rural Compensatory
    Education New Mexico State University
Junior Colleges University of California, Los Angeles
Counseling and Guidance University of Michigan
Disadvantaged Children and Youth Yeshiva University

Unpublished Theses and Dissertations

Two bulletins, published by the United States Department of Health, Education, and Welfare, reported on a number of unpublished master's and doctoral theses. Studies pertaining to high school programs, adult education, new products, and administration

---

[24]Sociological Abstracts. New York: Sociological Abstracts, 1966.

[25]Information Retrieval Division, The Center for Vocational and Technical Education, The Ohio State University, Columbus, Ohio 43212.

and supervision were drawn from those completed in the years 1955-1958.[26] The studies on the teaching of home economics in colleges and universities which were reviewed were for the years 1955-1956. They presented materials on evaluating college experiences while in college and after college, knowing students, planning and teaching realistically, and changing points of view.[27] In both bulletins, the appendix contains samples of interview questions, inventory forms, opinionnaires, pretests, questionnaires, and rating devices. These should be extremely valuable to anyone who is planning a research study.

Several sections of the American Home Economics Association have published selected bibliographies of theses and research related to their areas. For example, research related to design, family economics, and institution administration has been compiled.[28]

The most complete listing of unpublished master's theses and doctoral dissertations in home economics is found annually in the March issue of the Journal of Home Economics. It classifies theses in the following areas: art; child development; family economics--home management; family relations; food and nutrition; home economics education (administration, program planning, evaluation, methods and materials, teacher education); housing, equipment, and furnishings; institution administration; and textiles and clothing.[29]

Dissertation Abstracts will tell you whether or not a doctoral dissertation is available for purchase on microfilm. This publication gives complete bibliographical information and an abstract of dissertations that are available on microfilm. Unpublished theses that are not on microfilm may be available for interlibrary loan. Arrangements for a loan can usually be made through the librarian of your college or university.[30]

A precaution which you should take if you are planning to begin a research study is to find out whether or not someone else has a similar study underway. Doctoral dissertations that are currently in progress on educational topics are listed annually by Phi Delta Kappa in a monograph consisting of four sections: (1) doctoral dissertations underway; (2) doctoral dissertations completed during a given year; (3) author index; and (4) research methods bibliography. Subjects covered include:[31]

> 1 A. Philosophy of education, educational principles and trends
>   B. International education, intercultural education, United Nations
>   C. Religious education, religion and the schools
> 2 A. Educational administration--general, local; school boards, trustees, regents, reorganization
>   B. Supervision

---

[26] Studies of Home Economics in High Schools and in Adult Education Programs. 1855-58. OE-83005, Vocational Division Bulletin Number 286, Home Economics Education Series Number 32. Washington, D.C.: U. S. Department of Health, Education, and Welfare, Office of Education, 1960. 185 pages.

[27] Studies on the Teaching of Home Economics in Colleges and Universities, 1955-56. Vocational Division Bulletin Number 276, Home Economics Series Number 31. Washington, D.C.: U. S. Department of Health, Education, and Welfare, Office of Education, 1959. 144 pages.

[28] American Home Economics Association, Research Related to Design, Housing, and Equipment, Home Furnishings, and Interior Design. (Compiled by Jane K. Shearer) 1966. 70 pages.
Selected Bibliography of Theses and Research in Family Economics and Home Management. (Compiled by Sarah L. Manning and Marilyn Dunsing) 1965. 54 pages.
Home Economics Research in Institution Administration, 1965-1966. (Compiled by Beatrice Donaldson) 1966. 16 pages.

[29] "Titles of Theses: Home Economics and Related Fields, 1965-1966." Journal of Home Economics 59: 191-218; March, 1967.

[30] Dissertation Abstracts. Ann Arbor, Michigan: University Microfilms, 1961.

[31] Research Studies in Education. Bloomington, Indiana: Phi Delta Kappa, 1960. 133 pages.

	C.	Public relations, school and community relations
	D.	Recruitment
3		Finance
4		School plant (construction, space allotment, maintenance); pupil transportation
5		Educational legislation, school laws, court decisions
6		Educational history, biography
7		Child study, child psychology
8		Educational psychology, general psychology
9		Studies in adolescence, youth groups and problems
10		Measurement and evaluation, research
11		Teacher-education, in-service training
12		Audio-visual education
13	A.	Curriculum, co-curriculum activities, camping
	B.	Methods of teaching, teaching aids, libraries
14		Desegregation
15		Pre-school, kindergarten, elementary education
16		Secondary education, junior high school, high school
17	A.	Language arts (speech, writing, communications)
	B.	Reading, literature
	C.	Foreign language instruction
	D.	English in high school; English in the univeristy
18	A.	Science, aviation
	B.	Arithmetic, mathematics
19		Social Studies
20		Art, music
21	A.	Vocational education, industrial arts education
	B.	Business education
	C.	Vocational agriculture
22	A.	Guidance and counseling
	B.	Student problems--general, kindergarten to twelfth grade, beyond the high school
23	A.	Health
	B.	Physical education
	C.	Safety education, driver education
	D.	Recreation, athletics, sports
24	A.	Special education
	B.	Juvenile delinquency, rehabilitation
25		Home economics, family life education, consumer education
26		Rural education, conservation
27	A.	Teacher's problems--personal and personnel
	B.	Professional
28	A.	Undergraduate education--college and university
	B.	Graduate education--college and university
	C.	Junior college, extension, continuation
	D.	Adult education, veteran education
	E.	Accreditation, certification, professional education

SELECTED REFERENCES

Alexander, Carter and Arvid J. Burke. *How to Locate Educational Information and Data.* Fourth edition, revised. New York: Teachers College, Columbia University Press, 1958. Pages 23-56, 57-122, 168-180.

Good, Carter V. *Essentials of Educational Research.* New York: Appleton-Century-Crofts, Inc., 1966. Pages 130-143.

Mouly, George J. *The Science of Educational Research.* New York: American Book Company, 1963. Pages 111-140.

Rummel, J. Francis. *An Introduction to Research Procedures in Education.* Second edition. New York: Harper & Row Publishers, Inc., 1964. Pages 35-39.

PREPARATION OF A REVIEW OF LITERATURE

Since home economics is a relatively new field of research, students sometimes find little or no material related to the topic of their choice. The previously cited sources should help you to locate studies whether they are published or unpublished, completed or in progress, in the field of home economics or in related fields. However, no amount of reference help is sufficient in itself to enable you to prepare an adequate review of related literature. You must learn the art of discernment so that you will know what you are looking for and when you have found it.

Before reading extensively, take time to outline the types of literature which are related to your topic and that would guide you in your investigation. As an example, in her study of career information that was being made available to high school and junior college students, Palmer looked for literature pertaining to: (1) recruitment in home economics; (2) recruitment in other areas of education; and (3) the role of the counselor and vocational guidance programs. [32]

In cases where studies are in disagreement, you must make a special effort to present an unbiased review of the literature. As Beveridge said, "People whose minds are not disciplined by training often tend to notice and remember events that support their views and forget others." [33]

You may devote an entire chapter to a review of literature, or you may choose to combine it with other material in an introductory chapter. The review need not contain all of the material that is available on a topic. It should be comprehensive, but selective. Studies that are included may be presented chronologically, if that approach contributes to the readers' understanding, or they may be organized topically.

No one pattern can be followed in determining how much discussion should be given to each reference. When you are reviewing two or more studies in which similar approaches were used and comparable results were obtained, you may present them in the same paragraph. On the other hand, if their findings or conclusions were contradictory, you should mention both positions, and, if possible, give an explanation of the conflict.

Usually a brief summary of the study and a critical, but objective, view are sufficient. However, you may feel occasionally that a rather detailed review would be helpful to yourself and your readers, particularly when the study under consideration is unpublished or is not readily available to your readers and the approach or findings are of special importance to your field of study.

Good and Scates offered the following suggestions for criticizing studies:

> *In describing showy but unsound studies, attention may be directed to hidden weaknesses, assumptions that are not made explicit, crucial factors that are not controlled or measured, important points of procedure that are glossed over without proper reporting, and conclusions that do not follow rigorously from the facts.... Ordinary adjectives expressing approval or praise are omitted.... Where a study is unquestionably of outstanding merit, some indication of this fact is in order, but more by way of emphasis than direct commendation.* [34]

---

[32] Dorothy D. Palmer. "A Study of Information on Home Economics Careers That is Available to the Students of Secondary Schools and Junior Colleges in the Los Angeles Area." Unpublished report, University of California, Los Angeles, 1957. Pages 7-19.

[33] W. I. B. Beveridge, The Art of Scientific Investigation. New York: W. W. Norton & Co., Inc., 1950. Page 10.

[34] Carter V. Good and Douglas E. Scates, Methods of Research. New York: Appleton-Century-Crofts, Inc., 1954. Pages 85-86.

SELECTED REFERENCES

Borg, Walter R. *Educational Research: An Introduction.* New York: David McKay Co., Inc., 1963. Pages 326-345, 364-366.

Good, Carter V. and Douglas E. Scates. *Methods of Research.* New York: Appleton-Century-Crofts, Inc., 1954. Pages 84-86.

QUOTATIONS. FOOTNOTES, AND BIBLIOGRAPHY

References should be given to support any facts or opinions that are borrowed, whether or not they are quoted directly. Several different styles of footnotes and bibliography are in use. This section shows a few of the common styles and presents a discussion of their advantages and disadvantages. In selecting a style, you should adopt one that is recommended by your graduate school or by the publication for which you are writing. Whatever style you select, be sure to follow it consistently and accurately.

Quotations

A direct quotation may be used for several reasons. The most obvious use is in a situation where no change is possible for the sake of accuracy, as in a statistical formula, law, or official ruling. When a statement is unusually clear or beautiful, its exact wording may be the most effective way to present a significant thought. You might choose to use a direct quotation from a recognized authority as a means of adding strength to your paper.

Whenever a direct quotation is used, it must be reproduced exactly as it was contained in the original publication. Even though changes in spelling or punctuation might make a quotation more in keeping with modern usage, no corrections should be made. If you wish to omit part of the original quotation, you may use the ellipsis (...) to indicate the break. When the omission comes at the end of a sentence, a fourth dot is added to represent the normal punctuation at the break. If anything is added to a direct quotation, the addition should be placed in brackets [ ].

A short quotation, usually less than two sentences or four typewritten lines, is included in double quotation marks at its normal position within the paragraph. Poetry, or a short prose quotation for which emphasis is desired, may follow the style recommended for long, direct quotations.

A direct quotation of four or more typewritten lines is set apart from the regular text by single spacing and indentation. Style manuals differ in their recommendations on minor points of style-some suggest indenting the first line of a quotation exactly the same as other paragraphs are indented, while some treat the first line the same as the other lines in the quotation. Authorities differ in their recommendations as to the number of spaces to indent the entire quotation. One style, which is easy to follow and effective, is to indent regular paragraphs eight spaces and quotations four spaces. No quotation marks are necessary when quotations are set apart from the regular text by indentation and single-spacing. Either a footnote or bibliographical reference should be used to indicate the source of a direct quotation.

General factual information, which is common knowledge and is likely to be contained in many references, does not require documentation. However, another person's ideas that are summarized or restated should have footnote or bibliographical references so as to give credit to the one from whom they were borrowed. The reference number is usually placed at the end of the quoted or paraphrased material. However, when the author's name is mentioned, the reference may be placed immediately following his name.

Footnotes

Footnotes serve two purposes: (1) providing additional information; and (2) indicating the source of an idea. Hurt explained in further detail the uses of footnotes:

> *Footnotes may be employed to acknowledge the source of the information used, whether it be fact, theory, or opinion; to assign credit; to cite authority for controversial statements; to support arguments; to guide the reader to additional and related material; to identify quoted material; to interpret, limit, evaluate, describe, compare, or augment meaning within the text; or to refer to other pages or passages in the same text.*[35]

Occasionally information needs to be supplied to the reader, yet its inclusion with the regular text would tend to interrupt the continuity. This type of footnote should be avoided as much as possible, because it may detract from the text. However, it may be a desirable means of presenting such information as the names of persons who served on a committee, or references to additional material or to a more detailed explanation contained in another section of the report.

One purpose in giving the sources of facts or opinions is to be as helpful as possible to persons who wish to refer to the material. Complete and accurate information is essential. The importance of careful footnoting has been emphasized by Hurt:

> *The documentation of a work bears evidence of the author's indebtedness to others, of his discrimination and judgment in the collection and use of supporting data, and of his willingness to subject his sources to investigation. Footnotes should be used judiciously. The presence of numerous footnotes is not necessarily an indication of the good quality of a work, but the author's selection, evaluation, and interpretation of the supporting data, and its pertinence as cited, do serve as evidence of quality, and ought to show good quality.*
>
> *Honesty demands scrupulous care in the assignment of credit for borrowed materials; paraphrased, reworded, or rearranged statements do not evade this responsibility. Footnotes are the most important vehicle for conveying credit, but a precis or summary of the material, or a direct quotation, may be used and credited effectively within the text itself.*[36]

Footnotes are numbered consecutively throughout a chapter. The number is placed following the period at the close of a sentence and is raised one-half space above the line. At the bottom of the page, a short line should be typed below the last line of the text to separate the text from the footnote, or specially lined paper should be used. The footnote is indented the same number of spaces as paragraphs. Its number is placed one-half space above the line, followed immediately by the content of the footnote. When the footnote extends beyond one line, single spacing is used within the footnote with each succeeding line beginning at the left margin. Double spacing is used between footnotes.

The format of footnote references differs slightly from that used in a bibliography. The name of the author is placed in normal order and is followed by a comma. Only the page or pages that were used are listed. When a second reference to the same work is made on the same page or the following page, Ibid. (meaning "in the same place") is used. When other references have intervened between the two references to the same work, op. cit. (meaning "in the work cited") may be used following the author's name. Op. cit.

---

[35] Peyton Hurt, Bibliography and Footnotes. Berkeley: University of California Press, 1957. Pages 1-2.

[36] Ibid., pages 80-81.

should be used only when the references are close together, probably within three pages of each other. When two or more books by the same author have been used, the full reference should be repeated.

At least two styles are acceptable for indicating references. The more traditional form is the use of footnotes. A newer, but more simple technique, is the parenthetical style. From the standpoint of being most helpful to the reader, footnote references have an advantage over the parenthetical style of giving references. The name of the author; the title of the work; the time, place, and date of publication; and the page or pages that have been quoted or summarized are all contained on the page where the reference is made to the work.

The greatest advantage of the parenthetical reference over a footnote reference is that each source is typed only once--in the bibliography. The elimination of duplicate listings may amount to a considerable saving of space and time, thereby reducing the typing or printing cost.

Readers who are interested in looking up references may feel somewhat handicapped by having to turn to the bibliography to locate them. Probably many readers have no interest in going to the original source; perhaps the majority of readers who do have an interest would select only a few of the most outstanding references. When the author's name is mentioned in the text, persons who have some familiarity with the field have a basis for determining which references they would be interested to pursue further.

Another possible disadvantage of the parenthetical style is that the complete bibliography must be assembled and numbered before the manuscript is typed. When each reference is written on a separate card, the arrangement of the bibliography is simplified.
In preparing the first draft of a manuscript, you may leave a blank space after the author's name. The reference number can be inserted after the bibliography has been completed, as in the following example: "Good and Scates (: 866) .... " When two or more references by the same author are being included in the bibliography, you should indicate, when writing the first draft, how you plan to differentiate between them. For instance, if two books by Arny are included in the bibliography, you might temporarily call one "A" and the other "B". Each time a reference is made to Arny in the first draft of the report, the letter of identification can be inserted in the parentheses as follows: "Arny (B: 76) ..."

An effective arrangement of a bibliography is a straight, alphabetical listing by author. When the complete bibliography is assembled, a number is assigned to each reference. These numbers are inserted for each citation, immediately after the name of the author or organization. When reference is made to the whole work, only that one number need be given, as "Hurt (3) ..."

When specific portions of a work have been used, the page or pages should be indicated after the number that refers to the bibliography, as "Hurt (3: 80-81) ...." For a short quotation that is included in the text, the citation is given at the end: "Unless cited earlier, a cross-reference follows at the end of a quotation, but is not enclosed in quotation marks." (4: 866)

In the same manner, a citation is placed at the close of a longer quotation that is set apart from the text:

> *This device is used in certain periodicals and publications of the National Education Association. It will save the author a great deal of time in proofreading and will noticeably cut printing costs. Setting footnotes in small type, checking them, placing them on the right pages, and so forth, adds considerably to the cost of bookmaking. The absence of footnotes also means a larger page on which to present more material of immediate concern to the reader. (1: 144)*

Bibliography

A bibliography contains each reference that has been cited in a research report and additional selected references that would be helpful to others working in that problem area. In assembling a bibliography, a person should strive to have it complete, though not exhaustive.

The most frequently recommended bibliographical style is a straight, alphabetical listing by the last names of the authors. This style saves the writer's time in preparing the bibliography as well as the readers' time in using it. Other styles that are sometimes used, though not as widely accepted, include: (1) a chronological listing; (2) listing according to the type of publication--books, periodicals, unpublished materials; (3) listing in the order of their appearance in the report; and (4) listing by topics. Each of these styles has its own advantage, particularly for a certain type of research report, as is readily apparent in the use of a chronological listing for a historical study. The major disadvantage of each is that a reader must know in which section to look, or he will waste time going from one section to another in search of a reference.

The first part of a bibliographical entry is the author's name--surname followed by the first name and middle initial if these are available. If the author's name is not indicated, the first letter of the title--disregarding "a," "an," or "the"--should be used to place the reference in its alphabetical position. When two or more references have the same author, a line eight spaces in length may be used in place of repeating the author's name. For each entry, the first line begins at the margin and all lines after that are indented at least three spaces.

Various bibliographical styles are recommended by institutions of higher education and by writers of style manuals. Certain styles have the advantage of simplicity to prepare and use, but others are acceptable and correct. Whatever style is chosen, it should be followed consistently. The following sections show basic principles of bibliographical style and one recommended method of carrying them out.

BOOKS.--The title of a book is underlined in a typewritten manuscript and italicized in print. A capital letter is used for each main word in the title. Any further identification that might be necessary, such as the number of the edition or the name of the editor, is placed immediately following the title. Next comes the place of publication, which is usually the first city mentioned on the title page in case more than one is given. For most publications, the name of the city is sufficient. However, the state or country should be listed if the city is not well known, or if two or more states have cities with the same name. The publisher's name should be given exactly as it appears on the title page, followed by the year of publication. The specific pages applicable to your report should be listed. The total number of pages in the book may be included if the whole book is helpful and pertinent to your study. This would give your reader an idea of the cost of a book, or the amount of time he might need to spend if he were interested in reading it.

Examples:

Arny, Clara B. Evaluation in Home Economics. New York: Appleton-Century-Crofts, Inc., 1953. 378 pp.

Cottrell, Leonard S., Jr. "The Present Status and Future Orientation of Research on the Family," in Judson T. Landis and Mary G. Landis, editors, Readings in Marriage and the Family. Englewood Cliffs, New Jersey: Prentice-Hall, Inc., 1952. pp. 445-453.

Good, Carter V. and Douglas E. Scates. Methods of Research. New York: Appleton-Century-Crofts, Inc., 1954. Pages 84.86.

A Manual of Style. Chicago: The University of Chicago Press, 1949. 533 pp.

Spafford, Ivol. Fundamentals in Teaching Home Economics. Second edition. New York: John Wiley & Sons, Inc., 1942. 490 pp.

ARTICLES IN PERIODICALS. --Titles of articles are placed in quotation marks to indicate that they are part of a larger work. Since anyone requesting an article in the library would need to ask for the larger work, the name of the journal is underlined (italicized in print). Next the volume number is given either in arabic or roman numerals and the pages occupied by the article are indicated. Finally, the date of publication is listed. Usually the month and year are sufficient, but biweekly or weekly publications need more specific dates.

Examples:

Sister Mary Jeanne. "Should Parents and Students Help in Curriculum Planning?" Journal of Home Economics 48: 700-702; November, 1956.

Sneed, Ruth. "Values of Home Visiting for Teaching Homemaking." Journal of Home Economics 49: 177-181; March, 1957.

BULLETINS AND YEARBOOKS. --When an entire bulletin has been written by one author, it may be listed under that author's name. A government publication may be listed under either the author (if the name is given) or the department issuing the bulletin. If reference is made to only one chapter of a bulletin which was compiled by several authors, the listing should be under the author of the chapter, but reference should be made to the entire bulletin of which the chapter is a part. When using an entire bulletin which has been prepared by an association, you may alphabetize it by the title or by the name of the association publishing it.

Examples:

Hall, Olive A. What's the Next Move in Homemaking Education? Volume 24, Bulletin Number 2. Sacramento: California State Department of Education, April, 1955. 133 pp.

Home Economics in the Secondary School. Bulletin of the National Association of Secondary-School Principals, Volume 37, Number 196. Washington, D.C.: National Education Association, October, 1953. 236 pp.

McGinnis, Esther, et al. "The Measurement of Understanding in Home Economics." in Forty-Fifth Yearbook of the National Society for the Study of Education, Part I, The Measurement of Understanding. Chicago: The University of Chicago Press, 1946. pp. 253-269.

U. S. Department of Health, Education, and Welfare, Office of Education. Following Graduates into Teaching. Bulletin 1954, Number 6. Washington, D.C.: U. S. Government Printing Office, 1954. 45 pp.

UNPUBLISHED MATERIAL. --The title of an unpublished thesis is placed in quotation marks and is followed by the name of the institution and the year in which the thesis was completed. Mimeographed reports and those duplicated by other processes may be treated like books, with the addition of the method of processing at the end.

Examples:

Barkley, Margaret; Emma Whiteford; and Elizabeth Simpson. <u>Possible Clues for Recruit-</u><u>ment from Research</u>. Urbana, Illinois: Home Economics Education, College of Education, University of Illinois, June, 1957. 73 pp. (Mimeographed)

Porch, Louise W. "Home Economics: Trends and Developments, 1909-1952." Unpublished Doctor's dissertation, Stanford University, 1955. 275 pp.

Webber, Vivienne L. "The Performance of Home Economics and Non-Home Economics Teacher Education Majors at the University of California, Los Angeles, on the American Council on Education Psychological Examination for College Freshmen." Unpublished Master's thesis, University of California, Los Angeles, 1957. 93 pp.

Efficient use of the library, good study habits, and systematic procedures of note-taking are fundamental tools for anyone who is doing research or who is interested in keeping up to date with recent research findings. Selectivity and consistency are keys to assembling a useful bibliography. Specific questions on style will arise frequently, but these may be resolved by referring to a style manual such as the ones listed among the following references.

SELECTED REFERENCES

Campbell, William G. *Form and Style in Thesis Writing*. Boston: Houghton-Mifflin Co., 1954. Pages 12-14.

Dugdale, Kathleen. *A Manual of Form for Theses and Term Reports*. Bloomington, Indiana: Indiana University Press, 1962.

Good, Carter V. *Essentials of Educational Research*. New York: Appleton-Century-Crofts, Inc., 1966. Pages 121-127.

Hurt, Peyton. *Bibliography and Footnotes*. Berkeley: University of California Press, 1957. 167 pages.

A Manual of Style. Chicago: The University of Chicago Press, 1949. Pages 137-153.

Rummel, J. Francis. *An Introduction to Research Procedures in Education*. Second edition. New York: Harper & Row Publishers, Inc., 1964. Pages 288-293.

Turabian, Kate L. *Student's Guide for Writing College Papers*. Chicago: The University of Chicago Press, 1963. Pages 34-42, 90-121.

Williams, Cecil B. and Allan H. Stevenson. *A Research Manual*. Revised edition. New York: Harper & Row Publishers, Inc., 1951. Pages 118-148.

Chapter 4
BASIC PRINCIPLES OF RESEARCH DESIGN

Discovery should come as an adventure rather than as the result of a logical process of thought. Sharp, prolonged thinking is necessary that we may keep on the chosen path, but it does not necessarily lead to discovery.

--Theobald Smith

In his quest for knowledge, man has progressed from reliance upon authority and the use of logical reasoning to the method of scientific inquiry. The scientific process has helped greatly in the expansion of knowledge based upon facts and generalizations. The early procedures that were involved in obtaining authoritative answers, or in reasoning from a known to an unknown condition, are no longer considered dependable methods for solving problems, but they may still contribute to a basic understanding of research and the scientific process.

As you read Chapter 3, you learned about the importance of formulating a research problem carefully. Suggestions were given to help you specify exactly what your problem is and what information is relevant to its solution. Your next concern is to design a research study in such a way that you will be able to gather the necessary, meaningful, and accurate data with economy of effort. The present chapter should help you do this.

THE SCIENTIFIC METHOD

Long before we heard of research, or the scientific method of solving problems, man had developed ways of adding to his knowledge of the world about him. One method was to seek out an authority and rely upon his judgment. This approach was not entirely satisfactory because of such questions as these: Who is an authority? Have the authorities been able to discover all truth? Does knowledge remain static so that what the authorities have written on a given topic will continue to be true? What happens when the experts do not agree? If you are confronted with a problem on which you cannot find an authoritative answer, what can you do?

Reasoning

Various kinds of reasoning have been emphasized over the years. Principles of logic, deductive reasoning, and inductive reasoning still play an important role in the discovery and verification of facts. Logical thinking is based upon a belief that we live in an ordered universe, where everything operates according to definite laws of cause and effect. Logic, or clear thinking, is the process by which we study all the facts available and reach a conclusion based upon complete or partial evidence or by inference.

Deductive reasoning, i.e. from the known to the unknown, was popularized by Greek thinkers who used the syllogism. By this process they could test the validity of a given conclusion. If the major premise (first statement in the following illustrations) and the minor premise (second statement) could be accepted as true, then a reliable conclusion could be deduced from these premises. An example of a syllogism pertaining to home economics education is:

1. A year course on The Family is required of all senior women students at College X;
2. Mary Doe is a senior woman student attending College X;
3. Therefore, Mary Doe's program includes a course on The Family.

In the preceding illustration, the third statement (or conclusion) would be a reasonable deduction if the first two statements were true.

Sometimes a person makes a statement that is really a concluding step in this process of deductive reasoning, but he skips over some of the intervening steps. For example: "Since Jane Smith works such long hours, she should receive an increase in salary." The steps leading to this conclusion might be listed as follows:

1. Teachers who work long hours should receive an increase in salary;
2. Jane Smith is a teacher who works long hours;
3. Therefore, Jane Smith should receive an increase in salary.

Either of the first two statements might be questioned, thereby making the conclusion unreliable. Regarding the first premise: Are long hours a sufficient criterion for salary increases, or should the quality of work during those hours be considered? The second statement might be true according to the facts available; but, on the other hand, the evidence might indicate that her seemingly long hours are no more than those worked by the average teacher. You can see that shortcuts in the reasoning process might lead to conclusions that are not valid.

Another danger in the use of syllogistic reasoning is that of mistaking a part for the whole For example:

1. All teachers have patience;
2. Betty Jones has patience;
3. Therefore, Betty Jones is a teacher.

The major premise does not state the whole truth, since many persons besides teachers possess patience. The "proof" that Betty Jones is a teacher is not based on sound evidence.

From these examples of syllogisms, you can see some of the pitfalls inherent in the reasoning process as a means of solving problems and expanding knowledge.

Steps in the Scientific Method

The scientific method, which is characterized by its organized approach to increasing knowledge, is distinguished from other methods of learning in several ways: (1) conclusions are based upon facts; (2) facts are obtained through observation rather than by logical reasoning; (3) evidence is gathered systematically rather than by chance; and (4) objective measurement is employed.

Four general steps constitute the scientific method on which research is based. Each of these steps consists of two or more specific processes:

1. Defining the problem.

    The first step in becoming aware of a problem area is to be sensitive to the
    difficulties that you, and other home economics teachers, face in your work.
    Next, you should try to define a specific problem within the general area that
    you have chosen. This involves viewing the problem in the context of the total
    situation of which it is a part. Determining the nature of your problem before
    trying to find a solution is a fundamental aspect of scientific thinking.

2. Deciding on a tentative solution.

    You will need to select a frame of reference from which to view the problem and
    the facts that you gather. As an intermediate step between defining your prob-
    lem and determining how to proceed toward its solution, you can benefit from
    an investigation of the evidence that is already available. Next, you can decide
    on a tentative solution, or hypothesis. The problem may be broken down into
    a series of specific hypotheses to be tested. Each hypothesis should be ex-
    amined carefully so that you are convinced its solution would be acceptable and
    its results could be tested.

3. Obtaining evidence.

    At this point, you are ready to proceed with the design of a study that will en-
    able you to make a valid test of your hypothesis. When you have applied the
    necessary controls to enable you to study the phenomenon under consideration,
    you can proceed with the collection of data. Facts, in themselves, do not con-
    vey their full meaning until they are classified, analyzed, and summarized.

4. Appraising the solution.

    If your data are complete and convincing, you can draw conclusions on the basis
    of your evidence, or make generalizations in reference to a larger group similar
    to the sample you have studied. You may arrive at new hypotheses from a care-
    study even though its results fall short of the ultimate goal of research--that of
    developing valid generalizations. You must challenge your data and, if necessary
    retest in order to be confident in your conclusions and any generalizations you
    attempt to make beyond the specific situation you have studied.

SELECTED REFERENCES

Hillway, Tyrus. *Introduction to Research.* Second edition. Boston: Houghton Mifflin Co., 1964.
    Pages 5-13.
Whitney, Frederick L. *The Elements of Research.* Third edition. Englewood Cliffs, N.J.:
    Prentice-Hall, Inc., 1950. Pages 9-18.

COLLECTION OF MEANINGFUL DATA

As you read research literature from various disciplines, you will notice a number
of words that are used to describe various kinds of data. In this portion of the chapter
you will be introduced to some of these terms. You must realize that one bit of information can be classified in more than one way. There is overlapping among the classifications that are presented here, but it is important for you to understand what is meant
when we talk about research data.

Kinds of Data

Facts that describe a situation and from which conclusions are drawn are called data. Whitney pointed out the importance of data:

> Data are the things we think with. They are the raw material of reflection, until by comparison, combination, and evaluation they are stepped up to higher levels of generalization, where they serve as basic material for further and higher thinking.[1]

There are several classifications of data with which home economists should be familiar. These are presented with some examples in the following paragraphs.

ATTRIBUTES AND VARIABLES. --Whitney distinguished between attributes and variables in this way: "An attribute is usually considered to be a quality, trait, or function that is present or absent. On the other hand, a variable simply exists in different amounts."[2]

In home economics education, we deal with attributes when we classify data into discrete or distinct categories such as: sex (male and female), reimbursement of a home economics program (reimbursed and nonreimbursed), or location of schools by county.

Other types of data which we use in home economics research are variable, forming a continuous scale rather than fitting into discrete categories. For example, chronological ages, height, and test scores of students are variable data. Such data differ from time to time, from one place to another, or from one person or object to another.

QUANTITATIVE AND QUALITATIVE VARIABLES. --A continuous series of data is made up of items which vary in size and can be classified appropriately in the order of their size. When the variation among data is in the amount of the trait under consideration, we refer to quantitative differences (for example: weight, number of brothers and sisters, or test scores).

When our evidence deals with the kind of differences observed, we call the data qualitative. Qualitative data may be attributes, such as occupation, race, or sex. On the other hand, qualitative data may be variable, or related to a scale, as in the following illustrations: tall, medium, or short; bright, normal, or dull. Since measurement and classification of qualitative data present problems that are often greater than those involved in handling quantitative data, we sometimes quantify qualitative data by assigning numerical ratings which aid in interpreting the data.

STIMULUS, BEHAVIORAL, AND ORGANISMIC VARIABLES. --Psychological research makes reference to three kinds of variables. According to Edwards, stimulus variables may consist of simple factors (such as light, temperature, or sound) that can be quantified by measuring the physical intensity of the stimulus. On the other hand, they may consist of more complex factors (such as problem-solving situations and social situations) that are difficult to quantify, but sometimes judges can rate them according to their levels of difficulty. Other complex situations (such as the lecture method versus the discussion method of teaching) differ in kind rather than in degree and constitute a qualitative series. Treatment is the term used to refer to differences in conditions of stimulation in an experiment.[3]

---

[1] Frederick L. Whitney, The Elements of Research. Third edition. Englewood Cliffs, N.J.: Prentice-Hall, Inc., 1950. Page 133.

[2] Ibid., page 134.

[3] Allen L. Edwards, Experimental Design in Psychological Research. Revised edition. New York: Holt, Rinehart and Winston, Inc., 1960. Page 5.

Behavioral variables can be quite simple (such as finger flexions), or they may involve complex behavior patterns (such as motor behavior, withdrawal, aggression, dominance, leadership, and social adaptability). Any action of an organism is called behavior. Counting the number of responses, such as aggressive acts, during a brief period of observation (time sampling) is one means of quantifying a behavioral variable into discrete categories. Sometimes we assume that the data represent a continuous scale, perhaps with "1" rating a minimum degree and "5" a maximum degree of aggressiveness. Then, judges are asked to rate the degree of aggressiveness an individual shows in certain situations. [4]

Organismic variables arise from the *"physical, physiological, and psychological characteristics"* by which individuals vary. They may be qualitative differences (such as their sex or hair color) or they may be quantitative differences (such as those you could obtain by classifying individuals in terms of their height and weight, educational levels, or their satisfactory or unsatisfactory performance in a given job). Sometimes we use a response-inferred organismic variable--a classification that is based on a previous observation of response (such as IQ obtained from a standardized test). [5]

DEPENDENT AND INDEPENDENT VARIABLES. --In psychological research, an independent variable (or treatment variable) refers to the factor in an experiment that the investigator manipulates or varies while other conditions are held constant. Differences in treatment may be either quantitative or qualitative. When they are quantitative, or differences in degree, they are called levels of treatment. When they are qualitative, or differences in kind, they are known as qualities of treatment. The number of hours a certain method is used and the instructions for taking a test are examples of independent variables.

A dependent variable refers to the attribute or behavior that is measured to determine the effects of the independent variable. It is observed to see what happens when the independent variable is manipulated. Edwards stated it this way: *"As the independent variables are changed or varied, the investigator observes other variables to see whether they are associated with or related to the changes introduced. These variables are called the dependent variables."* [6]

An example of independent and dependent variables in a specific hypothesis might be: Students who have completed a home economics course in high school will make significantly higher scores on the test, Homemakers-of-Tomorrow, than students who have not had a high school home economics course. The independent variable in this instance is the completion, or lack of completion, of a home economics course in high school. The dependent variable is the score on the test, Homemakers-of-Tomorrow.

Plans for Classifying Data

Among the kinds of evidence that lend themselves to classification are the characteristics of respondents, responses, spatial units, time units, and geographical units. Categorizing is a useful technique for reducing the number of items to be studied, for revealing similarities among items, and in assisting you to generalize from the data. However, before you can classify data, you need to determine what relationships between factors are to be studied and whether it is necessary to retain a picture of individual cases or merely of the group as a whole. If your classification is functional, it will carry out the purposes of your particular research study. Categories should be small enough to insure the homogeneity of all cases falling within a single category, yet large enough to permit an observer to differentiate between cases in various categories.

[4] Ibid., pages 6-7.
[5] Ibid., pages 7-8.
[6] Ibid., page 10.

Plans for coding, classifying, and tabulating data should be made in advance to be sure the design will be workable. Usually, several classifications are possible, but the selection of any one plan should depend upon its fulfillment of the purposes of your specific study. For example, clothing might be categorized by its monetary value, condition of repair, design of the garment, type of fabric, or a number of other characteristics, depending upon the particular study. Can you decide on suitable classifications of clothing for a study dealing with self-help features in children's clothing? How would your classification differ from one that you might use in a study of the values that influence teenage girls in planning a clothing budget?

Facts about individual participants or schools might be placed on cards and coded in advance as a quick, flexible means of selecting a sample and for checking its representativeness. A code system can be worked out for each item, and a single number can be used to permit easy sorting on any of the facts. As an example, the coding plan for schools to be included in a survey might be set up as shown for items A - D in Figure 1:

A. The first number represents the county; the second number identifies the school within that county.

B. The total school enrollment is divided into five categories:

(1)   0 - 249
(2)   250 - 499
(3)   500 - 749
(4)   750 - 999
(5)   1,000 or more

C. Whether or not the school receives reimbursement for its home economics program from State and Federal vocational education funds is indicated as follows:

(1)   Reimbursed
(2)   Nonreimbursed

D. The number of home economics teachers in the school is classified in this way:

(1)   1 part-time (combines teaching of home economics with teaching of other subjects)
(2)   1 full-time (teaches only home economics courses)
(3)   2 or 3 teachers
(4)   4 or 5 teachers
(5)   6 or more teachers

Data on Participating Schools		
Name of school Roosevelt High	A.	24
County Saratoga		
Total high school enrollment 500	B.	3
Reimbursement Reimbursed	C.	1
Number of home economics teachers 1 full-time	D.	2
Etc.		

Fig. 1. Coding Plan for Characteristics of a School

Descriptive data can be simplified and handled more systematically by abstracting the essentials and coding them. Riley has pointed out that observation may be used as the basis of coding. For example, a family's social status may be coded as low, medium, or high depending on the kind of living-room furniture observed in the home. Each code designation is a measure by which an individual case is classified <u>relative</u> to other cases. [7]

Tabulating Data by Hand Methods

Before you start gathering data, you should have a plan for tabulating what you obtain. Techniques or instruments that lend themselves to the most convenient and accurate means of tabulation can then be developed.

The use of edge-punched cards, such as <u>Keysort</u> and <u>Hadley</u> cards, could assist you in sorting. These come in different sizes, with blank spaces in the center for listing items pertinent to a given study. One row of numbers runs consecutively around the four sides of the card. Another row of numbers repeats a set of four digits, 7 4 2 1, above every four numbers that are in the other row. With one or two punches, every possible combination between one and nine can be indicated with this group of four digits. A special U-shaped punch is used to punch holes along the edge of the cards. A long needle is placed through any numerical position, and the cards are held in such a manner that the punched ones fall off the needle. These cards can then be counted. Even though punching, sorting with a needle, and counting are all time-consuming, the process may represent a considerable saving of time and energy over hand sorting and tabulating. For large studies, a machine is available for punching and sorting these cards. Further information about these cards may be obtained from the companies producing them. [8]

You may find the following suggestions helpful when tabulating your data without the use of mechanical aids:

1. When your groups are fairly small, you may be able to tabulate the responses on blank copies of your questionnaire or another type of instrument.

2. Graph paper helps you to set up tabulation sheets easily.

3. A secure, yet flexible, type of notebook for the tabulations is recommended. A spiral binding is a precaution against loss of data. However, a loose leaf notebook permits various sections of the data to be compared readily.

4. Dividing the data into "bite-size" segments and tabulating each section on a separate page ($8\frac{1}{2}$ x 11) is usually the best plan. Sometimes you might wish to include several related items on a single large sheet (17 x 22), but sheets any larger than this are difficult to handle and to work on accurately.

5. Every tally sheet should be labeled carefully to identify the group and item it shows. Each factor that is being tabulated should be listed with an appropriate heading or coding system.

6. In addition to allowing sufficient space for tallying each item, you should make provision for "no reply" and miscellaneous responses. Space for both horizontal and vertical totals should be allowed.

---

[7]Matilda White Riley, <u>Sociological Research: A Case Approach.</u> New York: Harcourt, Brace & World, Inc., 1963. Page 331.
[8]Royal McBee Corporation, Port Chester, New York.
    Burroughs Corporation, The Todd Company Division, Rochester, New York.

7. Colored lines help to differentiate between sections.

8. Tallies should be placed horizontally when only one set of data is being tabulated.

9. When you analyze one item for its relationship with two or more other items, the column totals should be cross-examined for accuracy. For example, if you tabulate the ways in which freshmen, sophomores, juniors, and seniors indicated that home economics classes have helped them, you should find the same number of students for each year in the total columns as in any other item that involves an analysis by freshmen, sophomores, juniors, and seniors.

SELECTED REFERENCES

Association for Supervision and Curriculum Development. *Research for Curriculum Improvement.* Washington, D.C.: The Association, a Department of the National Education Association, 1957. Pages 94-107.

Edwards, Allen L. *Experimental Design in Psychological Research.* Revised edition. New York: Holt, Rinehart and Winston, Inc., 1960. Pages 1-12.

Rummel, J. Francis. *An Introduction to Research Procedures in Education.* Second edition. New York: Harper & Row Publishers, Inc., 1964. Pages 227-255.

Whitney, Frederick L. *The Elements of Research.* Third edition. Englewood Cliffs, N.J.: Prentice-Hall, Inc., 1950. Pages 133-137.

Electronic Data Processing

Recent advances in electronic data-processing systems can take much of the tedious work out of research and enable you to use your human talent for conceptualization and decision making. The traditional IBM card, $3\frac{1}{2}$ x 7 3/8 inches in size, contains 80 columns, each of which has space for punching up to 12 items. Cards having different numbers of punching positions are produced by Remington-Rand and Underwood Corporation. When using these cards, you might devote the first few columns to a code number that identifies the individual participant. Usually you can plan questions so that one column can handle each response, although programs can be worked out for tabulating more complex data. Subjective or qualitative data can be processed in this manner providing they lend themselves to classification and coding.

A computer system receives, stores, and returns information. It can perform complex mathematical and logical operations on large quantities of data within a few minutes. Its operation consists of three steps: input, processing, and output. Since the computer is simply a tool, someone must analyze the problem into its logical components and work out a routine for the computer to follow. This consists of translating the steps into a symbolic language or code. This program and the data to be processed are called the input.

The computer can receive punched cards, punched paper tape, or magnetic tape which represent the data and the program to be processed. The computer senses the pattern of the holes or magnetic spots and sends electrical impulses to designated locations in its storage or memory unit. This coded information is readily available for processing and it can be retrieved in a fraction of a second. Although the storage capacity of any memory unit is limited, additional data can be stored outside the central processing unit on cards or magnetic tape, disks, or drums. The central processor of a computer consists of thousands of logic circuits which perform the most basic operations of a computer.

When the computer has finished carrying out the instructions for processing the input data, it can print the results in readable form or produce output on tape, punched cards, drums, or disks. It can draw graphs or send data over telephone lines to another computer.

Grossman and Howe summarized the advantages of electronic data processing as follows:

1. Speed.

2. Accuracy. Some computers include self-checking. Even if they do not, they make verification easier and more positive, and machine errors are more easily detectable.

3. Reproduction. A test score that is punched on a card or recorded on magnetic tape may be converted io a normative score, used in a statistical summary, posted on records, and collated with other data.

4. Accessibility, internal and external. Stored data may be located rapidly. Such data are readily available for conferences, research, historical review, or transmittal.

5. Collating. Test scores, grades, teacher ratings, and other data can be assembled from a variety of sources.

6. Compactness. Data may be stored, transmitted, and referenced in highly condensed form.

7. Automatic processes. Although it takes time to develop programs for handling data, the programs are reusable and can be shared. Automation makes it easier to perform traditional tasks and also makes feasible a number of tasks that were formerly considered impossible.

8. Dividends. It is difficult to prove that out-of-pocket costs are reduced by the introduction of data processing systems. The real 'economy' is in the saving of valuable professional time, energy, and skill, as well as in the improvement of the speed and quality of the data processing itself.[9]

Goodlad pointed out another advantage of electronic data processing methods-- *the anticipated installation of a computer forces its users to think more precisely about their objectives and to specify them in exact terms.*[10]

The possibilities for using a computer have barely been tapped. Grossman and Howe suggested the following ways in which a computer could be utilized effectively:

1. Conducting a school census

2. Setting up student programs and schedules

3. Reporting students' grades

4. Evaluating students

[9] Alvin Grossman and Robert Howe, "Human Economy and Data Processing." Personnel and Guidance Journal 43: 336-347; December 1964.

[10] John I. Goodlad et al. "Application of Electronic Data Processing Methods in Education." Project No. F-026, Cooperative Research Program of the Office of Education, U. S. Department of Health, Education, and Welfare. Department of Education, University of California, Los Angeles, 1965. Page 3.

     5. Identifying and placing students

     6. Accounting for attendance

     7. Recording information and testing hypotheses

     8. Reporting [11]

     Among the problems educators have experienced is that they do not know how to pre-pare the data for the computer and they are unable to use data coming from the computer. Goodlad commented that the problems are not with the capabilities of the computer but with the *"human sophistication required in conceptualizing the data needed, collecting them effi-ciently, and translating them into terms appropriate for computer processing."* As a guide to the range of tasks for which electronic data processing might be appropriate, he summa-rized three levels: (1) processing of large quantities of data; (2) pulling out relationships among categories of data; and (3) formulating research designs and making major deci-sions (see Table 1). Levels 1 and 2 are already being carried on in business, industry, and many educational systems. Many of the master's theses and doctoral dissertations of the past have been centered largely around patterns of relationships which could be handled within a brief period of time by a computer. Goodlad urged graduate schools to involve students in research studies requiring a higher level of conceptualization that will challenge the student's talent and expand our understanding of significant educational problems. [12]

SELECTED REFERENCES

Borg, Walter R. *Educational Research: An Introduction.* New York: David McKay Co., Inc., 1963
    Pages 351-359.
Borko, Harold (editor). *Computer Applications in the Behavioral Sciences.* Englewood Cliffs, N.J.:
    Prentice-Hall, Inc., 1962. Pages 50-203.

BASIC RESEARCH DESIGNS

     A variety of approaches can be used to obtain research evidence. Later chapters in this book will provide detailed information about the purposes and techniques involved in various methods of research. The emphasis in this section is simply to give an over-view of the kinds of research studies that are useful in home economics education and to introduce you to some of the factors that you should consider in planning the design of a study.

Purposes of Research Design

     Research design has four main purposes: (1) to identify relevant variables; (2) to select variables that are important ones to be controlled; (3) to exercise control through appropriate selection of a sample and choice of conditions for carrying out the study; and (4) to guard against bias in observing, recording, analyzing, and synthesizing data.

     Basically, research design is a decision-making process. You attempt to eliminate those factors existing <u>prior</u> to the introduction of an experimental variable that might pro-duce a change in the dependent variable, which could erroneously be attributed to the

---

[11]Grossman and Howe, op. cit., page 346.
[12]Goodlad, op. cit., pages 35-36.

TABLE 1
PROBLEMS IN EDUCATION APPROPRIATE FOR ELECTRONIC DATA PROCESSING[13]

	Level 1 Raw Data	Level 2 Relationships Among Data	Level 3 Decisions and Research
General Policy and Administration	Codification and systemization of school laws, sources of funds, health and safety regulations, etc.	Effect of new policies on school health and safety records.	Studies into the relationship between policies and teacher and student effectiveness.
	Results of polls on citizens' expectations for their schools.	Patterns of relationships among sub-publics and types of expectations for schools.	
		Relationships among types of administrative problems and processes used in decision-making.	Conceptualization of possible new relationships and simulation of the consequences of effecting these relationships administratively.
Faculty, Staff and Students	Comprehensive inventories of teacher and pupil background.	Relationships among factors such as age, institution attended, credential, etc., and teacher retention in the system.	
	Long-term collections of data on student achievement, attendance, health, dropout, etc.	Relationship between factors in school achievement and factors in students' health.	Prediction of students' success in school from longitudinal data, followed by deliberate manipulation of the environment and analysis of the consequences.
Budget and Financial Support	Statistics on school costs broken down into budgeted categories.		
	Maintenance of assessed evaluation statistics and data pertaining to proportion of district's income going to education.	Relationship between financial support and various evidences of school productivity.	
			Decisions pertaining to school bond elections and building construction in relation to alternative predictions of population growth and financial support, together with calculations pertaining to how much new industry will be attracted by new and better schools.
Facilities	Cost statistics on all aspects of school construction and maintenance.	Relationship between costs of various types of construction and costs of maintenance.	Manipulation of facilities to test hypotheses growing out of observations at Level 2.
Curriculum, Instruction, and Materials	Numbers of students in various patterns of curriculum.	Relationships between students' high school curriculum and later academic and work careers.	
	Students' responses on programmed lessons and courses.	Relationship between responses and age, I.Q., past achievement, etc.	Studies into students' learning styles and various provisions for them such as different sizes and types of groups.
	Storage and retrieval of data on students' assignments to individual instruction, large groups, small groups, etc.	Relationship between students' assignments and various aspects of students' success.	Manipulation of the instructional-grouping environment to test hypotheses growing out of observations at Level 2.

[13]Ibid., pages 12-14.

experimental variable. Further, you attempt to eliminate or balance-out the effects of factors existing <u>during</u> the experiment which migh produce a change in the dependent variable and thus be attributed erroneously to the experimental variable.

Suppose you were interested in a comparison of two methods of gearing the instruction in clothing classes to the varying needs of students from different social classes. What are some of the decisions you must make? You would be confronted with both major and minor decisions relative to the selection of individual students, the concepts to be taught, teaching materials, instructions, sequence of events, making observations, recording data, and the analysis and interpretation of the data. Decisions would be involved in relation to each of these points. For example, you would need to plan appropriate teaching materials for the study: (1) What steps in clothing construction should be illustrated with actual fabrics? (2) What verbal material should you include? (3) Toward what level should the verbal material be directed? (4) How should the materials be made available to the students? (5) How can the materials be kept in usable conditions? (6) What size should the materials be? (7) What will be the cost of preparing the materials? (8) Who will pay for the necessary materials? (9) Who will prepare them? and (10) How much time will be required for their preparation? Perhaps you can think of others.

One of the major questions with which educators are concerned is: What happens to different kinds of students who are subjected to different kinds of learning experiences? The basic design for such a study might include such factors as these:

Antecedent Factors $\longrightarrow$ Mediating Factors $\longrightarrow$ Behavioral Changes

Test scores	The curriculum	Self-concept changes
High school grades	Student's living condition	Value changes
Personality	Etc .	Success in college
Education of parents		
Etc.		

Models of Research Design

There is always a danger inherent in the use of a model. Presumably the model helps to clarify the kind of situation for which it is suited, but, at the same time, it may limit the learner's thinking to situations which fit into only one particular pattern. This should be kept in mind as you read these illustrations and you should try to see beyond them. Here is an opportunity for you to do some creative and critical thinking. Try to think of other examples of the kinds of variables which are described, and visualize exciting ways in which their effects on, or relationships with, each other might be studied.

The following cases have been adapted from Edwards' illustrations of how a psychologist deals with problems of predicting behavior. His ideas have proven to be adaptable and meaningful for home economics education studies. [14]

CASE 1: $O_x \rightarrow O_y$ (relationship between two organismic variables)

Example: Do boys grow in height at the same rate as girls between the ages of two and five?

---

[14]Allen L. Edwards, Experimental Design in Psychological Research. New York: Holt, Rinehart & Winston, Inc. , 1950. Pages 9-12.

CASE 2: $B_x \rightarrow B_y$ (relationship between two behavioral variables)

Example: Are the grades obtained in student teaching related to the ratings of performance during the first year of teaching?

CASE 3: $O_x \rightarrow B_y$ (relationship between an organismic variable and a behavioral variable)

Example: Do adults who are classified according to their educational level differ in their opinions about allowances for teenagers?

CASE 4: $B_x \rightarrow O_y$ (study of the behavioral differences between organisms in an attempt to relate these to an organismic variable)

Example: Can we predict from scores on the Graduate Record Examination which candidates will be "successful" and which ones "unsuccessful" in fulfilling the requirements for a master's degree?

CASE 5: $B_x \rightarrow S_y$ (attempts to predict the nature of the stimulus from observations of behavior)

Example: When teenage girls break into laughter during a home economics class, what was the cause of their reaction?

CASE 6: $S_x \rightarrow B_y$ (relationship between a stimulus variable and a behavioral variable)

Example: Do students differ in their acceptance of programmed material that is presented by a teaching machine and similar material that is presented in the form of a "tutor-text"?

CASE 7: $S_x \rightarrow O_y \rightarrow B_z$ (attempt to predict a behavioral variable from a stimulus variable operating in conjunction with an organismic variable)

Example: (A) More than one independent variable related to one dependent variable

When a self-instructional method of teaching is used with slow, average, and rapid learners, do the students of varying levels of ability make similar gains in achievement?

(B) Effects of one independent variable on several dependent variables

As problems of increasing difficulty are presented to slow learners, what effects are observable in their attitudes, motivation, and achievement?

You can think of many other illustrations of two-variable studies similar to those in Cases 1 - 6. Case 7 is concerned with more complicated research designs, where several variables are studied in one experiment. Methods of factorial design enable you to study the effects of two or more treatments and their interactions. These methods are beyond the scope of an introductory book on research methods, but you may obtain helpful information from some of the references at the end of this chapter.

Findings are considered only tentative until they have been replicated. When a large population is available, both the experimental and control groups can be divided to provide a test of the reliability of the findings with the other half. Replication helps to establish the extent to which a finding can be generalized.

Table 2 shows a model for an experiment in which two groups, experimental and control, are studied. Although this is just one of many possible variations of research design, you may learn from this example some of the procedures to consider when planning the design for a study in which you are interested.

TABLE 2

MODEL FOR AN EXPERIMENT

Procedure	Experimental Group	Control Group
Prior selection	Yes	Yes
"Before" measurement	Yes: E_I Test on scientific applications in the home	Yes: C_I Test on scientific applications in the home
Exposure to experimental variable	Yes A unit of study that emphasizes applications of science to the home through lectures, discussions, audio-visual materials, and laboratory experiments	No
Exposure to uncontrolled events	Yes	Yes
"After" measurement	Yes: E_{II}	Yes: C_{II}
Change (diff. = D)	$D_e = E_{II} - E_I$	$D_c = C_{II} - C_I$
Test for significant change	$D = D_e - D_c$	

Research Approaches

Research evidence can be obtained in a variety of ways. The major research methods and techniques will be discussed in detail in the next few chapters. They are merely being introduced in this chapter to give you an idea of various kinds of approaches that are useful in home economics education research.

An easy way to remember the major emphases of research methods is to think of them in terms of the view they take: (1) Has the event already happened? (2) Is the study concerned with a present event? or (3) Will the situation be created and studied in the future?

EVENTS OF THE PAST. --The purpose of historical research is to examine evidence from previous experience. To uncover valuable information, or to discover knowledge that has been overlooked, are worthy motives in themselves, but, in addition, historical research may help you to interpret a present problem.

Philosophical studies are not discussed in great detail in this book. However, they enable us to go beyond an analysis of what happens under certain circumstances and to discover how it happens. Many significant theories are developed through a philosophical process. We could benefit from more attempts to conceptualize in terms of the content and process of home economics education.

Ex post facto studies also take a look at the past in one of two ways: (1) to determine what has caused some behavior that is observed at the present time; or (2) to start with some condition in the past and study its effect on present behavior. The investigator is not able to actually manipulate factors that have operated in the past; he uses indirect means of manipulation by selecting and studying those persons or objects that he wants from the past.

PRESENT EVENTS. --Studies of current behavior or practices are referred to in this book as descriptive studies. These include the well-known opinion polls, questionnaire studies, and depth interviews through which respondents express their opinions or give factual answers. Questions may be objective in nature, or they may encourage the respondents to answer freely, with as much detail as they desire to give.

Normative survey studies involve the use of tests to determine the present standing of individuals in relation to a group, such as high school seniors in a particular school district. Sometimes it is possible to compare the performance of an individual or a group with norms that have been established on a citywide, statewide, or national basis.

Analytical studies are penetrating studies of an individual or event, looking back into the past but with emphasis on a thorough analysis of the present. Analytical or diagnostic studies include such problems as case studies of individuals or institutions, studies of trends in the development of courses of study, and detailed analyses of teaching materials.

PROJECTED EVENTS. --Controlled experimental studies enable you to compare the effectiveness of given procedures by trying them out under conditions that are set up particularly for this purpose. The emphasis in experiments is on the future, where non-relevant variables can be held constant and the experimental variable can be studied.

LONGITUDINAL STUDIES. --These represent an approach with which you should be familiar, one which takes a long-range view, following the same individuals over a long period of time. Genetic or longitudinal studies have definite advantages over the short-range studies that use a cross-sectional approach. For example, a cross-sectional approach could include the administration of a test on family values to a sample of home economics freshmen in a particular college and also to a sample of seniors in the same college. Perhaps the two groups were quite different as freshmen, so it is difficult to know how much of the change in family values can be attributed to college experiences. A longitudinal approach, on the other hand, would involve giving the test to a sample of the freshmen and then repeating that test with the same individuals when they become seniors.   However, the time and expense involved in keeping track of individuals over a period of years tend to discourage many investigators from undertaking longitudinal studies.

The Central Regional Co-operative Research Project in Home Economics Education employed both a cross-sectional and longitudinal approach.   In one part of this research, Ford studied attitudes of home economics teachers toward children.   The high attrition rate of a longitudinal study was revealed when her sample of 724 freshman subjects was reduced to 68 persons who completed the home economics education curriculum, taught one year, and for whom data were available.   She also studied a group of students who transferred into the institution as juniors.   They were measured again as seniors and first-year teachers.[15]

As you think back over this chapter and attempt to summarize it, keep in mind that the design of your research is a master plan to guide you throughout your study.   Sound principles of logic and basic steps in the scientific process help you to steer your course. Simple techniques that are involved in classifying and tabulating data act as road signs to point out economical ways of reaching your destination.

SELECTED REFERENCES

Hillway, Tyrus. *Introduction to Research.*   Second edition.   Boston: Houghton Mifflin Co. , 1964.
    Pages 99-106.
Townsend, John C.   *Introduction to Experimental Method.*   New York: McGraw-Hill Book Co. , Inc. ,
    1953.   Pages 52-88.
Whitney, Frederick L.   *The Elements of Research.*   Third edition.   Englewood Cliffs, N.J.: Prentice-
    Hall, Inc. , 1950.   Pages 131-151.
Zimny, George H.   *Method in Experimental Psychology.*   New York: Ronald Press Co. , 1961.   Pages
    158-186.

---

[15]Roxanna R. Ford, "Attitudes of Home Economics Teachers Toward Children." Journal of Home Economics 54: 466-469;
    June, 1962.

Chapter 5
HISTORY AND DEVELOPMENT OF HOME ECONOMICS

Perhaps nobody has changed the course
of history as much as the historians.
-- Franklin P. Jones

As mentioned in previous chapters, one of the early steps in formulating the design of a research study is to find out what has been done previously on your topic or in a related field. A survey of related literature, as it is frequently called, should give some background information about the development of your topic and may be, to a very limited degree, a form of historical research. However, historical research is much more penetrating and involves different techniques than those used in reviewing related literature. Good clarified the meaning of historical research in this way:

> *Viewed as research, history may be defined as an integrated narrative or*
> *description of past events or facts, written in the spirit of critical inquiry, to find*
> *the whole truth and report it.*[1]

DESCRIPTION AND VALUES OF HISTORICAL RESEARCH

Historical research has as its purpose the discovery and recording of significant events that took place in the past, the interpretation of trends in the attitudes or events of the past, and the suggestion of generalizations from these past events that might guide present or future behavior. Although historical research can help us to avoid repeating the same mistakes, its greatest value is that it provides a perspective for the future.

Types of Studies

Brickman has suggested several topics that lend themselves to the methods of historical research.[2] For example, in applying his suggestions to home economics, you might study the history of home economics, or some phase of it in a geographical region, a period of time, or an institution. If you choose to study the life of an individual, it is called biographic research. The development of home economics might be studied through an analysis of the trends revealed in its curriculum, teaching materials, finance, architecture, administration, or influence. Although the classification of research methods in this book is a convenience, it is important to remember that a research study may include more than one approach, but one usually predominates.

The following paragraphs illustrate how the methods of historical research have been applied in a few studies that pertain to home economics education. These are classified according to Brickman's list of possible topics.

[1]Carter V. Good, Essentials of Educational Research. New York: Appleton-Century-Crofts, Inc. , 1966. Page 145.
[2]William W. Brickman, Guide to Research in Educational History. New York: New York University Bookstore, 1949. Pages 5-6.

INNOVATIONS. --In 1954, Craig wrote a narrative account, tracing the history of home economics from early attempts in the seventeenth century to train girls for their home activities through the introduction and development of home economics education in the public schools, colleges and universities, and extension programs. She pointed out the contributions of cooking schools, World's Fair exhibits, land grant colleges, public schools, and Lake Placid Conferences to the early development of home economics. The role of legislation, research, and literature in extending the influence of home economics was revealed. As a supplement to her topical organization of historical events, she included a chronological summary of the "Milestones in Home Economics."[3]

BIOGRAPHY. --The American Home Economics Association published a tribute to its first president in the form of a biography, presenting the life of Ellen H. Richards from her childhood through her college years, her marriage, and her professional activities. In response to a request for material, first-hand information was obtained from her relatives, classmates, college friends, faculty associates, and professional organizations. The biography quoted from her diary, from letters written by her, and from testimonies of her personal friends.[4]

ORGANIZATION. --The American Home Economics Association made another contribution to the history of home economics by tracing the "forerunner movements," Lake Placid Conferences, and the founding and growth of the American Home Economics Association. The history included mention of the early leaders, the constitution and structure of the American Home Economics Association, and its special projects. The final chapter and appendix gave a concise, chronological summary of important dates and events as far back as 1821. In addition, the appendix listed the time, place, and attendance at the annual meetings; names of the elected officers; recipients of scholarships and fellowships; and statistics on the budget and membership of the American Home Economics Association.[5] A supplement has been prepared on the more recent history of this organization.[6]

PERIOD. --For her doctoral dissertation, Porch identified some of the trends and developments in home economics between 1909 and 1952. She showed parallel social changes that affected the American home and family during the same period of time. She traced these changes in terms of general socio-economic conditions affecting the family, changing functions of the family, and social thought influencing change. The changes that took place in home economics education were discussed in terms of philosophies and purposes, and the achievement of proposed objectives. All of her information about home economics was gathered from the Journal of Home Economics. She pointed out the possibility that we tend to accept things with which we are happy, so the things that were written about may indicate areas of dissatisfaction.[7]

INSTITUTION. --On the occasion of the fiftieth anniversary of the beginning of home economics at Michigan State University Gilchrist wrote a history of its first 30 years. She traced back to the organization of the Michigan Agricultural College and the entrance of women into the institution. She discussed the pioneer years of developing the women's course and equipping the Women's Building. In addition, she discussed the names and contributions of the personnel, the expansion of the curriculum, the opening of the new Home Economics Building, and the influence of related developments of student life.

---

[3]Hazel T. Craig, The History of Home Economics. New York: Practical Home Economics, 1945. 45 pages.

[4]Caroline L. Hunt, The Life of Ellen H. Richards. Washington, D. C.: American Home Economics Association, 1942. 328 pages.

[5]Keturah E. Baldwin, The AHEA Saga. Washington, D.C.: American Home Economics Association, 1949. 108 pages

[6]Mary Hawkins, The American Home Economics Association 1950-1958. Washington, D. C.: American Home Economics Association, 1959. 52 pages.

[7]Louise W. Porch, "Home Economics: Trends and Developments, 1909-52." Unpublished Ed. D. dissertation, Stanford University, 1955. 270 pages.

Direct quotations were made from such sources as an article in the Detroit Post, a letter from a student, copies from the Owasso Press, a commencement program, a report of the president to the Board of Regents, an address made by one of the professors, and course descriptions as outlined in the college catalogs.[8]

Benefits

The study of significant movements in the development of home economics inspires respect for the early leaders, develops understanding of the relationship between home economics and the society of which it is a part, gives insight into past mistakes that might be avoided, contributes to an understanding of contemporary problems, and may even be suggestive of new approaches that might be used in solving current problems.

SOURCES AND EVALUATION OF DATA

Source materials that are used in historical research are commonly divided into two types: (1) primary, or original sources--the person describing the event was actually present to observe it; and (2) secondary--the person describing the event was not actually present, but he took his description from someone else who may or may not have been present. As an illustration of this difference, a study of the nutritional values of school lunches might include a series of physical examinations recorded by the doctor who made the examinations. His records would be a primary source of data. If this doctor spoke to some organization about his research findings, a newspaper editor who was in attendance might review the lecture in one of his editorials. The newspaper editor is one step removed from the original materials, and no matter how accurately he presents the findings, his editorial would be a secondary source.

Primary sources which are useful in home economics studies include such materials as the following:

1. Oral--legends, folktales, family stories, personal observation or testimony of one who was present at the event, language

2. Written documents--records of state and local boards of education, reports of professional associations, committee reports, minutes of meetings, courses of study, or other documents that contain a first-hand description of the event

3. Physical remains--pottery, utensils, houses, furniture, equipment, costumes, textiles, and other museum pieces

4. Personal records--paintings, photographs, diaries, autobiographies, letters, manuscripts, or other records that were intended to convey information either for that time or for posterity

5. Motion picture or other films, recordings, drawings, paintings

Sometimes primary sources are not available or are difficult to locate, but they should be obtained whenever possible. Secondary sources are helpful in providing background and in presenting a full account of a situation. However, they should be selected carefully so that they represent only those documents which are based upon primary sources.

---

[8] Maude Gilchrist, The First Three Decades of Home Economics at Michigan State College, 1896-1926. East Lansing: Michigan State College, 1896-1926. East Lansing: Michigan State University, 1947. 92 pages.

Whether primary or secondary sources are used, the documents should be examined for their genuineness or authenticity (known as external criticism) and their meaning or credibility (known as internal criticism). The processes of external and internal criticism may overlap and be carried on simultaneously. External criticism seeks to answer questions such as the following: Why, where, when, and by whom was the document written? Is this document consistent in style with the writer's previous works, establishing him as the author? Did the author write about events or places which would be familiar to a person living in that period?

Internal criticism seeks to answer such questions as: What was the writer's intent (his real meaning, not the literal meaning)? Was the author capable of reporting accurately? Are there evidences that the writer was biased or illogical in his thinking? Were reliable sources used as the basis for his writing? Inaccurate reporting might stem from such factors as emotional stress, poor health, lack of intelligence, writing about an event after a lapse of time, political or other types of personal bias.

The person who writes historical research has seldom witnessed the original events about which he is writing, and these events cannot be reproduced. Therefore, he must strive to determine the reliability of the evidence he obtains. The evidence may be incomplete, deliberately biased, or otherwise defective. Since an individual tends to record only what he considers to be of interest or value, or what he chooses to make known to others, great expenditures of time and money are often required to locate complete and accurate information.

TREATMENT OF HISTORICAL DATA

Historical writing is not merely a compilation of all the facts you can accumulate on a given topic. Brickman summarized very succinctly the steps involved in synthesizing this kind of data:

> *The research worker must endeavor to be thoroughgoing in his search for sources, conscientious in his evaluation, cautious and fair-minded in his interpretation, and skillful in his synthesis.*[9]

In searching for historical sources, you must attempt to uncover all of the important material. Your selection of what to include in your report will be based upon such factors as the relevance of the data to the main headings in your outline and the size and cost of the final report.

Conscientious evaluation involves the presentation of sufficient supporting evidence to enable your reader and yourself to make a correct interpretation. In your interpretation, you must guard against reasoning from analogy or attempting to interpret some point on which the evidence was silent.

A report of historical research is not just a series of quotations or brief summaries of a vast amount of material. A skillful synthesis of historical information is essential in order for your reader to relate the facts you have gathered to each other and to understand the whole setting. The following suggestions are offered to assist you in writing historical research:

1. A topical organization of the data enables you to relate events pertaining to various topics, but this should usually be supplemented by a chronological listing of the most important events.

---

[9] Brickman, op. cit., page 189.

2. Resemblances or <u>analogies</u> in the events may be pointed out to make the report interesting and to form the basis for generalization.

3. <u>Relationships</u> between any single event and other events that preceded it or followed it should be noted. However, you must be cautious about assuming that one was caused by the other.

4. <u>Trends</u> may be pointed out by comparing the facts over a period of time or during two periods of time. The existence of a trend, however, does not necessarily make that trend desirable.

5. <u>Hypotheses</u> may be formulated after a thorough and critical study of the data. They are tested by re-examining the evidence and searching for further information from the past that deals with the relationships between parts of an event, or between a particular event and others that preceded or followed it. Good has cautioned against forcing data into a particular frame of reference, but he said that a hypothesis *"may become a central thesis, unifying theme, or principle of interpretation."*[10]

6. Some historians feel that their responsibility goes beyond that of hypothesizing about a single, unique event. As Van Dalen expressed it:

    They believe that it is important to study the past for the lessons it teaches, for the broad generalizations or laws that can be derived from a study of historical facts....   They believe historians can discover and formulate the fixed laws that govern human events just as scientists have discovered natural laws that govern phenomena in the physical world.[11]

SELECTED REFERENCES

American Home Economics Association. *Home Economics Research 1909-1959.* Washington, D.C.: American Home Economics Association, 1960. 58 pages.

Borg, Walter R. *Educational Research: An Introduction.* New York: David McKay Co., Inc. 1963. Pages 188-201.

Good, Carter V. *Essentials of Educational Research.* New York: Appleton-Century-Crofts, Inc., 1966. Pages 145-189.

Hillway, Tyrus. *Introduction to Research.* Second edition. Boston: Houghton Mifflin Co., 1964. Pages 141-164.

Scott, M. Gladys (editor). *Research Methods in Health, Physical Education, Recreation.* Second edition. Washington, D.C.: American Association for Health, Physical Education, and Recreation, 1959. Pages 465-481.

Whitney, Frederick L. *The Elements of Research.* Third edition. Englewood Cliffs, N.J.: Prentice-Hall, Inc., 1950. Pages 203-207.

---

[10]Carter V. Good, <u>Essentials of Educational Research</u>. New York: Appleton-Century-Crofts, Inc., 1966. Page 182.

[11]D. B. Van Dalen, "The Historical Method" <u>in</u> M. Gladys Scott, <u>Research Methods in Health, Physical Education, Recreation.</u> Second edition. Washington, D. C.: American Association for Health, Physical Education, and Recreation, 1959. Page 468.

Chapter 6

DESCRIPTION OF THE PRESENT STATUS OF HOME ECONOMICS

Knowledge comes from noticing
resemblances and recurrences
in the things that happen around us.
-- Wilfred Trotter

The type of educational research with which most persons are familiar has as its principal purpose the description of present achievement, opinion, method, or other specific characteristics. Descriptive studies may be analytical in nature, attempting to discover what elements comprise a given situation and how each part functions. Other studies, which we classify as descriptive-survey, are conducted as a means of learning common characteristics or behavior, status of a group or institution, widely accepted opinion on a given topic, or trends in any of these factors.

DESCRIPTIVE-ANALYSIS RESEARCH

If you were to engage in an analytical study, you would view some event or behavior thoroughly with the intention of discovering its components. In addition, you would study the structure or manner in which the factors fit together to give the over-all effect. Presumably, characteristics that were observed to be closely related to one group but not to the other might have some causal relationship to the factor on which the groups differ. From a careful analysis, clues might be revealed that would point toward the desirability of further studies on cause-effect relationships. Present goals might be clarified and new ways of reaching goals might be discovered.

Illustrative Studies

Analytical description might be helpful in situations such as the following, which have been chosen from studies in home economics.

DIFFERENTIATING CHARACTERISTICS OF PERFORMANCE. --As part of an article on the importance of research for home economics teachers, Hatcher summarized briefly a study that was planned cooperatively by members of the state research committee for home economics education in Michigan. The purpose of the study was to contribute toward an understanding of the differences that characterized the teaching performance of superior home economics teachers and of teachers who were experiencing difficulties. The sample included 21 home economics teachers, 20 school superintendent, 114 high school home economics students, and 78 mothers of these students. Basically, the same questions were used with all of the groups. Information was obtained chiefly through individual and group interviews, although it was supplemented by college records and records of the State Board for Vocational Education. In reviewing the findings, Hatcher listed seven characteristics of superior teachers. She suggested that teachers be encouraged to compare their own characteristics with those of the superior teachers and to strive for improvement. [1]

TEXTBOOK ANALYSIS. --Nelson felt that junior high school students experienced difficulty in reading and understanding printed materials. She studied the vocabulary of widely-used books to determine the extent to which junior high school girls were familiar with the meaning of the words. Her analysis covered nine books in their entirety and sections of five other books, including more than 3,500 pages. She recorded each technical term and the number of times it appeared. Two equivalent test forms, containing multiple-choice items from all areas of home economics, were developed to measure students' knowledge of the meaning of these technical terms. The tests were given in 27 schools, one of which was in a large city and the others were selected at random from Minnesota towns with a population of 4,000 or less. A total of 1,911 girls in grades 7, 8, and 9 took the tests both in September and again near the end of the semester. They also filled out the Sewell Socio-economic Status Scale. Her analysis related the test scores and three types of background information: (1) size of the town in which they attended school; (2) amount of instruction they had had in home economics; and (3) scores on the Socio-economic Status Scale. [2]

CLASSIFICATION OF OBJECTIVES. --A major contribution in classifying educational objectives was made by Bloom and others in Taxonomy of Educational Objectives. [3] This book deals with the classification of objectives in the "cognitive domain" -- those concerned with the recall and recognition of knowledge. Affective goals, concerned with interests, attitudes, appreciations, and values, can also influence what is learned in home economics, as in other subject areas. Bloom's classification is useful in any field of study and is not specifically directed to home economics education. A classification of the objectives and content of home economics could be a real contribution to our profession. It must have a sound research base and not be merely a representation of one person's opinion.

COURSES OF STUDY. --Merritt and Harap have made a series of studies pointing out trends in the production of teaching guides. Their analysis of courses of study which were published from 1951 through 1953 covered 796 guides from 185 school systems. They summarized trends under the following headings:

Output: Type of school system, grade level, and subject

Format: Rating of typography, index, margins, spatial arrangement, illustrations, mimeographed versus printing, length, covers

Leadership in Curriculum Development: Committee procedures, teachers, supervisors, consultants, workshop groups, lay persons

Role of Experimentation and Research: Number tried in classroom before publication

Scope of Introductory Treatment: General objectives of the subject, stages of child development, basic views of education, suggestions to teacher

Organization into Units of Work: Subdividing into functional, lifelike activities

---

[1] Hazel M. Hatcher, Characteristic Differences among Homemaking Teachers of Varying Proficiency. Bulletin No. 288. Lansing, Michigan: State Board of Control for Vocational Education, 1944. (As found in Hazel M. Hatcher, "What Research Offers to the Homemaking Teacher." Journal of Home Economics 35: 151-153; March, 1943.)

[2] M. Joyce Nelson, "Technical Vocabulary in Texts used in Junior High Schools." Journal of Home Economics 45: 658-659; November, 1953.

[3] Benjamin S. Bloom et al., Taxonomy of Educational Objectives. New York: David McKay Co., Inc., 1956. Pages 201-207.

Use of Community Resources: Field trips, tours, excursions, interviews

Adjusting Instruction to Individual Differences: Levels of difficulty and interests of the students

Evaluation of the Results of Learning: Suggested evaluation procedures and techniques in terms of goals, sample tests.[4]

JOB ANALYSIS.--For her master's thesis, Halstead developed a checklist to clarify the responsibilities carried or shared by home economics teachers in the high school. A class of graduate students from seven states compiled a list of activities in which they had participated as home economics teachers. The leaders in home economics education from the University of Minnesota, Purdue University, University of Nebraska, and Michigan State University gave additional suggestions. The checklist was divided into three sections: classroom, school, and community activities. The questionnaire was mailed to the vocational home economics teachers in Michigan. Replies, which were received from 182 teachers, indicated their degree of participation in each responsibility as well as their enjoyment of it. Descriptive data on the size of school and the amount of teaching experience were provided also.[5]

A job analysis may be approached by having persons with a strong general background and good judgment analyze their concepts of the position. Another approach is to review written materials which describe the duties of workers in that position. A third approach is to ask persons who are engaged in the work what they actually do, and what proportion of their time is devoted to the various phases of their work. Roskie incorporated these steps in planning a home economics program for beginning teachers when she: *(1) formulated a list of characteristics of high school programs based on a review of literature; (2) derived and tried out a checklist with several types of persons who had been associated with a home economics program; and (3) had 14 beginning teachers try out the program that was judged to be desirable.*[6]

CONCEPT.--The American Vocational Association studied job satisfaction of teachers --the factors that influenced home economics teachers to remain in or to leave the teaching profession. The nationwide study of secondary school home economics teachers was conducted in February, 1947. Regional and state research chairmen were chosen. At regional conferences, state supervisors and teacher educators compiled lists of reasons for teachers to be satisfied or dissatisfied with teaching. From their experience with teachers and the results of previous studies, they assembled 196 statements which were classified into seven categories: salary, living conditions, community conditions, marriage and family, school conditions, teaching load, and profession. Descriptive information was obtained concerning the community in which the teacher was employed, her residence, family responsibilities, salary, and teaching experience. In addition, four statements were adapted from the Job Satisfaction Blank by Hoppock to obtain the teacher's general reaction to her job.

The instruments were tried out first by teachers from 41 states, who criticized the items for their clarity and suggested additional items which were important in their satisfaction with teaching. Reliability coefficients between the odd and even items of the entire scale and each of the seven categories were determined. The revised forms were sent to

[4] Eleanor Merritt and Henry Harap, Trends in Production of Curriculum Guides. Nashville, Tennessee: Division of Surveys and Field Services, George Peabody College for Teachers, 1955. 43 pages

[5] Georgia Halstead, "Determining the Activities for which Home Economics Teachers Carry or Share Responsibility in the High School." Unpublished Master's thesis, Michigan State University, 1945. 53 pages.

[6] Gertrude Roskie, "The Homemaking Program for Beginning Teachers." Unpublished Doctor's dissertation, Stanford University, 1953. (As abstracted in Journal of Home Economics 46: 199-200; March, 1954.)

each home economics teacher in states having fewer than 126 teachers, and to a systematic sampling of teachers in states having more than 125 teachers. A total of 4,668 answer sheets were returned; a sub-sample of 971 was drawn as a basis for the statistical analysis. The Douglass formula was used to compute teaching load.[7]

General Procedures

If you are planning to do an analytical type of study, you will first want to be sure that the necessary materials can be made available for your use. These might include textbooks, magazines, newspapers, courses of study, or other types of documents.

Next, you will need to decide on what characteristics you plan to consider and then define them carefully. Good pointed out *that earlier forms of documentary analysis dealt primarily with measuring such aspects as sentence length, word difficulty, picture content, topics, space allotment, grade placement, and vocabulary load. Since approximately 1940, more complex analyses have appeared: analysis of propaganda in films, radio, and print in relation to truth and responses sought from individuals; dominant images in Shakespeare's plays, values in American plays compared with German plays of the same period, treatment of minority ethnic groups in short stories, manner in which motion pictures reflect popular feelings and desires.*[8]

Good outlined the variety of possible applications of content analysis:

Characteristics of Content: Substance

Characteristics of Content: Form

> *To expose propaganda techniques; to measure readability; to discover stylistic features*

Producers of Content

> *To identify the intentions and other characteristics of the communicators; to detect the existence of propaganda*

Audience of Content

> *To reflect attitudes, interests, and values (cultural patterns) of population groups*

Effects of Content

> *To reveal the focus of attention; to describe attitudinal and behavioral responses to communication.*[9]

Forming suitable categories will aid you in classifying your data. Good listed the following primary uses of classification which he defined as: *"the recognition of similarities and differences among experiences."*

> *1. To provide codified data, as in dividing the data of the United States census or school census according to sex, age, place of residence, nationality, and the like*

---

[7]American Vocational Association, Factors Affecting the Satisfactions of Home Economics Teachers. Research Bulletin No. 3. Washington, D.C.: American Vocational Association, 1948. 96 pages.

[8]Carter V. Good, Essentials of Educational Research. New York: Appleton-Century-Crofts, Inc., 1966. Pages 266-268.

[9]Ibid., pages 272-273.

2. To form useful classes according to kind, as in classifying and reporting frequencies for the reasons high-school pupils give for leaving school before graduation

3. To afford logical order and system, as in cataloguing books in the library according to a system

4. To develop the meaning of class concepts, as in examining court decisions to determine the meaning of the category "discretionary powers of school boards"

5. To create cases through delimitation, as in studying parent-child relationships by taking different cultures (probably in different parts of the world) as representing varying categories of parental behavior

6. To standardize observations that describe, as in studying the behavior of mothers during their visits to pediatricians working in clinics

7. To select and categorize scale indicators, as in determining that the manner of a particular pediatrician is positive and reassuring (rather than negative, disturbing, and offensive) by counting the number of instances of detailed behavior classified under these different categories.[10]

SELECTED REFERENCES

Good, Carter V. *Essentials of Educational Research.* New York: Appleton-Century-Crofts, Inc., 1966. Pages 266-274.
Rummel, J. Francis. *An Introduction to Research Procedures in Education.* Second edition. New York: Harper & Row Publishers, Inc., 1964. Pages 163-173.
Whitney, Frederick L. *The Elements of Research.* Third edition. Englewood Cliffs, New Jersey: Prentice-Hall, Inc., 1950. Pages 175-182.

DESCRIPTIVE-SURVEY RESEARCH

Surveys have become so common that they are frequently held in disrepute. Nevertheless, purposeful surveys which are well-planned and analyzed have an important place in home economics education. Their principal contribution is in describing current practices or beliefs with the intent of justifying existing practices or making intelligent plans for improving educational conditions or processes in a local situation. Sometimes an investigator not only ascertains present status but determines its adequacy by comparing it with selected standards or norms. A normative-survey study is concerned with identifying "norms" of behavior under certain conditions, as in the standardization of a test that indicates the raw scores or percentiles of a representative sample of boys and girls to whom it was administered early in its preparation.

Davis described the purposes and possible limitations of a survey as follows:

The general purposes of the survey are to reveal current conditions, to point up the acceptability of the status quo, and to show the need for changes. If the survey involves the help of several persons in addition to the surveyor and if they are not interested in conducting careful research or in carrying out the purposes of the survey, the pertinent facts remain either undiscovered or unreported. Furthermore,

---

[10]*Ibid.*, page 195.

some surveys are financially supported by persons who, when they see the findings, resolutely object to a certain finding and demand that no report be made of it. . . . These unfortunate possibilities do not eliminate the survey as a method worthy of consideration in conducting some research. [11]

As a teacher or administrator, you may support a proposed change in the home economics program by reporting upon typical patterns and their success in other institutions. Needs that have been overlooked may be brought to light as you compare your practices with those of other teachers or institutions. A group whose practices are well above average can give leadership in helping others identify ways of improving their programs. Frequently, a survey opens up new vistas that aid in meeting current problems.

Suitable Topics

A survey may be an appropriate means of making a follow-up study of the graduates of a home economics program; describing the characteristics of students, teachers, or some other group; discovering opinions about a home economics program or any part of it; determining the trends in enrollment, course offerings, or teaching methods; or comparing a group or individual with norms established by testing.

Van Dalen categorized the kinds of information sought in most school surveys. A study may explore several areas or probe intensively into specific aspects of one area.

1. The setting for learning--legal, administrative, social, physical, board of education rulings, bonded indebtedness, per-pupil cost, school plant, health and safety conditions, cafeteria, library; size, length, and frequency of classes; social structure in the classroom, home, or community that may influence learning.

2. The characteristics of educational personnel--sex, age, nationality, education, degrees, socio-economic background, group memberships, income, residence, certification, tenure, retirement status; behavior of instructional personnel in the classroom, their department, and in the community; physical fitness; attitudes on various questions; nature and number of their contacts with colleagues, students, and community; levels of expectation they hold for themselves, students, school, and community; their duties and amount of time devoted to each.

3. The nature of students--their behavior patterns in classrooms, with peers, at home, and in the community; family's socio-economic status; health, attitude, knowledge, skills, academic achievements, intelligence, aptitudes, work or study habits, likes and dislikes, extracurricular activities, work or travel experiences, play and recreational activities, reading habits, health practices, diet, attendance, drop-out records, number and type of handicapped or other exceptional students, number and nature of disciplinary incidents.

4. The educational process--what is and is not included in the curriculum; time allotments for various aspects of each activity; nature and amounts of various types of content in textbooks and instructional materials; nature and number of school services--health, library, guidance, research, adult education; kinds and degrees of acceleration or retardation among students in various subjects and on different academic levels. [12]

---

[11] Elwood C. Davis, "The Survey." in M. Gladys Scott, <u>Research Methods in Health, Physical Education, Recreation</u>. Second edition. Washington, D.C.: American Association for Health, Physical Education, and Recreation, 1959. Page 253.

[12] Deobold B. Van Dalen and William J. Meyer, <u>Understanding Educational Research</u>. New York: McGraw-Hill Book Co., Inc., 1962. Pages 189-190.

A few studies from home economics education have been chosen to illustrate some of these uses of descriptive surveys.

ATTITUDES. --The California cooperative study of attitudes toward home economics education sought answers to three questions: (1) why students do or do not enroll in home economics classes; (2) how home economics helps students, schools, and communities; and (3) what can be done to strengthen the home economics program in California public schools.

A pilot study was conducted to determine the procedures that might be used to greatest advantage. A systematic sample of 49 schools was chosen from an alphabetical listing of all the public secondary schools in California that offered home economics courses. In each school, a regional supervisor from the California State Department of Education held an individual interview with the home economics teachers, counselors, principal, district superintendent, and a school board member. The regional supervisor also led two group conferences in each school--one conference was for parents, and the other conference was for teachers of subjects other than home economics. In addition, questionnaires were given in regular class periods to the home economics students, and, in other classes, to selected students who were not enrolled in home economics courses. Questionnaires were mailed to former students who had taken home economics when they were in high school and who had graduated within five years prior to the study.

Each group of participants provided certain types of descriptive data, such as information about marital status, occupation, education, home and community activities. Basically, the questions about home economics were similar for each group, including such questions as: Should every high school boy and girl take home economics? Why don't more high school students take home economics courses? How do home economics classes help high school students the most? What could the home economics department do to give other students and people in the community a better understanding of what it does? What could the home economics department do to make its classes more enjoyable? [13]

PRACTICES. --The University of California, Los Angeles, sponsored a study to discover the nature and extent of home economics education for boys in California and to ascertain the problems confronting administrators and teachers in providing such home economics programs. A questionnaire was mailed to the principal of each school whose annual report to the California State Department of Education indicated that classes had been available for boys during the preceding year. The principals were asked what led their schools to offer home economics for boys, what difficulties had been encountered, how effective they considered various types of programs, and what they would recommend for strengthening the preparation of teachers. The head of each home economics department provided information about the background of the school program, the type of curriculum offered to boys, and the teacher's preparation for teaching boys. In addition, each home economics teacher who had boys in her classes was asked what types of programs she thought were suitable for boys and what experiences were most beneficial in the background of the teacher. Completed questionnaires were returned by 35 administators, 31 heads of home economics departments, and 46 home economics teachers. [14]

ACHIEVEMENT. --Minnesota conducted a five-year study of the effectiveness of the home economics programs in its high schools, the factors that appeared to be related to their effectiveness, and ways of improving the home economics programs. Twenty participating schools were chosen within a radius of approximately 100 miles of St. Paul.

[13] Olive A. Hall, What's the Next Move in Homemaking Education? Bulletin 24, No. 2. Sacramento: California State Department of Education, 1955. 133 pages.

[14] Olive A. Hall, "Homemaking Education for Boys in California." California Journal of Secondary Education 30: 391-395; November, 1955.

When it was possible, the schools whose departments were receiving reimbursement from vocational funds were matched with those that did not receive reimbursement. Size of community, size of school, per cent of nonresident students, economic level, and school support were some of the factors considered in selecting the schools. Visits were made to each school in the fall and spring of the first four years and in the spring of the fifth year. Workshops and conferences at the University supplemented the visits. Tests, score cards, check lists, and record forms were constructed and employed. Pencil-and-paper tests, practical tests of meal preparation, the scoring of garments made during the year, checklists indicating students' activities and opinions, and records of foods eaten for one week were among the evaluation techniques used. Statistical analyses included the average, variability, significance of differences between groups, and correlation. Regression equations were developed for predicting achievement at each grade level. [15]

PROBLEMS. --Gillaspie analyzed unsolicited letters that were received by Good Housekeeping Magazine from July, 1944 through June, 1945. She assumed that the questions asked in these letters indicated the needs of typical consumers and that the letters resulted from their initiative in trying to find answers to their problems. Each question was placed on a card, together with any identification data that were available, such as: sex of the person asking the question, whether or not the person was married, the month in which the question was asked, the size of community, and the state from which the question was received. The questions were classified and interpreted according to the major area of interest they represented: housing, household care, home laundry, and special management problems; foods and nutrition; personal appearance and grooming; babies and small children; special occasions and recreation; health and safety; and vocational interests. [16]

INTERESTS. --Johnson reported a preliminary study that was planned as the first of a series to develop a special vocational interest inventory in home economics. The trial form consisted of 448 items that were grouped in three sections: (1) abilities to be rated on a five-point scale according to the extent of one's like or dislike; (2) job characteristics and environmental factors to be rated on a five-point scale according to the extent to which the respondent considered them desirable; and (3) miscellaneous statements to be ranked in order of preference. Of the 1,884 inventories that were mailed to persons employed in 14 home economics professions, 1,175 replies were received. Since too few returns were received from four groups, only 10 occupational analyses were made. Chi square was used to select the items that would differentiate among the occupational groups. Further investigations were suggested for developing scoring keys for the occupations that were not included in this study and for developing norms for each occupational group. [17]

UNDERSTANDING OF CONCEPTS. --Burton studied the opinions students held toward home economics courses and professions. The Information Inventory contained questions which were designed to find out how interesting, challenging, and functional the person considered the home economics curriculum to be and how much understanding the respondent had of the scope, working conditions, qualifications of workers, responsibilities, and satisfactions derived from home economics professions. The professional categories included teaching and home demonstration work, research, child development and nursery school education, hospital dietetics and public health nutrition, and home economics in business. Responses of 71 specialists in home economics professions were compared

[15] Clara B Arny, The Effectiveness of the High School Program in Home Economics. Minneapolis: University of Minnesota Press, 1952. 319 pages.

[16] Beulah V. Gillaspie, Consumer Questions and Their Significance. No. 947. New York: Bureau of Publications, Teachers College, Columbia University Press, 1949. 129 pages.

[17] Hildegard Johnson, "Development of a Home Economics Interest Inventory." Journal of Applied Psychology 36: 338-341; October, 1952.

with those of 607 freshman women from five institutions of higher learning in Arizona. The students included both home economics majors and non-home economics majors. The t test was used to evaluate the significance of obtained differences.[18]

Conducting a Survey

If you are planning to conduct a survey, you might benefit from answering the following questions before you start gathering data:

1. What is my main purpose, and what are my subpurposes?

2. Have I defined the scope and nature of my study adequately?

3. Can I be objective in approaching this problem?

4. Are my assumptions well-founded and my hypotheses testable?

5. Do I have the personal qualifications and the time to conduct this survey?

6. Am I familiar with what other researchers have found when they have conducted surveys on topics similar to mine?

7. Is a survey the best way to obtain the desired information?

8. If the assistance of other persons would be necessary, is it likely that I could find available persons who are qualified and interested in this study?

9. Have I consulted my superiors and any colleagues whose cooperation would be essential or desirable in carrying out my study?

10. Are there any regulations or customs that might affect my freedom in obtaining the kinds of information desired?

11. Are adequate supplies, equipment, and facilities available?

12. Have I allowed for a pilot study or pretest to try out my instruments and determine the feasibility of the approach I plan to use?

13. Do the respondents know the information I am seeking to obtain?

14. Is it reasonable to ask informants to provide the kinds of information which are necessary?

15. What source or sources of information would be best in helping me to fulfill my purposes? Are they available?

16. What methods of collecting data will be best from the standpoint of validity and reliability of the data within the limits of the time and other resources available?

17. Do I have adequate financial resources to complete the study--to gather the necessary data, analyze and interpret it, and prepare a report of pertinent facts?

18. Is there a likelihood, or even a possibility, that changes could be made if certain changes should be recommended as a result of my proposed study?

---

[18] Byrd Burton, "A Study of Opinions of College Freshman Women about Home Economics and Related Professional Fields." Unpublished Doctor's dissertation, Pennsylvania State University, 1954. (As abstracted in Journal of Home Economics 47: 202-203; March, 1955.

Cook has given illustrations of analytical, developmental, predictive, and survey studies. Each report is followed by a critical analysis, which would help a beginning researcher to avoid common pitfalls.[19]

SELECTED REFERENCES

Hillway, Tyrus. *Introduction to Research.* Second edition. Boston: Houghton Mifflin Co., 1964. Pages 187-195.

Parten, Mildred B. *Surveys, Polls, and Samples.* New York: Harper & Row Publishers, Inc., 1950. Pages 48-50.

Scott, M. Gladys. *Research Methods in Health, Physical Education, Recreation.* Second edition. Washington, D.C.: American Association for Health, Physical Education, and Recreation. 1959. Pages 252-264.

CASE STUDY AND GENETIC METHODS

The descriptive methods that have been presented thus far enable you to obtain a picture of a group. For some purposes, you might prefer a penetrating study of an individual rather than a survey of many persons. As Hillway pointed out, the survey and case study methods can supplement each other:

> *When human beings constitute the subject matter of a study, actual examples of the experiences and the development of individual histories add reality to the picture. Quantitative data tend generally to make the description abstract; case histories can make it human.*[20]

A case study, or intensive investigation of one person, can provide insight into the characteristics of an exceptional person, such as a gifted learner, slow learner, underprivileged, maladjusted, delinquent, highly successful or unsuccessful person. Through a careful, thorough study of an individual, you can learn about factors that are associated with high or low achievement in home economics courses.

The case method is useful in studying an institution or community as well as with an individual. One widely-known example is the community case study by Hollingshead.[21] It can be used also to study a family, school, college, organization, or other community institution.

As Good pointed out, case and genetic studies have common interests in growth and development. The case study looks backward whereas the genetic study moves forward.[22] The genetic method is similar to a case study except that the observations are repeated with the same individuals at specific intervals, usually covering a long period of time. A classic illustration of a genetic study may be found in Terman's comprehensive report of gifted children and their development.[23] He studied a large number of cases and included a variety of characteristics. A later investigation followed these same individuals into their adult lives.[24]

---

[19]David R. Cook, A Guide to Educational Research. Boston: Allyn & Bacon, Inc., 1965. Pages 39-101.

[20]Tyrus Hillway, Introduction to Research. Second edition. Boston: Houghton Mifflin Co., 1964. Pages 238-239.

[21]August B. Hollingshead, Elmtown's Youth. New York: John Wiley & Sons, Inc., 1949. 480 pages.

[22]Carter V. Good, Introduction to Educational Research. Second edition. New York: Appleton-Century-Crofts, Inc., 1963. Page 391.

[23]Louis M. Terman et al., Genetic Studies of Genius: I. Mental and Physical Traits of a Thousand Gifted Children. Stanford, Calif.: Standard University Press, 1925. 648 pages.

[24]Louis M. Terman and Melita H. Oden, Genetic Studies of Genius: IV. Twenty-Five Years' Follow-Up of a Superior Group. Stanford, Calif.: Stanford University Press, 1947. 448 pages.

Sources of data for a case study or genetic approach are similar to those used in historical and descriptive studies. You might include personal interviews with the subjects, observations, personal documents such as diaries and letters, newspaper records, health examinations, standardized test scores for psychological and social measures, school records, and records from community agencies. You may endeavor, through sources such as these, to obtain information about an individual's home and family background, his habits and interests, the neighborhood in which he lives or has resided, his present status, diagnosis of difficulties he is having and their causes, physical status and growth, mental test scores, and personality traits. Your emphasis in doing this type of study is the individual. You describe and explain the principal factors which have contributed to his present status and their causes.

The analysis of data for a case or genetic study probably will be in terms of identifying patterns or events rather than in terms of statistical analyses. Although you cannot generalize from single cases, you can draw meaningful conclusions from replications when the individuals have been selected at random.

SELECTED REFERENCES

Good, Carter V. *Essentials of Educational Research.* New York: Appleton-Century-Crofts, Inc., 1966. Pages 310-344.
Hillway, Tyrus. *Introduction to Research.* Second edition. Boston: Houghton Mifflin Co., 1964. Pages 238-245.
Scott, M. Gladys (editor). *Research Methods in Health, Physical Education, Recreation.* Second edition. Washington, D.C.: American Association for Health, Physical Education, and Recreation, 1959. Pages 264-276.
Whitney, Frederick L. *The Elements of Research.* Third edition. Englewood Cliffs, N.J.: Prentice-Hall, Inc., 1950. Pages 172-175.

Chapter 7

EXPERIMENTATION ON THE TEACHING OF HOME ECONOMICS

Leave the beaten track occasionally and dive into the woods. You will be certain to find something you have never seen before.

-- Alexander Graham Bell

In everyday conversation, people frequently say that they are going "to try" something. A creative homemaker makes a miniature research laboratory out of her home-- she experiments with new recipes or variations of old ones, she tries a new method of washing the floor, she discovers the easiest way to remove soil from the children's clothes, she strives to show her love for her children and yet help them to develop independence and a sense of responsibility. In these, and many other ways, she is experimenting. She is trying to discover the relationships between certain causes and their effects and to develop new and improved ways of doing her job as a homemaker.

Teaching also affords many opportunities for an alert, creative person to experiment with new and improved ways of understanding students, stimulating their interest in learning, and helping them to understand what they study. Within the limits set by the school environment and its resources, a teacher who is interested may try new approaches for solving the problems which arise daily. Merely trying something different, however, does not mean that a teacher is doing research. Experimentation is distinguished by control. Designing a study involves planning and making decisions in anticipation of the situations that are expected to arise. To receive optimum value from meaningful experimentation, a teacher must possess considerable skill and understanding of research procedures. Carefully controlled experiments contribute significant information in the highest levels of research studies; without careful control, an experiment is little more than a survey conducted on a small scale.

According to Rummel:

The major purpose of experiments is to describe the effect of certain treatments upon some characteristic of a group or population and to test some hypothesis about this effect. In planning experiments it is not only necessary to consider how to describe or measure the desired effect, but it is also necessary to consider how to test its significance.[1]

Zimny defined an experiment as:

Objective observation of phenomena which are made to occur in a strictly controlled situation in which one factor is varied and the others are kept constant.[2]

---

[1] J. Francis Rummel, An Introduction to Research Procedures in Education. Second edition. New York: Harper & Row Publishers, Inc., 1964. Page 179.

[2] George H. Zimny, Method in Experimental Psychology. New York: Ronald Press Co., 1961. Page 18.

The major emphasis in this chapter is on controlled experimental research, the purpose of which is to test hypotheses about the effects of certain treatments on specific characteristics of a group.   However, the latter part of the chapter presents information on an uncontrolled approach, known as action research.   As a teacher, you can make constructive use of this approach in finding solutions to the practical problems you face daily in your classroom.   Action research is specific and valuable for its contributions to one teacher or a group of teachers.   On the other hand, a controlled experiment can be repeated by another investigator, or by the same investigator on another occasion, with nearly identical results.

CONTROLLED EXPERIMENTAL RESEARCH

When you experiment in a natural or operational setting, such as a school, you can not expect to achieve the high degree of control that would be possible for a scientist to achieve in a laboratory.   Nevertheless, if you plan carefully, you can obtain data from which you can estimate the degree of error which may affect your findings, and you can test the significance of any differences which occur.   In some instances you can achieve a high degree of control prior to starting the experimental treatment.   Sometimes you exert measures of control while you are conducting the experiment or during the statistical analysis of the data.

Control can be achieved either by: (1) holding constant the variables that are extraneous to your hypothesis to prevent them from changing; or (2) deliberately causing a variable that is pertinent to your hypothesis to change in a prescribed manner.   You manipulate the independent variable and study its effects on the dependent variables.   The purpose of control is to help you answer the question, "How certain can I be that I really know what I think I know?   The level of certainty at which you accept or reject a hypothesis is a function of the accuracy with which you can identify, measure, and manipulate the relevant variables.

Errors and Their Control

As an experimenter, you have the opportunity and the responsibility to take definite steps to insure unbiased results of your study.   You need to understand what kinds of errors can produce differential effects on the groups you are studying, what steps you can take to insure a random distribution of errors, and what tests of significance are appropriate for you to use under the particular circumstances of your study.   More important than a knowledge of what to control and how to exercise the necessary control is the judgment as to what level of control should be attempted.   At times an inadequately controlled study may suggest leads to a more penetrating study.   Preoccupation with controls may cause you to select a problem for its ease of investigation rather than for its significance.

ERRORS AFFECTING EXPERIMENTS. --Scientifically controlled experiments enable you to study the relationships between phenomena under conditions which eliminate, as far as possible, the effects of extraneous influences.   From an ideal standpoint only one factor is varied at a time, and all other conditions are held constant throughout an experiment.   From a practical viewpoint, we know that there are many kinds of errors that can affect the results we obtain, even in carefully planned experiments.   These errors are of several types:

1. Errors arising from variable characteristics in the subjects

    As you will see later in this chapter, sometimes an attempt is made to equate two groups by pairing each individual in Group I with an individual in Group II.

This procedure may take considerable time and may not be effective in controlling some of the less tangible factors that are relevant to learning. For example, if individuals were paired on the basis of intelligence test scores and pretest achievement scores, other important variables might be left uncontrolled. These include such aspects as personality traits, physical condition, aptitudes, familiarity with the learning procedures, age, sex, race, and cultural background. To further complicate educational research is the fact that individuals change while they are being studied.

2.   Constant or group errors

Sometimes a factor affects all members of a given group in a way that is consistently different from the treatment being given to another group. For example, teacher differences (in ability, enthusiasm or other personality factors, sex, age, and instructional techniques) may mean that one class has a better teacher than another class. Other differences which could affect an entire group include the amount of practice a class is given, the time of day when a class meets, presence in the group of a "neurotic" child, classroom facilities, the instructions given to the students who are taking a test, the timing allowed for test responses, the physical setting, and distractions.

3.   School or replication errors

In some experimental designs, two or more groups, drawn from different subpopulations of the total universe, receive the same treatment. The classes or schools that receive a given treatment may vary in such factors as instructional materials, size of classes, curriculum plans, administrative organization, school plant and equipment, and community resources. Such errors affect all members of one replication (such as the participants from one school or community) but they probably do not affect all of the groups receiving one treatment (for example, the influence of a particular film may be studied in four different schools or communities). Borg illustrated this by pointing out that a democratic classroom atmosphere may lead to better success of a method in a school where the environment and previous training make this method appropriate, than in a school accustomed to an authoritarian, teacher-centered atmosphere. He suggested further research to identify the conditions leading to the success of a method in one replication and its failure in another.[3]

4.   Indeterminable errors

Many of the errors which have been described can be controlled by keeping the conditions constant. However, Zimny pointed out that many factors must remain unknown because we cannot determine their size or the extent of their effects. Among these indeterminable factors, he mentioned season of the year, amount of ozone in the air, radioactive fallout. Yet, even factors with only minor differential effects must be controlled, or otherwise accounted for, so that only one factor is permitted to vary at a time.[4]

TECHNIQUES FOR ACHIEVING CONTROL. --The more you understand the many kinds of errors that can affect your results, the more you may be inclined to think that it is impossible to conceive of an experiment in which all variables, except one, are held

---

[3]Walter R. Borg, Educational Research: An Introduction. New York: David McKay, Co., Inc., 1963. Page 292.
[4]Zimny, op. cit., page 53.

constant. Techniques of control can help you solve this dilemma. Zimmy defined control in this manner:

> *To control is to exert direction of influence. As employed in experimentation, the direction or influence can be exerted upon the factor itself and hence upon its effects or upon the effects alone.*[5]

1. Control of factors

In order to achieve control through the factors themselves, you would need to keep many factors constant throughout the experimental period. For example, the instructions would need to be given with the same tone of voice and degree of encouragement; the individual participants would have to possess comparable physical health, emotional health, personal characteristics, and learning ability; any equipment used in the study would have to be appropriate and in good condition; all materials would have to be meaningful and in good condition; and the physical setting would have to be controlled in such respects as room temperature, ventilation, lighting, comfort of chairs, and amount of noise.[6] Sometimes control over factors is attained through indirect means. For example, the participating groups are selected in such a way as to be comparable in learning ability and other factors which may be important to the study.

2. Control of effects

Zimny described the rationale for random selection of subjects for an experiment by saying that some factors can be kept constant only by controlling their effects. Random selection of the individuals results in random selection of factors present in those individuals. The purpose of random selection, then, is to distribute the varying amounts of any factor among the groups in such a way that the effects of this factor tend to cancel out.[7]

Although simple randomization cannot give assurance that unknown or unwanted factors have been controlled, it does make it likely that each group is affected to the same extent by such factors. Further, it enables us to estimate the degree of probability that our control methods have been effective. By computing the level of significance of our findings, we can estimate the likelihood that any differences we obtain are true differences, not differences that could have arisen merely from chance factors such as the selection of the groups or the effects of errors operating in the groups.

Underwood described ways of balancing "progressive factors" that might affect research. He defined a progressive error as *"any change in behavior which occurs as a consequence of continued experience or successive trials with a given task."* Sometimes an individual performs better in successive trials because of the "practice effect." On the other hand, his performance might become worse because he gets tired or doesn't try as hard (fatigue effects). Since progressive errors will occur, he suggested ways of designing an experiment so the effects of practice *"will not differentially influence the results (the behavior) which we wish to attribute to differences in our independent variable."* Two of his suggestions were these:

1. Counterbalancing. This technique is used to present two conditions so the effects of the progressive error will fall equally on the two conditions.

---

[5] Ibid., page 57.
[6] Ibid., pages 52-53.
[7] Ibid., pages 59-63.

Counterbalancing may be expressed as abba, where a and b symbolize the two conditions of the experiment. If there were four conditions, they would be presented in the following sequence: abcddcba.

2.　Complete randomization. The logic of this technique is that the effects of the progressive error will influence all conditions by an equal amount. The appendix of Underwood's book contains tables of random sequences which might be used in determining the order in which to present certain conditions to the subjects. [8]

TECHNIQUES FOR EQUATING GROUPS OR CONTROLLING VARIABLES. --In many kinds of experimental designs, a control group is important to help an investigator determine whether the amount of change which occurred between two measurements could be attributed to the experimental variable, or whether it might have resulted from other factors. The experimental variable is introduced to the experimental group but not to the control group. The first part of this section deals with methods of achieving control by equating groups through precise matching or through the frequency-distribution method. In order to do either of these successfully, you must have considerable knowledge of factors. The method of randomization does not necessitate previous knowledge of relevant factors and does enable you to apply statistical methods to eliminate the effects of an unwanted variable.

1.　Precision control

Precision control involves the matching of each individual in one group with an individual in another group. When using stringent criteria, you need to start with a large number of cases in order to have enough individuals from whom to select your matched pairs. It is particularly difficult to match subjects at the high and low extremes where there are few cases to start with. When you lose a disproportionate number of extreme cases, you restrict the range and make the sample less comparable to the population from which it was drawn.

Brown suggested a procedure for pairing students on two or three factors. If three factors are used for this plan, one of them should either be dichotomous or capable of being placed within three categories. For example, when one of the factors is sex, all of the girls may be tabulated on one sheet and the boys on another. On each sheet, a cross-tabulation can be made on the other two variables, using one color (or a circle) to depict individuals in one group and another color (or square) to depict those in another group. If a symbol is used, each individual's number is placed inside or beside the group symbol. A circle is drawn around each matched pair, representing one person from each group. The matched pairs should be as close together as possible on both variables. When pairs are not in juxtaposition, an individual may be paired with one who is higher, providing this difference is balanced by another individual who is lower than his partner on that characteristic. [9]

When more than three variables are used in pairing, the data about each individual should be written on a card. Cards are flexible enough to permit an investigator to select pairs who are matched on two or three factors and then to check other factors to be sure the pairs are reasonably matched on other important characteristics. Precise matching on more than two or three variables

[8]Benton J. Underwood, Experimental Psychology. Second edition. New York: Appleton-Century-Crofts, Inc., 1966. Pages 32-39, 118.

[9]Clara M. Brown, Evaluation and Investigation in Home Economics. New York: Appleton-Century-Crofts, Inc., 1941. Pages 292-298.

is difficult to achieve. Probably you should set definite standards as to the range of differences which you consider acceptable for paired individuals. After you have matched a pair of subjects, you should use a random method of assigning one individual to the experimental group and the other to the control group.

2.   Frequency-distribution control

Your primary concern in many studies is for similar groups rather than in matched pairs of individuals. In such instances, you need not spend the time nor risk the loss of the number of individuals which might have to be sacrificed in an effort to achieve precision control. You can equate groups by comparing their means and standards deviations to be sure that they are not significantly different on important variables at the beginning of your study. If you are using classes which are already formed, and there are a few extreme cases who prevent the groups from being comparable, you may simply drop these cases out from all of your measurements. Even though it is easy to omit the scores of extremely superior or inferior students, you cannot really eliminate the effects these students may have on the rest of the group.

Selltiz cautioned that groups are not necessarily similar because their averages are similar: *"It would be possible to have in one group young people with high income and older people with low income and in the other group just the opposite combination."*[10]

Chances for errors to affect experimental results occur unless you give attention to a number of factors when you are equating groups. These were discussed earlier in this chapter, but they are important enough to merit further emphasis through a brief summary by Good of the characteristics which require consideration when groups are being equated:

> *In educational experimentation the characteristics that require consideration include intelligence, age, achievement in the particular field of experimentation, study habits, personality traits, physical conditions, sex, and possibly race. The factors relating to the teachers include instructional techniques, classroom-management procedures, interest or zeal for the experimental factor, personality traits, physical condition, sex, and age. The more general school factors involve the instructional materials, time devoted to learning activity, characteristics of the particular class as a group, size of class and school, school organization and supervision, and the school plant. The extraschool factors that may affect an experiment include participation in extracurricular activities, the pupil's home life, and the community interest in and attitude toward the school. The approximate equating of groups or pupils may be less difficult than it appears, since many of the factors are positively correlated.*[11]

3.   Randomization

Precision matching and frequency control assume considerable knowledge of factors that might be relevant to a study as well as the ability to match effectively. Since these two goals are difficult to achieve, randomization is usually recommended as a method of control.

[10]Selltiz, op. cit., page 107.

[11]Carter V. Good and Douglas E. Scates, Methods of Research. New York: Appleton-Century-Crofts, Inc., 1954. Page 708.

Selltiz pointed out that:

> The chance assignment of individuals to the different conditions precludes the possibility of systematic or nonramdom differences between the groups selected. This does not mean that the experimental and control groups will be exactly alike, but rather that whatever differences exist before the introduction of the experimental variable are the result of chance alone.[12]

A randomized block design is one in which treatments are given to groups that have been matched on a variable or variables related to the study. Treatments are then assigned to the groups at random. Presumably the various groups would be more alike in their responses than if random sampling alone were the basis for forming the groups. For example, you might classify students into high, medium, and low ability groups and then draw at random from each ability level to form the experimental and control groups.

Whenever chance is the basis for selection, a poor sample may be chosen. However, when fairly large groups are selected at random and assigned to treatments on a chance basis, differences have an opportunity to nullify each other.

4.   Analysis of covariance

When intact groups are used, or when it is not possible to match groups or individuals prior to the introduction of the experimental variable, a statistical technique of control, called analysis of covariance, may be used.

One home economics study in which analysis of covariance was used was reported by Meshke. In her comparison of the effectiveness of home economics instruction that included direct utilization of community resources and instruction that was limited to classroom activities, Meshke selected communities having similar types of stores and electrical services. She limited her study to ninth and tenth grade classes. The experimental schools were selected to be accessible for several visits during the year; the control schools were visited only once. Procedures involved three classifications: (1) "store classes" had an exploratory excursion of the teacher and students to acquaint them with the local stores, followed by individual and group trips during class time; (2) "classroom classes" used specially prepared materials to supplement class discussions; and (3) "control classes" were taught as the teacher desired and for any length of time. Data consisted of pretest scores, retest scores, intelligence test scores, and socio-economic ratings. Since entire classes were used, homogeneity was established through statistical techniques of analysis of variance and analysis of covariance.[13]

Variations of Experimental Design

A chapter such as this cannot begin to cover all of the intricacies of experimental research design. Here you will find a blending of some of the traditional concepts of simple group designs with a suggestion of some of the newer approaches. You will learn about the importance of measurement at appropriate times, and you will be introduced to a few techniques that have been used to equate groups or to control the effects of variables upon the groups.

---

[12]Selltiz, op. cit., page 99.

[13]Edna D. Meshke, "The Effects of Utilizing Selected Community Resources in Ninth-Grade and Tenth-Grade Homemaking C Classes." Journal of Experimental Education 12: 1-9; September, 1943.

Lindquist listed the following essential characteristics of a good experimental design.

   1. It will insure that the observed treatment effects are unbiased estimates of the true effects.

   2. It will permit a quantitative description of the precision of the observed treatment effects regarded as estimates of the "true" effects.

   3. It will insure that the observed treatment effects will have whatever degree of precision is required by the broader purposes of the experiment.

   4. It will make possible an objective test of a specific hypothesis concerning the true effects; that is, it will permit the computation of the relative frequency with which the observed discrepancy between observation and hypothesis would be exceeded if the hypothesis were true.

   5. It will be <u>efficient</u>; that is, it will satisfy these requirements at the minimum "cost," broadly conceived.[14]

SIMPLE GROUP DESIGNS. --Although some kinds of studies involve very complex designs, the type of group experimentation most likely to be undertaken by a beginning graduate student would probably fit into one of the following categories: one-group technique, parallel-group technique, rotation-group technique, or factorial design. Following the discussion of each classification, one illustration of its use is given.

1.   <u>One-group technique</u>

In conducting an experiment with one group, an initial test of the experimental factor is made, the experimental factor is applied, and another test is given. The differences between the preliminary measurement and the final results are determined. Interpretation of these changes poses a problem unless you have knowledge of the normal performance which might be expected without application of the experimental factor. The paradigm for a one-group method is:

$Test_1$ .... Apply the Independent Variable .... $Test_2$.
Test for significant change: $D = Test_2 - Test_1$.

Arny used the one-group technique in determining the most suitable grade levels for teaching various aspects of home economics. To do this, she found out *"what the majority of the girls knew before any school instruction in home economics; what was learned primarily at specific grade levels, and what the majority of them had not learned by the time they had completed the course offered in the last two years of high school."* She assumed that *"the reduction in the percentage of error on a test item from one grade level to the next indicated the extent to which learning had taken place at each level."* The students were divided into four groups: (1) those entering grade nine--no previous home economics instruction; (2) those completing grade nine--including ninth grade home economics; (3) those completing grade ten; and (4) those completing the course for grades eleven or twelve. The per cent of error made by the students at the four grade levels was determined for each item. The subject matter with which these items dealt was analyzed according to the per cent of the items learned at the following levels: prior to school instruction, mostly in grade 9,

---

[14]Everett F. Lindquist, <u>Design and Analysis of Experiments in Psychology and Education</u>. Boston: Houghton Mifflin Co., 1953. Page 6.

mostly in grade 10, mostly in grades 11 and 12, at either of two grade levels, and by fewer than a majority of the students at the end of grade 12. [15]

The one-group technique might be useful in determining how much the students have learned from the introduction of new audio-visual material or a new method of teaching a certain aspect of home economics. A test would be given prior to instruction and again following the instruction. In classroom projects, the students might use the one-group technique to study the effect of varying one factor, such as an ingredient in custards. A panel would rate the custards on such characteristics as color, consistency, and flavor.

Because it need not interfere with the regular program of a teacher or class, the one-group technique has the advantage of simplicity. However, its results are likely to have low validity, because a satisfactory basis for comparison is difficult to obtain. You cannot be sure how much of the change might have taken place as a result of maturation or other experiences, without the introduction of the experimental variable. Improvement may result from such factors as practice in taking a test, changes in attitude, or normal acceleration in the early stages of learning something new. When little change results, you cannot be certain whether this is because of the ineffectiveness of the experimental variable or whether it is due to the effects of some extraneous factor, such as discouragement or carelessness on the part of the students.

Borg summarized the only conditions under which a single-group design should be used: *"When the dependent variable is reasonably stable, when the interval between the pretest and post-test can be kept short, and when it is impossible to obtain a control group."* [16]

2.   Parallel-group technique

The parallel-group approach is sometimes referred to as the "equivalent-group" technique. Ideally, two or more groups should be chosen so as to be nearly equivalent, but, in actual practice, it is not always feasible to match the groups precisely. A random assignment of the individuals to each group would enable you to control the effects of any factors that vary between the groups. The group which is subjected to the experimental treatment is known as the "experimental" group, and the other group serves as a "control" group.

The paradigm for a parallel-group design is:
Randomization: Subjects are assigned to experimental or control group at random.
Application of experimental variable:
    Experimental group: $Test_1$ .... Apply experimental variable .... $Test_2$
    Control group: $Test_3$ .... No application of variable .... $Test_4$
Difference within each group: D_e(Experimental group)   = $Test_2 - Test_1$
                                 D_c(Control group)   = $Test_4 - Test_3$
Test for significant change: D(Experimental - Control) = $D_e - D_c$

The use of parallel groups was illustrated in a study of *"the nutritional status and diet of children with and without a school lunch...in two selected elementary schools in Cumberland, Md."* The control school did not have a plate lunch

[15]Clara B. Arny, The Effectiveness of the High School Program in Home Economics. Minneapolis: University of Minnesota Press, 1952. Pages 189-198.
[16]Walter R. Borg, Educational Research: An Introduction. New York: David McKay Co., Inc., 1963. Page 295.

available during the first year but did serve one during the second year of the study. The experimental school had served a noon meal for several years. The children in these schools were divided into three groups according to the extent of their participation in the lunch program: regular, occasional, and no participation. The control and experimental schools were similar in the number of students enrolled and the economic status of their families. In the fall of 1946, tests were made of the children who participated regularly and those who did not participate in the school lunch program. The tests were repeated in the spring of 1947 and again in the spring of 1948, six months after the school lunch program had been started in the control school. The characteristics which were studied included: changes in height, weight, selected physical signs suggestive of nutritional deficiencies, the level of certain blood constituents of the children, and the dietary patterns of the children in the two schools and of their families. The physical examinations were made without the clinicians's knowledge of whether or not the child participated in the school lunch program. A valuable contribution of the report of this study is the discussion of its limitations and suggestions for future studies in which certain of these limitations might be overcome.[17]

The parallel-group technique is applicable in many educational research studies, particularly those which are attempting to determine the effectiveness of a teaching method or teaching material. By selecting similar groups at the beginning of an experiment, you could study the effects of various methods of presenting subject matter on the achievement of the students during, and following, a unit of study. In addition to comparative studies of student achievement, you could use parallel groups in studying student interests and changes in practices, attitudes, and values.

3.   Rotation-group technique

When parallel groups are used, other factors besides the variable under consideration may contribute to the increased scores of either the experimental group or the control group. Such factors as the initiative, industry, or interest of the students in the two groups may have varied, without the researcher being conscious of the effects they have upon the measurements. At times, the matching of groups is not as precise as you might desire, especially when regularly scheduled classes must be used so as not to upset the rest of the school's program.

To overcome these limitations, the rotation-group technique is sometimes suitable. It involves the reversal of the groups during the study so that the group to whom the experimental variable was applied serves as a control group, while the experimental variable is applied to the other group. When using rotation groups, you must be careful to consider the carry-over effects from one procedure to the other. In a school situation, it is hard to prevent a previous treatment from having some effect on a later treatment that is given to the same individuals. When they have already learned something, another method of teaching them the same material would have little meaning.

The paradigm for using a group as its own control is: Application of experimental variable: (Group A) $Test_1$ .... No experimental variable .... $Test_2$ .... Apply experimental variable .... $Test_3$. Test for significance of difference: $D_e = Test_2 - Test_1$; $D_e = Test_3 - Test_2$; $D = D_e - C_c$

---

[17]Clarence Velat et al., Evaluating School Lunches and Nutritional Status of Children. Circular No. 859. Washington, D.C.: U. S. Department of Agriculture, 1951. 85 pages.

To have further control over the effects that might be related to changes in time or to the time of the year, another group might be used in rotation as follows: (Group B) Test$_4$ .... Apply experimental variable .... Test$_5$ .... No experimental variable .... Test$_6$.

You will notice in the following illustration that Harrell controlled carry-over effects by rotating about half of the pairs between the experimental and control groups while keeping the other half of the pairs in the same group throughout the study.

Harrell was interested in testing the hypothesis that children gain efficiency in certain mental activities as their thiamine intake increases. Her sample consisted of 120 children who lived in an orphanage where their living conditions and dietary regimen would be nearly identical. During the first year, the 60 experimental children received daily a tablet containing 2 milligrams of thiamine, while the 60 control children received daily a placebo which could not be distinguished by either the children or the adults from the thiamine tablet. Preliminary measures indicated that the groups had similar means and standard deviations on the tests at the beginning of the study. Since the study was conducted during war conditions, an unusual number of children were withdrawn from the institution before the study was completed. However, 27 pairs of children continued for a second year to receive the same kind of tablet they had received during the first year. A reversal of tablets was achieved for 20 pairs during the second year of the study. A series of graphs was used to compare the measurements on various activities at the beginning of the study, at the end of the first year, and at the end of the second year for the groups whose supplementation was maintained for two years, and for the groups whose supplementation was reversed after one year. The t ratio was used to determine the probability that the superiority of the thiamine-fed group over the control group was due to chance.[18]

4.   Factorial designs

One of the promising newer types of experimental designs, known as factorial design, enables you to have more than one variable at a time. In the earlier kinds of design, you would have to decide which of several factors might be most important and then proceed to control all but that single variable. In subsequent studies, that variable might be controlled while the effects of another variable were studied. With factorial designs it is possible in a single study to determine which treatment is the most promising and to find out whether there is an interaction between the factors.

The subjects for this type of study should be assigned at random to the various treatment groups. At the end of the treatment period, measurements of progress are recorded and analyzed by the t test or analysis of variance.

A factorial approach is useful when comparing the effect on achievement of two different teaching methods as used by two different teachers. Cook has summarized the procedure as follows:[19]

Teacher 1		Teacher 2	
Group A	Group B	Group C	Group D
Method X	Method Y	Method X	Method Y

[18]Ruth F. Harrell, Further Effects of Added Thiamine on Learning and Other Processes. Number 928. New York: Bureau of Publications, Teachers College, Columbia University, 1947. 102 pages.

[19]David R. Cook, A Guide to Educational Research. Boston: Allyn & Bacon, Inc., 1965. Page 110.

Observations:

1. Differences due to method: AC - BD
2. Differences due to teacher: AB - CD
3. Differences between groups: A - B - C - D
4. Difference due to interaction of teacher and method is what remains when
   No. 1 and No. 2 are subtracted from the between-groups differences, No. 3,
   or (A - B) - (C - D).

More complicated factorial designs permit the use of any number of factors
with more than two variations of each.[20]

TIME OF MEASUREMENT. --Measurement is essential in an experiment. You need
to know what to measure, when to obtain the measurements, and what the measurements
mean. This portion of the chapter discusses various times for taking measurements.
You will find suggestions on what to measure, and how to interpret your results, in later
chapters.

The time or times that you select for measurement will be dependent upon the type
of study you are planning, how you plan to select the groups for your experiment, and how
you plan to compare the groups on the experimental variable. Usually one of the following
times for measurement lends itself better than the others for a specific study:

1. "Before-after" measurements

    If you use the one-group technique, you would probably need to compare the
    initial status of individuals within the group with their status following the ap-
    plication of the experimental treatment. When you use parallel or rotation
    groups, the "before and after" measures enable you to compare the progress
    made by the experimental groups with the progress made by the control groups.
    You can also note changes made within each group.

    The use of measurements before and after the introduction of an experimental
    variable is illustrated in a study by Walters. For his study of attitudes of col-
    lege women, he selected white, female, single home economics majors at
    Oklahoma Agricultural and Mechanical College. They were between 17 and 24
    years of age and had been reared in the United States. Seventy-six women in
    the experimental group were matched with 80 control subjects on socio-economic
    status, year in college, intelligence, and academic achievement. He tested the
    women at the beginning and end of a semester, using the University of Southern
    California Parent Attitude Survey and the Child Guidance Survey (measures of
    attitudes concerning the guidance of children). The experimental group had an
    introductory three-hour course in child development and guidance, including
    laboratory observation in a nursery school-kindergarten program. Gains in
    the experimental and control groups were compared and differences in mean
    scores were studied for possible relationship to socio-economic status, intelli-
    gence, rural and urban residence, size of family, ordinal position in the family,
    and academic achievement.[21]

---

[20]Lindquist, op. cit., pages 20-23, 207-219.

[21]James Walters, "Attitudes Concerning the Guidance of Children: A Study of the Differential Effects of an Introductory Course
   in Child Development on the Attitudes of College Women." Unpublished Doctor's dissertation, Florida State University. (As-
   abstracted in Journal of Home Economics 47: 208-209; March, 1955).

Although knowledge of initial and final status enables you to make a more thorough and reliable analysis of the changes, Selltiz warned that:

The attempt to measure the subjects' attitudes before the experiment begins may crystallize the attitudes; it may exhaust the good will of the subjects, etc. The second, or "after," measurement may introduce other problems: the subject may be bored and therefore unwilling to respond; he may try to give responses that are consistent with his previous responses (thus minimizing the apparent change); or he may try to make his responses "interesting" by varying them from one interview to the next (thus increasing the apparent change).[22]

2. "After-only" measurement

To overcome the possible disadvantages inherent in measuring both before and after an experiment, Selltiz suggested the "after-only" design.

As in all experimental designs involving control groups, the experimental and control groups are selected before the introduction of the experimental variable (X), and the variable is introduced either specifically for the purpose of the experiment or at a specified time and in a specified manner known in advance to the experimenter.[23]

In an abstract of her dissertation, Lippeatt mentioned the "before-after" control of factors that would assist her to understand the effectiveness of two methods of directing home experiences. She said: *"Much attention was given to the selection of the sample and to the factors comparable in the two groups so that comparisons of effectiveness of the two methods would have optimum significance."* Her study, which covered one academic year, included ninth grade home economics students in 16 high schools of Arkansas. The experimental method consisted of integrating and enriching the home economics curriculum by planning it in the light of students' needs and interests, whereas the control method used home experiences as supplemental to classroom activities. Comparisons of the experimental and control groups were based upon data which were obtained from home experience logs, individual student records, interviews with students and parents, teacher evaluations, and representative case studies.[24]

3. "Ex post facto" measurement

You may wish to study the causes or effects of a certain factor even though you cannot create an experimental situation in which you could observe that factor. When existing records show the variable under consideration, you can match records to obtain control and experimental groups which are similar except for the crucial variable.

Chapin has called such experiments ex post facto, because the investigator studies an effect that has already occurred, as distinguished from projected experiments in which the investigator plans and stages an event that will give evidence relevant to his hypothesis.[25]

---

[22] Claire Selltiz et al, Research Methods in Social Relations. Revised edition. New York: Holt, Rinehart and Winston, Inc., 1959. Page 115.

[23] Ibid., pages 108-109.

[24] Selma F. Lippeatt, "An Experimental Study to Determine the Relative Effectiveness at the Secondary Level of a Home Experience Program Planned as an Integral Part of the Homemaking Curriculum and a Home Experience Program Used as a Supplement to Classroom Activities." Unpublished Doctor's dissertation, Pennsylvania State University. (As abstracted in Journal of Home Economics 46: 198-199; March, 1954.)

[25] F. Stuart Chapin, "Design for Social Experiment." American Sociological Review 3: 786-800; December, 1938.

The basic difference between an ex post facto experiment and an "after-only" experiment is this: In an ex post facto experiment, groups are equated and studied after the experimental variable has occurred, whereas an "after-only" design equates the groups on related factors before the introduction of the ex-perimental variable and measures the effects of the experimental variable following the period of study.

Greenwood classified ex post facto experiments in two groups: "cause-to-effect" and "effect-to-cause"[26] In the following illustrations, the Gingles study started with a cause and studied its effects, while the Leahy study began with an observed effect and analyzed possible causes.

Gingles was interested in comparing the personal adjustment of home economics college freshmen at the University of Nebraska who came from differing resi-dential background. Her sample included 307 girls: 145 from farm background, 72 from towns (up to 10,000 population), and 90 from city homes. She used the Heston Personal Adjustment Inventory which gave a quantitative score in six personality components: *"analytical thinking, sociability, emotional stability, confidence, personal relations, and home satisfaction."* Differences on each of the six components among the three residential groups were tested by analysis of variance. When significant differences were found, the t test was used to determine which two of the groups differed. [27]

The approach in Leahy's study was to identify the home economics majors who withdrew from the University of California, Los Angeles, during 1951. Twenty-seven (73 per cent) of these drop-outs replied to a questionnaire which covered three categories: *"general (marriage, socioeconomic factors, unsatisfactory grades, inadequate counseling, lack of interest in home economics), home eco-nomics curriculum, and instruction (in home economics and other courses)."* To determine whether the opinions of the drop-outs would be supported or re-futed by another group, she selected a group of home economics majors who were in attendance during the spring semester of 1952. Her criteria for match-ing students in residence with those who had dropped out of college were: *"(1) age, within 6 months; (2) number of units achieved within plus or minus 6; (3) grade point average, plus or minus 0.5 point; (4) English entrance exemption; (5) home economics major; (6) employed or not while attending UCLA; (7) soror-ity membership; (8) marital status; and (9) residence distance from UCLA."*[28]

Barnes cautioned that ex post facto studies involve the same problems of matching that would be encountered in projective designs. Another possible disadvantage is that adequate records may not be available after a lapse of time. The major advantage is that the effects of many years of experience can be studied now, without having to wait for the experience to take place.[29]

---

[26] Ernest Greenwood, Experimental Sociology: A Study in Method. New York: Morningside Heights: King's Crown Press, 1945.

[27] Pages 64-71.

[28] Ruby H. Gingles, "Personal Adjustment of College Students." Journal of Home Economics 50: 194-200; March, 1958.

[29] Dorothy M. Leahy, "Why Drop-outs in College Home Economics?" Journal of Home Economics 45: 651-653; November, 1953.
Fred P. Barnes, Research for the Practitioner in Education. Washington, D.C.: National Education Association, Department of Elementary School Principals, 1964. Pages 69-71.

SELECTED REFERENCES

Barnes, Fred P. *Research for the Practitioner in Education.* Washington, D.C.: National Education Association, Department of Elementary School Principals, 1964. Pages 68-73.

Borg, Walter R. *Educational Research: An Introduction.* New York: David McKay Co., Inc., 1963. Pages 289-312.

Good, Carter V. *Introduction to Educational Research.* Second edition. New York: Appleton-Century-Crofts, Inc., 1963. Pages 443-483.

Ray, William S. *An Introduction to Experimental Design.* New York: Macmillan Co., 1960. Pages 1-25.

Rummel, J. Francis. *An Introduction to Research Procedures in Education.* Second edition. New York: Harper & Row Publishers, Inc., 1964. Pages 178-197.

Selltiz, Claire et al. *Research Methods in Social Relations.* Revised edition. New York: Holt, Rinehart and Winston, Inc., 1959. Pages 80-143.

Townsend, John C. *Introduction to Experimental Method.* New York: McGraw-Hill Book Co., 1953. 220 pages.

Underwood, Benton J. *Experimental Psychology.* Second edition. New York: Appleton-Century-Crofts, Inc., 1966. Pages 110-131.

ACTION RESEARCH

Corey defined action research as *"the process by which practitioners attempt to study their problems scientifically in order to guide, correct, and evaluate their decisions and actions."*[30] Other terms that are used to describe this process are <u>cooperative</u> <u>research</u> and <u>operational</u> <u>research</u>.

In order to conduct a scientifically acceptable study in the traditional point of view, a person had to be a specialist or expert in research. Many research specialists were college teachers or administrators who were removed from direct contact with classroom problems. They conducted studies which were of theoretical interest or value in expanding educational understanding, but classroom practices usually were not affected by these advances in general knowledge. Action research has increased in recent years as a means of stimulating classroom teachers to identify problems and use creative techniques for solving problems of immediate, practical concern in their teaching situations.

Description and Characteristics

The characteristics of action research might be summarized briefly as follows:

1.   The problem is one of immediate concern to the individual or group planning the study.

     Corey believed that: *"A teacher is most likely to change his ways of working with pupils when he accumulates and interprets information about these pupils because he wants to work more effectively with them."*[31] The philosophy underlying action research is that a teacher's educational practices are more likely to be influenced by guiding him to select and solve his own problems rather than by merely informing him of recommendations based upon the research studies carried out by specialists. Of course, a teacher should also use the results of experts to supplement and broaden his own experiences. Perhaps the very process of engaging in a study of practical importance to him will stimulate a teacher's interest in reading about the research of others.

---

[30]Stephen M. Corey, <u>Action Research to Improve School Practices</u>. New York: Teachers College, Columbia University, 1953. Page 6.

[31]<u>Ibid.</u>, page 9.

2. The sample is a particular group of subjects chosen without regard for the principles of random selection or generalization to the total population. Usually they are students in the class of the teacher doing the research.

Corey compared the kind of generalizations that might result from traditional and action research:

> ... *investigators engaged in action research are not attempting to establish generalizations applicable to groups of school children or teachers in other school systems. They are busy discovering generalizations that they hope will help them work more effectively with present and future populations of school children or teachers in the same situation as that in which the studies were conducted.... In a real sense action research studies are undertaken not to make possible lateral extensions of generalizations but to make possible vertical extensions, with the vertical line going into the future.*[32]

3. The design is often developed cooperatively and is subject to modification as the study develops.

Although an individual can plan a study by himself, action research frequently develops in a cooperative setting with a group of teachers and research specialists working together. Ability to work with others, an appreciation of democratic values, and an understanding of group dynamics are qualities which contribute to the success of a cooperative project. The process of working together in solving problems of common interest can be as rewarding an experience as that of reaching conclusions based upon the research data. A better study may result because of the greater variety of talent directed toward it and the moral support an individual gains from knowing that others support the basic ideas of the project.

In carrying out a controlled experiment, details are planned in advance and carried out in a scientific manner, even though ways of improving the plan might be revealed as the study progresses. On the other hand, action research operates within the dynamics of a classroom. It encourages evaluation at appropriate times and alteration of the research design as a study progresses so that successive stages of the study will make optimum contributions. The possibility of changing his initial design can increase a person's sensitivity to the effectiveness of various parts of a study.

4. The value of a study is measured by improved practice in the particular situation.

Since the basic purpose of action research is to enable practitioners to solve their own problems, this goal is fulfilled when teachers discover improved ways of dealing with immediate educational problems and then change their practices in these directions. As improvement is made in an individual school or classroom, the community also receives social and educational benefits. Although we may hope that similar improvements will be made ultimately in other communities where they would be appropriate, these wider applications in no way determine the value of action research.

---

[32]Ibid., page 14.

Procedures

Taba discussed the following steps in the development of action research projects:[33]

1. Identifying problems

    Along with problem identification, a research consultant needs to understand the teacher's perspective of the problem and the teacher's capacity to deal with it.

2. Analyzing problems and determining some pertinent causal factors

    Problem analysis includes *"an analysis of causes and consequences of the difficulties mentioned, an examination of the assumptions made, a study of the research data available, or securing some preliminary data in order to clarify the issues or to change teachers' perspective on the problem."*[34]

3. Formulating tentative ideas about the crucial factors

    "Focusing hypotheses" help a person to eliminate unworthy ideas and to decide on relevant and appropriate techniques for obtaining data.

4. Gathering and interpreting data to sharpen these ideas and to develop action hypotheses.

    Taba pointed out that *"experimentation needs to carefully guided."*[35] Teachers need help in planning procedures, practice in developing new skills, and a healthy attitude about what changes to expect.

5. Evaluating the results of action

    Careful records are necessary of the procedures and materials used, changes in students' responses, and objective records of performance or test data. These records should indicate status, both before and at the completion of a study.

Brown and Abernathy summarized the steps in action research as follows:[36]

Identifying the Problem

1. *Consider your situation. Select a problem or problem area about which you, or you and other members of the groups, are concerned--an area in which you believe change is needed.*
2. *Consider whether or not the problem has the same meaning for everyone in the group.*
    (a) State the problem or problem area.
    (b) Describe the ideal state of affairs in relation to the problem area.
        * Identify what the group members desire the situation to be.

[33]Hilda Taba and Elizabeth Noel, Action Research: A Case Study. Washington, D.C.; Association for Supervision and Curriculum Development, a Department of the National Education Association, 1957. Pages 12-27.

[34]Ibid., page 15.

[35]Ibid., page 26.

[36]Camille Brown and Ruth Abernathy, "Action Research." in M. Gladys Scott, Research Methods in Health, Physical Education, Recreation. Second edition. Washington, D.C.: American Association for Health, Physical Education, and Recreation, 1959. Page 463.

* Use examples of concrete evidence to describe what the desired situation should be.

3. Determine what the situation is as related to what is desired by the group.   The problem is stated as the difference between what the group or individual desires a situation to be and what the situation actually is.

Stating the Action Hypothesis

1. Consider possible action procedures which may solve the problem.
2. Select the action procedure which is most apt to solve the problem.
3. State the action procedure as an action hypothesis to be tested in the solution of the problem.

Making the Research Design

1. Decide what evidence is needed to determine the degree to which the problem may be solved through the action being taken.
2. Determine the tools and techniques needed to collect the evidence.
3. Plan for recording and treating data.
4. Make a plan for carrying out the action and evaluating the results.

Testing the Action Hypothesis

1. Gather evidence.
2. Record the data.
3. Treat the data.

Deriving Conclusions

1. Analyze the results; determine the relationship between the action hypothesis and the goal or problem.
2. Make generalizations or derive inferences from the evidence.

Setting Next Steps

1. Retest the generalizations resulting from the first action, or state a new action hypothesis to be tested.
2. Define a new problem.

Suitable Topics

A variety of approaches may be used in action research. A few of these are suggested and illustrated in the following paragraphs:

SURVEY. --Cameron investigated the ability of college students at Ohio State University to apply generalizations on home management and basic facts in making a managerial decision. Her study contributed to an evaluation program being carried out by the School of Home Economics. Her instrument consisted of two parts:

Part I, which appraises the student's ability to see logical relations in applying management generalizations and basic facts in relation to solutions given for six homemaking problems; and Part II, which measures knowledge of such generalizations and facts.[37]

---

[37]Anne Cameron, "The Development of an Instrument to Evaluate the Ability of College Home Economics Students to Apply Home Management Generalizations and Facts in the Solution of Homemaking Problems." Unpublished Doctor's dissertation, Ohio State University. (As abstracted in Journal of Home Economics 47: 203-204; March, 1955).

Face validity was promoted by having core teachers and specialists check the generalizations for accuracy, importance in management, and use with students. The instrument was given to 60 home economics education seniors. Results were analyzed for their item discrimination, reliability of both parts of the test, and correlation with percentile rankings on The Ohio State Psychological Examination.

CASE DIAGNOSTIC. --An intensive analysis of the program in home and family living at Chico State College was made by Carlson as a basis for improving the program. She studied four areas: *"Preparation of individuals for wage-earning, the development of interdivisional services, the contribution of the department of home and family living to the community, and the availability of opportunities in the community as resources for the enrichment of the program."* The study was a co-operative one involving approximately 100 persons: *"national and state home economists in various careers, college personnel, students, homemakers, principals of high schools, and alumnae."*[38]

EXPERIMENTAL. --Huntzicker experimented with her first-year home economics classes at Yakima Senior High School to compare the effectiveness of selected clothing construction methods. Four classes, with a total of 88 students, participated in her study. Two classes were taught in the first semester and two in the second semester. She outlined detailed procedures to show the essential differences between Plan A and Plan B in cutting, marking, and construction of a blouse. Her instruments included a background questionnaire, test of factual information (used as a pre-test and post-test), time chart showing students' daily progress, score sheet for evaluating quality of the finished blouses, and an attitude questionnaire. Each instrument was reviewed by another clothing teacher at Yakima High School and by a college teacher.[39]

Among the problems which Taba suggested might be studied by action research are these:

1. Selection and organization of curriculum content: development of sequences of learning, implications of social class structure for learning, implications of psychological life needs, and guides to curriculum content.

2. Interpersonal relations, grouping and leadership: patterns of grouping, impact of psychological climate on learning.

3. Meeting heterogeneity: varying content and standards of achievement to meet needs of heterogeneous groups (socially, culturally, intellectually), adequacy of program for slow learners, challenge for faster and creative learners.

4. Forms of control in classroom: methods of nondisciplinary group control, developmental levels of group controls, cultural factors in styles of effective controls.[40]

Evaluation from a Research Standpoint

Should action research really be considered as research? This question has been raised by some writers who feel that it would be more appropriate to view action research

---

[38] Gwendolyn Wagner Carlson, "Improving the Program in Home and Family Living at Chico State College." Unpublished Doctor's dissertation, Teachers College, Columbia University. (As abstracted in Journal of Home Economics 50: 225; March, 1958).

[39] Jane Huntzicker, "The Effectiveness of Selected Methods of Clothing Construction Used in Teaching First Year Students at Yakima Senior High School." Unpublished Master's thesis, Oregon State College, 1957. 120 pages.

[40] Taba, op. cit., pages 3-5.

as a method of in-service education rather than as research. Good expressed his opinion in this manner:

> *The major contribution of action or cooperative research is to in-service training and stimulation of teachers rather than as a basic research methodology paralleling the historical, descriptive-survey, experimental, case-clinical, and developmental techniques. All of these fundamental methods of investigation are available for cooperative research on the part of field workers, with the assistance of research specialists.*[41]

What have been the major contributions of action research and what difficulties have been encountered by those who engaged in action projects? Good made the following evaluation:

> *Many of the reports of action studies include statements to the effect that teachers have found cherished prejudices challenged, leadership developed, lines of communication made clearer, interest in research engendered, curriculum change facilitated, and success in incorporating the action approach both in the training of teachers and in the teaching of public-school classes. . . .*

> *Certain problems or difficulties in conducting action or co-operative research studies have included the reluctance of teachers to undertake research because of their concept of formal research, lack of time to conduct studies, difficulty of communication, and inadequate training for research activities. Suggestions for facilitating co-operative investigation have mentioned the need for a climate in the schools favorable to study and experimentation, ways to provide time for teachers to participate, and leadership and consultative help for the workers.*[42]

SELECTED REFERENCES

Association for Supervision and Curriculum Development. *Research for Curriculum Improvement.* 1957 Yearbook. Washington, D.C.: The Association, a Department of the National Education Association, 1957. Pages 32-40.

Borg, Walter R. *Educational Research: An Investigation.* New York: David McKay Co., Inc., 1963. Pages 313-325.

Corey, Stephen M. *Action Research to Improve School Practices.* New York: Teachers College, Columbia University, 1953. Pages 1-18, 25-41.

Good, Carter V. *Essentials of Educational Research.* New York: Appleton-Century-Crofts, Inc., 1966. Pages 262-266.

Scott, M. Gladys (editor). *Research Methods in Health, Physical Education, Recreation.* Second edition. Washington, D.C.: American Association for Health, Physical Education, and Recreation, 1959. Pages 453-463.

Shumsky, Abraham. *The Action Research Way of Learning.* New York: Teachers College, Columbia University, 1958. 210 pages.

Taba, Hilda and Elizabeth Noel. *Action Research: A Case Study.* Washington, D.C.: Association for Supervision and Curriculum Development, a Department of the National Education Association, 1957. Pages 1-27.

---

[41]Carter V. Good, Introduction to Educational Research. New York: Appleton-Century-Crofts, Inc., 1959. Page 242.
[42]Ibid., pages 242-243.

Chapter 8

DATA-GATHERING INSTRUMENTS

If we want to know how people feel: what they
experience and what they remember, what their
emotions and motives are like, and the reasons
for acting as they do--why not ask them?
-- Gordon W. Allport

Research data may be obtained in a variety of ways, such as observing someone's behavior, asking him to discuss his opinions or feelings orally, or presenting him with a questionnaire on which he writes his own answers. Each of these techniques has an important place in home economics research providing it is appropriate for the particular investigation and is effective in its style, content, and administration.

Among the considerations when choosing any measuring instrument are its validity, reliability, and certain practical aspects.

1. Validity

    When you are choosing a test or other measuring device, the most important factor is its validity--its ability to do what you are trying to accomplish. Validity is concerned with WHAT the test measures and HOW WELL it fulfills its function. When you study a test manual, you will not be able to find an answer to the question, "Is this a valid test?" Rather, you should be seeking an answer as to how valid this test is for the decision you wish to make.

    The American Psychological Association defined four types of validity, each of which is involved in making a different kind of judgment:[1]

    Content validity is used to determine how an individual would perform at the present time in a given universe of situations of which the test constitutes a sample. The questions or situations included in the test must represent the content areas or behavioral patterns to be assessed. They must be appropriate for the individuals under study and for the circumstances in which they are being used. Content validity is determined by a logical process, by examining the representativeness of the test content. The test content can be examined systematically and compared with an analysis of the textbook, a description of the universe of items, or the opinions of authorities. The degree of validity is indicated by the extent to which the method of collecting evidence (or obtaining scores) agrees with the specifications that were set up in advance (such as definitions, a body of content, or opinions of authorities). Content validity is used in achievement tests that are designed to measure how well an individual has mastered a specific skill or course of study.

---

[1] American Psychological Association, Technical Recommendations for Psychological Tests and Diagnostic Techniques. Supplement to the Psychological Bulletin 51: 28; March, 1954.

Predictive validity is used to predict future success or behavior from the re-sults of a present measurement. This form of validity is useful when hiring job applicants to predict their success in a particular job on the basis of a test battery. Also, it is used in selecting students for admission to college and to professional schools. The method involves administering the test, waiting for the events the test is attempting to predict to occur, and then correlating the test scores with some measure of performance appropriate to the event. Academic achievement, performance in specialized training, and on-the-job performance are among the criteria for validating scores on a predictor (such as a scholastic aptitude test or a test battery).

In an attempt to offer better guidance to students who indicated interest in pre-paring to teach home economics, Chadderdon obtained data for prediction dur-ing the first two years of college by employing inventories to measure the student's vocational interests, temperament, social and psychological charac-teristics, academic ability, and achievement in certain courses. She employed four criterion measures as evidence of teacher effectiveness: *mean class gains to show the ability of students to apply generalizations in solving problems, a measure of the students' estimate of teacher concern, observation and tape recordings of teacher and pupil classroom behavior on such areas as classroom management and cognitive behaviors at various levels, and ability to relate satisfactorily with members of the community and school personnel.*[2]

Concurrent validity is used to estimate an individual's present status on some variable other than the test. For example, concurrent validity would be con-cerned with the question, "Is Mary neurotic?" rather than with the prediction of future behavior ("Is Mary likely to become neurotice?").

Construct validity refers to the adequacy of the theory or concept underlying a specific instrument. A construct is a theoretical, imaginary mechanism or theory to account for behavior as it is observed. Most theories involve con-structs. From the theory, predictions can be made about the attributes that account for variation of scores between persons or on different occasions. Data can then be gathered to confirm these predictions. Construct validity is valuable for scientific purposes rather than immediately practical purposes. It is more complex than the other types, since it involves developing a theory about what a score means psychologically and what causes a person to get a certain score. Construct validity is important in measuring abilities, attitudes, personality characteristics, and complex behavior patterns.

Cronbach illustrated a theory of anxiety that might be accepted and tested by an experimenter:

> *If persons are exposed to a threat of electric shock, their anxiety will increase.*
> *Neurotics are more anxious than nonneurotics.*
> *Anxiety is lowered by administration of a certain drug.*
> *Anxious persons have a high level of aspiration.*[3]

---

[2] Hester Chadderdon, "Study of Prediction of Teaching Success of Home Economics Graduates, Iowa State University." Project No. 1413, Iowa Agricultural and Home Economics Experiment Station, in cooperation with the Vocational Division, Iowa State Department of Public Instruction. (As contained in mimeographed "Notes of Some Home Economics Education Research and Studies Now in Progress." U. S. Office of Education, 1964. Pages 10-11.)

[3] Lee J. Cronbach, Essentials of Psychological Testing. Second edition. New York: Harper & Row Publishers, Inc., 1960. Page 105.

2. Reliability

Tools that are used for research purposes must be dependable. If results can be verified by impartial, independent observers or if you could repeat the testing process and obtain similar results, you have evidence of the test's reliability. All measurement contains some error and so a test is never perfectly reliable. Evidence that is considered to be reliable is relatively free from errors. The American Psychological Association has recommended the following ways of referring to the major types of reliability coefficients:[4]

Coefficient of internal consistency--based on a single trial of a test, obtained by dividing the test into equivalent halves (split-half method) or by the analysis of variance method (Kuder-Richardson technique).

Coefficient of equivalence--based on scores from two parallel forms of the test administered at approximately the same time.

Coefficient of stability--based on retesting with the same test, following an intervening period of time.

3. Practical considerations

Among the factors to consider when selecting a test are the complexity of administering it, the amount of time required to respond to the items, the cost, the possibility of using the test booklets again, the time required for scoring and the special skills or equipment necessary for scoring, the type of norms and their appropriateness to your group, the availability of a comparable form at the same level of difficulty, the possibility of a series of parallel forms at different levels of difficulty to permit following the growth of the same group during later years.

QUESTIONNAIRES

A questionnaire is a form that is used to elicit responses to specified questions and is filled out by the respondent. Although a questionnaire is often used as a means of reaching persons who are difficult to contact personally, it can be given also to groups under supervision. Administering a questionnaire requires less skill than interviewing demands; the approach is impersonal, and the instructions can be uniform. Questionnaires have the further advantages of being less expensive than interviews and of permitting the respondent to take as much time as he wishes to think about his answers without feeling under pressure to respond. Unusual or personal kinds of activities may be discussed more freely through questionnaires than in interviews. There may be less desire on the part of the respondent to try to impress the investigator, and he may think through his answers more carefully than would be possible in an interview.

Among the disadvantages of questionnaries are the diversity of meaning attributed to a question by various respondents, the amount of education that may be required of a person in order to understand the questions and procedures, the difficulty of securing valid personal or confidential information, and the uncertainty of receiving an adequate number of responses to represent the population. Also, the respondent may reread the entire questionnaire and then make changes in his replies to some of the earlier items.

---

[4] American Psychological Association, op. cit., page 28.

The researcher must keep in mind two "philosophic objections" to the use of questionnaires as stated by Galfo and Miller: *(1) "The fallacious belief that what is should be; and (2) The notion that the truth of a fact is directly proportional to the number of people who accept its accuracy."* [5]

Kinds of Questions

Questions may be asked in two forms: closed or open. In the <u>closed</u> form, possible answers are suggested. The respondent checks those with which he agrees, or he responds to each item indicating whether or not he agrees with it. When answers are of the "yes-no" type, provision should be made for a person to say that he is uncertain or that he has no opinion about an item. A checklist should include most of the answers that a person might wish to give, but provision should be made for writing some additional response if he so desires. Ease of response and tabulation are major advantages of closed questions or checklists.

The following question is an example of one that requires simple checking and includes some provision for adding responses which do not appear in the checklist:[6]

What would have made your homemaking classes more enjoyable?

(1)	*I was satisfied with them as they were*	(1)_____
(2)	*Having an attractive and conveniently arranged room*	(2)_____
(3)	*Teaching us the variety of homemaking responsibilities*	(3)_____
(4)	*Having equipment at school like we have at home*	(4)_____
(5)	*Having both boys and girls in the same class*	(5)_____
(6)	*Learning things we haven't already had in Junior High School or at home*	(6)_____
(7)	*Planning for better use of class time*	(7)_____
(8)	*Working on projects that would be of practical value in our homes*	(8)_____
(9)	*Making homemaking interesting to students of all nationalities and family backgrounds*	(9)_____
(10)	*Teacher-pupil cooperation in solving problems*	(10)_____
(11)	*Having an understanding and impartial teacher*	(11)_____
(12)	*Other . . . .*	

"Open-end," or free-response questions, permit an individual to respond in his own words. Tabulating these responses can be time-consuming and expensive, but the information written by the respondent may give insight into his feelings, background, hidden motivations, interests, or decisions. Free-response questions can stimulate a person to think about his feelings or motives and to express what he considers to be most important. In this manner, some of the disadvantages of a checklist type of questionnaire are overcome, for where unequivocal replies are sometimes demanded a respondent's thinking may be conditioned by the suggestions or limited by an incomplete list.

The American Association of University Women used the following "free-response" question in its study of college graduates:[7]

As you think over your college education, in what ways do you feel it is of value in your life today? In the light of your later experiences, what kinds of improvements or changes would you now suggest? Please use this and the following page for your answer.

---

[5] Armand J. Galfo and Earl Miller, <u>Interpreting Education Research</u>. Dubuque, Iowa: Wm. C. Brown Co., 1965. Page 26.

[6] Olive A. Hall, <u>What's the Next Move in Homemaking Education?</u> Bulletin 24, Number 2. Sacramento: California State Department of Education, 1955. Page 116.

[7] "What do you think about your college education?" <u>American Association of University Women Journal</u>, 42: 32; October, 1948.

Two types of information are likely to be sought through a questionnaire: personal data and items pertaining to the subject of the investigation. <u>Personal</u> or identifying data might include the name of the respondent, although many questionnaires make this optional. Parten pointed out: *"Evidence suggests that for most survey topics asking for the informants' signature does not affect returns greatly."*[8] Other items on personal and family background which might be significant to an investigation in home economics include age, grade in school, marital status, education, occupation or vocational preference, family size and composition, home and community activities. Such information may be obtained through a checklist or through "open-end" questions, as in the following examples from a study of the graduates of Mount St. Mary's College:[9]

Check the statement that describes the highest level of education completed by your husband: ·

(1) High school	*(1)*_____
(2) Two-year college program	*(2)*_____
(3) Four-year college program with B.A. or B.S. degree	*(3)*_____
(4) A Master's degree	*(4)*_____
(5) A Doctor's degree	*(5)*_____
(6) Other	*(6)*_____
(describe) _____	

How many times did you change your major after enrolling at M.S.M.C.?

_____

Questions pertaining to the <u>subject</u> <u>matter</u> of the survey might cover a variety of information, such as:

FACTS. --When planning factual questions, you should be certain that the information you are requesting is not already available to you (for example, in the school's permanent record system). Next, you should be sure that the respondents have had an opportunity to acquire the information they are being asked to provide. A good plan is to include a basic question to find out whether or not the respondent knows about the particular subject before asking him for specific information about it. Facts about himself and his environment are only as accurate as the ability of the respondent to remember and recall them. Parten summarized the principal factors in remembering as follows:[10]

Recency	-- We remember more recent events readily.
Primacy	-- We remember the associations which were formed first.
Frequency	-- We remember experiences which are repeated frequently.
Duration	-- We remember what we have been exposed to over a long period of time.

[8] Mildred B. Parten, Surveys, <u>Polls, and Samples</u>. New York: Harper & Row Publishers, Inc., 1950. Page 165.

[9] Chapla, Sister Marie Stephen. "A Study of the Personal, Social and Professional Development of the Graduates from the Department of Home Economics and Other Departments of Mount St. Mary's College." Unpublished Master's thesis, University of California, Los Angeles, 1960. Page 91.

[10] Parten, <u>op. cit.</u>, pages 179-180.

Vividness   -- Personal experiences are generally more vivid than experiences of others.

Interest   -- Interesting experiences are remembered more easily.

Meaningfulness   -- Comprehensible experiences are recalled more easily than meaningless ones.

Setting   -- Appropriate environment aids recall.

Set   -- Readiness to remember and sympathetic encouragement are important.

Mode   -- Recognition of what is present is easier than recall without clues.

FEELINGS, BELIEFS, OR ATTITUDES. --Selltiz recommended:

Frequently, before asking questions about the <u>nature</u> of a person's beliefs, it is desirable to find out whether he <u>has</u> any beliefs or information relevant to the topic under investigation. For example, it makes little sense to inquire, except "projectively," about a person's beliefs about the United Nations if he does not know that the organization exists.[11]

A three-point rating scale was used to obtain the points of view of graduates from the Department of Home Economics, University of California, Los Angeles:[12]

As you recall your college program, which of the following best expresses your point of view? Write 1, 2, or 3 according to this scale:
    1 -- seldom or never
    2 -- occasionally
    3 -- most of the time

_____ *(1) Did you have freedom in the choice of your courses?*
_____ *(2) Were there discussion groups in which each student could participate?*
_____ *(3) Did you look up your own material in a library rather than depend upon lecture notes?*
_____ *(4) Were you expected to do independent research in an area of particular interest to you?*
_____ *(5) Were you encouraged to extract all the possible values from a course rather than just "cover the ground"?*
_____ *(6) Did you have opportunities to get to know your teachers in conferences?*
_____ *(7) Was your college work a challenge to you?*
_____ *(8) Were you more interested in grades than in actual achievement?*
_____ *(9) Were the problems presented in class the problems that seemed important to you?*
_____ *(10) Were you encouraged to evaluate your own progress in relation to your goals?*

Differences may exist between what a person believes <u>should</u> be done and what he thinks he actually <u>would</u> do in a practical situation. Eckert took this into consideration

[11]Claire Selltiz et al, <u>Research Methods in Social Relations</u>. Revised edition. New York: Holt, Rinehart and Winston, Inc., 1959. Page 246
[12]Olive A. Hall, "A Questionnaire for Home Economics Graduates of the University of California, Los Angeles," 1959.

when he wrote the directions for the SOCIAL INSIGHT QUESTIONNAIRE on which respondents were to answer each question from three standpoints:

> *Each question in this test has the implied beginning, "TO WHAT EXTENT...."*
> *and is to be answered in three ways. SHOULD PEOPLE represents how you think*
> *it would be ideal for people to think or act--for example: To what extent SHOULD*
> *PEOPLE enjoy sports. Having decided that, you next say, "To what extent DO*
> *MOST PEOPLE enjoy sports. And finally you say "DO I," which means, of course,*
> *the way you personally feel about it.*[13]

Emotional reactions and intensity of feelings may be revealed through free-response
questions, such as the sentence-completion items. The use and interpretation of information obtained through any kind of projective technique demands special skill and education.
An example of a sentence-completion item is:

At home I enjoy_____.

PRESENT OR PAST BEHAVIOR. --Educational surveys are made to determine current status on such matters as teacher selection, nature of teaching training, length of
service of teachers, duties performed, size of classes, salaries, or average expenditure
per student. An example of a closed form of question, as used in the national study of
teacher satisfaction, is:

> *School provision for operating expenses of home economics department*
> *(1) No definite amount set aside.*
> *(2) Definite amount set aside yearly.*
> *(3) No school funds for this purpose.*[14]

Characteristics of Effective Questionnaires

Good cautioned users of the questionnaire technique, for it is a technique which has
been overworked and abused:

> *Perhaps the first thing for the young or inexperienced worker to get in mind*
> *regarding the questionnaire technique of gathering data is that it is not a quick, easy,*
> *and facile method of investigation. It is relatively slow, requires a large invest-*
> *ment of time on the part of the investigator, and often gives results that are highly*
> *disappointing, because of their incompleteness, indefiniteness, and the generally*
> *hostile attitude of recipients toward the flood of appeals made for cooperation in*
> *answering questionnaires.*[15]

Before sending out a questionnaire, you should answer the following questions to
estimate how effective this instrument will be:

1.   Is the questionnaire valid? A valid questionnaire is one that fulfills the basic
     purposes of your study clearly and without ambiguity. In addition, it is admin-
     istered to people who are qualified to answer the questions or who are given an
     opportunity to separate the answers in which they express firm convictions from
     those in which they have little or no feeling. Results from a valid questionnaire

---

[13]Ralph G. Eckert, "Social Insight Questionnaire."

[14]American Vocational Association, Factors Affecting the Satisfactions of Home Economics Teachers. AVA Research Bulletin
No. 3. Washington, D. C.: American Vocational Association, 1948. Page 90.

[15]Carter V. Good and Douglas E. Scates, Methods of Research. New York: Appleton-Century-Crofts, Inc., 1954. Page 605.

are usually consistent with other information available on the topic. If they differ from what is reasonable to expect, you should attempt to ascertain reasons for the inconsistency.

2. Is it <u>objective</u>? If your questionnaire is objective, its questions are not colored by your bias or your sponsor's viewpoint. Responses are called for which are definite throughout and can be given rather simply, often with check marks.

3. Are the instructions and questions <u>clear</u>? The purpose of the questionnaire should be made clear, instructions should be simple and effective, and the questions should be geared to the respondent's level of comprehension. Understandable and familiar words contribute to clarity. Each item should be numbered. Precoding of a questionnaire may simplify the transfer of information to cards for electronic sorting and tabulating.

4. Has the questionnaire been carefully formulated and <u>tried</u> <u>out</u>? Usually a questionnaire is submitted first to an individual or a group of persons who have expert knowledge of its subject matter and who understand questionnaire construction. Revisions are made, and then it is tried out, as a pilot study, with persons similar to the ones who will participate in the major part of the study. Further revisions are usually necessary before administering the questionnaire to the sample selected for the major study.

5. Does the questionnaire have a neat and attractive <u>appearance</u>? Are the questions arranged logically and spaced appropriately? Ample margins should be allowed so the questionnaire does not seem crowded. For ease of tabulation, the possible replies for a checklist item should be placed in columns.

If you can afford to have printed questionnaires, the respondents may be impressed favorably by the effort and money you have invested in the study. However, multilithed or mimeographed questionnaires can be prepared very neatly at less cost, particularly for small studies. Generally, questionnaires should be no larger than $8\frac{1}{2}$ x 11 inches because of the difficulty of handling and filing larger sizes. White or light colors are attractive and readable. When several forms of a questionnaire are used in the same study, each form can be printed on paper of a different color to enable you to locate and sort them readily. Face appeal is important to attract the interest of the reader. You may use photographs or drawings to make a questionnaire sufficiently interesting so that your respondents will answer promptly. Photographs may have "nostalgic value" in a survey of school or college alumnae. Nevertheless, the value of photographs in relation to their cost should be weighed carefully.

6. Is the <u>length</u> of the questionnaire suitable? A questionnaire must be long enough to obtain the desired information, and yet not so long as to discourage people from replying or giving careful answers. Trivial questions, those that are only of remote interest or those on which information is available from other sources, should be removed in an effort to keep a questionnaire as brief as possible. The scope of the remaining questions should be broad enough to make the study valuable.

7. Is it <u>reasonable</u> to expect a busy person to complete the questionnaire? A questionnaire must seem important enough to a respondent to merit the time and effort he would spend in completing it. Furthermore, the problem should be of interest and importance to the professional field, not just to the investigator. Not only must the respondent be in a position to have the information, but he

must also feel free to answer truthfully without endangering his position or self-regard. Superficial replies are a waste of time, both for the respondent and the investigator. Whenever possible, your questions should provide for some depth of response.

8. Does a suitable <u>letter</u> <u>of</u> <u>transmittal</u> accompany mailed questionnaries? A cover letter should state the purpose and importance of the study in a sincere, persuasive manner. One of the most effective ways of inducing the respondent to return a questionnaire is to make him aware that he has an important contribution to make to a study that will affect him personally. Some indication may be given as to the basis for selection of the persons to whom the questionnaire is being sent. Respondents should be given assurance that their replies will be kept confidential. The investigator should give his name, address, and position. In the case of a graduate student, the adviser's name and position might add prestige to the study. If some institution or foundation is sponsoring your study, you might want to mention the sponsor's name. A self-addressed, stamped envelope is usually enclosed as a courtesy. You may ask the respondents to check a specific item if they are interested in having a summary of the results of your study. If you make such an offer, you must be sure to fulfill your promise and send a specially-prepared summary or a reprint of a published report.

Even though you have developed and administered an effective questionnaire, your data might fail to be significant because of a low per cent of returns. When you send a questionnaire to a small, interested group with whom you have good rapport, you can reasonably expect a high per cent of returns. If a group is less-highly selected, relatively disinterested, or not aware of the importance of the study, a lower per cent of response may result. Although you should be very concerned about the per cent of responses you obtain, the extent to which the respondents represent the total population is of even greater importance.

It is impossible to set a definite standard as to an acceptable per cent of replies for any type of study. In general, the higher the per cent, the more likely the responses are to represent the total group to whom the questionnaires were given. You might wish to compare certain objective characteristics of respondents and nonrespondents for which information is available. If the two groups are not significantly different on these important factors, you can feel confident in proceeding with the analysis of data based upon your group of respondents.

In many studies, an attempt is made to follow up the persons from whom no reply has been received. Various procedures are used. A common one is to send a card or letter within a few weeks after sending the questionnaire. The follow-up letter should state in a direct, straightforward manner the significance of the study and the need for obtaining a reply from each person who received the questionnaire. You might suggest your willingness to send a duplicate questionnaire in case the other copy is no longer available.

Even in studies where the replies are anonymous and confidential, an identifying number is necessary on each questionnaire or return envelope if a follow-up notice is to be sent only to the nonrespondents. As each reply is received, the respondent's name is checked off. Follow-up cards or letters are sent only to the persons from whom no reply has been received by the suggested deadline, or within a week following the deadline. Just in case a person has sent his reply while your follow-up letters are being addressed or mailed, you might word the letter something like this: "If you have not already returned your completed questionnaire ...."

If a follow-up letter fails to bring the desired response, you must decide whether to rely on the information you have received or try to obtain more responses. One factor to consider in reaching this decision will be the effect of urging or forcing people to participate in a study in which they apparently are not interested. Sometimes investigators interview a selected group of the nonrespondents to find out why they did not respond. Another technique is to send the nonrespondents a short form of the questionnaire to see if they will cooperate in supplying the most essential data for the study.

SELECTED REFERENCES

Good, Carter V. *Essentials of Educational Research.* New York: Appleton-Century-Crofts, Inc.,
    1966. Pages 213-227.
Hillway, Tyrus. *Introduction to Research.* Second edition. Boston: Houghton Mifflin Co., 1964.
    Pages 201-210.
Parten, Mildred B. *Surveys, Polls, and Samples.* New York: Harper & Row Publishers, Inc., 1950.
    Pages 157-189, 198-217.
Rummel, J. Francis. *An Introduction to Research Procedures in Education.* Second edition. New
    York: Harper & Row Publishers, Inc., 1964. Pages 111-162.
Spafford, Ivol. *Studies of Home Economics in High School and in Adult Education Programs 1955-58.*
    Vocational Division Bulletin No. 286, Home Economics Education Series No. 32. Washington, D.C.
    U. S. Department of Health, Education, and Welfare, 1960. Pages 123-178.
Spafford, Ivol. *Studies on the Teaching of Home Economics in Colleges and Universities 1955-56.*
    Vocational Division Bulletin No. 276, Home Economics Series No. 31. Washington, D.C.: U. S.
    Department of Health, Education, and Welfare, 1959. Pages 83-138.

INTERVIEWS

Kahn and Cannell defined an interview as: *"a specialized pattern of verbal inter-action--initiated for a specific purpose, and focused on some specific content area, with consequent elimination of extraneous material."*[16]

The importance of the interview method in home economics research was summarized by Burchinal and Hawkes:

> *Where the focal data of the investigation are the attitudes, perceptions, or in-terests of persons, the direct and often most fruitful approach to obtaining the pertinent data is to ask the individuals themselves. The interview is a face-to-face method of obtaining this information by means of conversation carried on by the interviewer and the respondent.*[17]

The Interview as a Research Tool

For certain types of studies, the interview method has advantages over the questionnaire. In some studies, interviewing a small sample of respondents provides worthwhile supplementary information to a questionnaire study. As is true of any research instrument, interviews have both advantages and limitations with which you should be familiar if they are to be used with optimum value.

ADVANTAGES. --Among the major advantages of an interview is the possibility of obtaining information that very likely could not, or would not, be obtained by any other method. For example, a person might be willing to talk about certain family problems on which he would not wish to comment in writing. A person may be willing to spend more time giving information when he has direct personal contact than when he is asked to take time to complete a questionnaire. In some instances, the personal contact encourages co-operation from persons who might neglect to respond to a questionnaire.

---

[16]Robert L. Kahn and Charles F. Cannell, The Dynamics of Interviewing. Third printing. New York: John Wiley & Sons, Inc.,
    1959. Page 16.
[17]Lee G. Burchinal and Glenn R. Hawkes, "Home Interviews with Families." Journal of Home Economics 49: 167; March, 1957.

Furthermore, an interview may yield more accurate information and greater depth of response than could be obtained through a questionnaire. This is true particularly when respondents are poorly educated or when they are from a low socioeconomic area. These people might have difficulty reading or understanding the questions, or they may not be able to express themselves clearly. An interview can be somewhat flexible and adapted to the level of understanding of the interviewee. An interviewer may clarify the questions, follow up leads in the responses, or probe more deeply to obtain a clear picture of the interviewee's ideas. Since questions are hidden from the respondent, later questions cannot affect earlier replies.

The interview situation can be controlled if you wish to administer standardized tests. Visual materials can be incorporated easily and inexpensively.

And finally, the interviewer has an opportunity for personal growth through contacts with many types of home or community situations different from those with which he is most familiar. Through observation of the environment and personal characteristics of the interviewees, an interviewer can gain deeper insight into factors related to the research problem.

LIMITATIONS. --Possible limitations of interview data arise from three sources: the interview situation, the respondent, or the interviewer.

First, the interview situation may be a very expensive one, especially if a random sample is selected from a wide geographic area in which transportation costs are high. In a comparative study of the cost of mailed questionnaires and interviews, the investigators reported that, for every dollar spent on questionnaires, interview procedures cost $60.[18]

The process of interviewing is time-consuming. In addition to the time actually spent in personal contact with the interviewees, you must allow transportation time, time to arrange in advance for an appointment, or time to return to homes where the person to be visited was not available when first contacted. Evening or weekend hours often must be used in reaching persons who are employed full time.

The respondent may be a limiting factor because of his inability to understand the questions or to express himself clearly, lack of information or unwillingness to reveal what he does have, unreliable memory of events, suppression of facts or memories, rationalization or deliberate distortion in order to make a good impression, or the poor quality of his judgment concerning relationships between causes and effects.

An interviewer may be a source of bias, directly or indirectly. Errors introduced by him may be of several types: omitting a question, rewording questions, giving insufficient time for a respondent to express his ideas, failing to probe when necessary or to probe adequately, not listening carefully, giving his own interpretation of what the respondent says, using inadequate or inappropriate motivation, and actually cheating in recording answers to questions he did not ask.

On the other hand, the interviewer may be helpful by clarifying a question, probing for a more thorough answer, or even persuading someone to answer a question that he would skip if he were responding to a questionnaire.

---

[18] Robert M. Jackson and J. W. M. Rothney, "A Comparative Study of the Mailed Questionnaire and the Interview in Follow-up Studies." Personnel and Guidance Journal 39: 569-571; March, 1961.

The Effective Interview

The success of an interview depends upon many factors, among which are the interviewer's qualifications, the kinds of questions being asked, and the manner in which the interview is conducted.

THE INTERVIEWER. --Besides the necessary training, experience, and interest in the problem, the interviewer's personal qualities contribute much to the success of an interview. These basic qualities include a real interest in people, the ability to meet people easily and to win their confidence at the first contact, friendliness, and tact. Hymen discussed two types of involvement that are crucial to an interview: *"task involvement"* which refers to the respondent's involvement with questions and answers; and *"social involvement"* which refers to his involvement with the interviewer as a personality. He said that rapport may be a function of total involvement, but validity increases with task involvement.[19]

Learning in advance about the culture and background of the groups under study enables the interviewer to appreciate their way of living and to gain their confidence. If he is to obtain significant responses, an interviewer must strive to be adaptable in meeting many different kinds of situations, patient in trying to encourage people to respond, honest in his handling of information, and objective in recording responses. He must guard against letting his own attitudes or beliefs influence the way he asks questions or records answers.

The interviewer's appearance and manner should be pleasing and businesslike. He should be able to speak clearly and enunciate properly. As Burchinal and Hawkes pointed out, an interviewer should be a good listener, trying to see the hidden feelings that may not be expressed in words:

> *Interviewers, however, should not be too talkative: talking unnecessarily wastes interview time; but, more serious, it may reveal opinions or attitudes of the interviewer which introduce biasing factors into the interview.*[20]

Enough time should be allowed for an interviewee to express his ideas. If the respondent goes off on a tangent, the interviewer should attempt to bring him back to the subject. Since the interviewee is likely to be a busy person the interviewer must be careful not to waste his time by asking unimportant questions, by studying insignificant problems, or by allowing unnecessary pauses while he takes notes.

THE INTERVIEW SCHEDULE. --The form of questioning varies with the purpose and type of interview. Several types of interview are applicable in home economics education research.

1. The structured interview is one *"in which both the questions and the alternative responses permitted the subject are predetermined."*[21] Selltiz pointed out the advantages of fixed-alternative questions as *"being 'standardizable,' simple to administer, quick and relatively inexpensive to analyze."*[22] The major disadvantages are in seemingly forcing an individual to state an opinion. If the possible choices are specified, a complete list of the essential responses from which an interviewee may choose should be included.

---

[19] Herbert H. Hyman et al., Interviewing in Social Research. Chicago: The University of Chicago Press, 1954. Page 138.

[20] Burchinal and Hawkes, op. cit., page 168.

[21] Claire Selltiz et al, Research Methods in Social Relations. Revised edition. New York: Holt, Rinehart, and Winston, 1959. Page 255.

[22] Ibid., page 171.

2.   In the *"open-end"* interview, as in the "open-end" questionnaire, the questions *"merely raise an issue but do not provide or suggest any structure for the respondent's reply...."*[23] The individual's responses reflect his motivation and his estimation of which factors are important.

Among the difficulties encountered in this technique are the inflexibility of following a rigid set of questions in a predetermined sequence, and the difficulty of analyzing the responses.

Cannell and Kahn have suggested a *"funnel approach"* as a desirable sequence for questioning. In this approach, the most general question is asked first, followed by a series of more restricted questions. *"The purpose of the funnel sequence is to prevent early questions from conditioning those which come later and to ascertain from the first open questions something about the respondent's frame of reference."*[24] This approach might be adapted to a home economics study in the following way:

QUESTION 1: How do you think home economics is getting along as a profession?

QUESTION 2: How do you think we are doing in the enrollment of home economics majors at the college level?

QUESTION 3: Do you think that we ought to be doing differently in college level home economics programs?

QUESTION 4: (If yes) What should we be doing differently?

QUESTION 5: Some people say that we should change the name, "Home Economics," and others think this name is still our best choice. How do you feel about it?

3.   The focused or depth interview is one in which the persons are known to have been involved in a particular experience (such as viewing a film, reading a pamphlet, or attending a conference). The investigator has analyzed the significant elements or patterns and has developed a set of hypotheses concerning their meaning for those who have been exposed to the pre-analyzed situation. The framework for the interview focuses on the subjective experiences of the persons exposed to the situation--such as identifying the points of special interest and aspects that were not effective. Advance planning would enable the investigator to distinguish between the responses of various subgroups in the sample. The interviewer has freedom to frame questions and to time them in ways that encourage the respondent to explore his reasons and express himself completely. The focused interview is helpful in identifying which aspects of a specific experience seem to be related to changes in attitude.

Questions involving varying degrees of structure may be used in focused interviews. Merton gave the following examples:[25]

Unstructured question: (stimulus and response free)

What impressed you most in this film?

---

[23]Ibid., page 257.

[24]Charles F. Cannell and Robert L. Kahn, "The Collection of Data by Interviewing." In Leon Festinger and Daniel Katz, Research Methods in the Behavioral Sciences. New York: Holt, Rinehart and Winston, Inc., 1953. Page 349.

[25]Robert K. Merton; Marjorie Fiske; Patricia L. Kendall, The Focused Interview, A Manual of Problems and Procedures. Glencoe, Ill.: The Free Press, 1956. Pages 15-16.

Semistructured question:

(response structured and stimulus free)

What did you learn from this pamphlet which you hadn't know before?

(stimulus structured, response free)

How did you feel about the part describing Joe's discharge from the army as a psychneurotic?

Structure question: (stimulus and response structured)

Judging from the film, do you think the German fighting equipment was better, as good as, or poorer than the equipment used by the Americans?

In her doctoral study, Paolucci had a group of beginning home economics teachers record the decisions they made in classroom management during a two-week period. She used a focused interview with each of these teachers to probe more deeply into their decision-making.[26]

A depth interview is useful in understanding what motivates a person, although an investigator must realize that a person may not be aware of his real motives or may not be able to describe them adequately.

4. The nonstructured or nondirective interview, which is used frequently in clinical situations, permits the interviewee to express his feelings with a minimum of questioning or guidance. The interviewer *"encourages the respondent to talk fully and freely by being alert to the feelings expressed in the statements of the respondent and by warm, but noncommittal, recognition of the subject's feelings. Perhaps the most typical remarks made by the interviewer in a nondirective interview are: 'You feel that. . . .' or 'Tell me more' or 'Why?' or 'Isn't that interesting?' or, simply, 'Uh huh.'"*[27]

PILOT STUDY. --The three types of interview situations which have just been described demand careful advance planning on the part of the investigator. Usually an interview schedule is developed, consisting of a specific set of questions which have been worded appropriately for the respondent. Generally it is important to try out the questions and procedures on a small scale in order to determine whether or not the purpose of the research will be fulfilled. This preliminary or exploratory study is called a pilot study. It enables you to do a preliminary testing of your hypotheses and to appraise the statistical techniques you plan to use. Sometimes a pilot study will raise questions about the advisability of expending large amounts of time and money on a major study that will yield very little.

Sometimes two or more approaches are tried in a pilot study and then the more effective one is used in the major study. The California study of attitudes toward home economics education employed both individual interviews and group conferences. The basic questions for the individual interviews with home economics teachers, counselors, and administrators were similar to those used in the group conferences for parents and teachers of subjects other than home economics. Two approaches were tried in the pilot

[26]Beatrice Paolucci, "Decision-making in Relation to Management in Classes of Home Economics by Beginning Teachers." Unpublished Doctor's dissertation, Michigan State University. (As abstracted in Journal of Home Economics 49: 225; March, 1957).
[27]Selltiz, op. cit. , page 268.

study for the group conferences: (1) conducting the interview first to obtain the participants' ideas in free discussion prior to the introduction of possible suggested answers
(each individual completed a checklist type of questionnaire at the close of the interview);
and (2) having each individual fill out a questionnaire first to indicate his own feelings
before he was influenced by the group discussion. The latter approach was adopted for
the major study and proved to be fruitful in raising questions and establishing a framework for the group discussion. The interview schedule was designed to enable interviewers
to check quickly and inconspicuously the responses as they were given. Questions for the
interviews were "open-end" and they were worded in a manner similar to those on the
questionnaires. Neither the questions nor the possible answers were given verbatim on
the interview schedule; only key phrases were used. The schedule was divided into three
sections so that it could be folded and held inconspicuously during an interview (see Figure 2). [28]

A group interview may be used with groups including from six to twelve respondents. By listening to others, an individual may be able to discuss his own problems and
needs more freely. This technique has been employed successfully with juvenile delinquent gangs, prison inmates, and in the solving of other social problems. Its major
disadvantages as a research technique are: (1) You cannot tell whether an individual is
expressing his own feelings or reflecting those of group leaders; and (2) You do not obtain comparable data from each individual.

THE INTERVIEW PROCESS. --In most educational surveys where interviewing is
used, preliminary contacts are made to explain the purpose and scope of the study and to
arrange a convenient time. The interview is opened with a pleasant greeting and perhaps
a further word about the reason for the study or assurance that the information will be
confidential. When interviewees are selected at random and are visited in their homes,
the interviewer may need to be concerned with the conditions under which a favorable interview can be held and the techniques of approaching people. Parten discussed these
factors and gave specific suggestions about introductory remarks and ways of overcoming
objections:

> These introductory remarks should be brief, but should satisfy most informants
> that a harmless 'study' is being made. Words such as 'Survey,' 'Statistics,' 'Popu-
> lation,' 'Opinion Poll,' 'Research,' and phrases such as 'not interested in names,'
> 'University research,' and 'families in cities all over the country are giving this
> information' (if such is the case), may convey the desired impression of a statistical
> survey which will not harm the interests of the informant. [29]

Once the cooperation of the interviewee has been established, the interviewer pro-
ceeds to ask the questions according to the plan. Usually a fixed order of questioning is
followed, which may, of course, be altered if a respondent happens to give information
pertaining to another question out of sequence. Every question must be included, and the
exact wording of a question should be used. If a respondent does not understand a question,
mere repetition might make it clear. Definite instructions should be prepared in advance
regarding permissible ways to change the wording of questions with which an interviewee
has difficulty. Parten suggested that, "It may be desirable to supply the interviewer with
various explanatory phrases or substitute wordings suitable for different educational
levels." [30]

---

[28] Olive A. Hall, What's the Next Move in Homemaking Education? Volume 24, Number 2. Sacramento: California State
Department of Education, 1955. Page 112.

[29] Mildred B. Parten, Surveys, Polls, and Samples. New York: Harper & Row Publishers, Inc. , 1950. Page 350.

[30] Ibid. , page 358.

I. WHY PUPILS TAKE HOMEMAKING?	II. WHAT HOMEMAKING PROGRAM IS DOING?	III. HOW COULD PROGRAM BE STRENGTHENED?

I. WHY PUPILS TAKE HOMEMAKING?

A. Who or what influences them?
____ 1. Boy friend
____ 2. Counselor
____ 3. Girl friend
____ 4. Homemaking teacher
____ 5. Mother or father
____ 6. Own interest
____ 7. Principal
____ 8. Sister or brother
____ 9. Work experience

B. What do pupils want to learn?
____ 1. Boy-girl, marriage preparation
____ 2. Caring for sick at home
____ 3. Caring for children
____ 4. Cooking, family food
____ 5. Dressing properly
____ 6. Entertaining easily
____ 7. Everything for family living
____ 8. Furnishing a home
____ 9. Getting along with others
____ 10. Saving time, energy, money
____ 11. Sewing

C. Why don't others enroll?
____ 1. Don't know what it contains
____ 2. Don't like teacher
____ 3. Don't want more after Junior High School
____ 4. Friends don't recommend it
____ 5. Homemaking too easy
____ 6. Learn in clubs
____ 7. Learn in homes
____ 8. Not interested
____ 9. Only for girls
____ 10. Programs full
____ 11. Pupils not their nationality

II. WHAT HOMEMAKING PROGRAM IS DOING?

Now doing / Could do better

A. How does it help students?
____ 1. Appreciate family   1. ____
____ 2. Cook or sew better   2. ____
____ 3. Get along with others   3. ____
____ 4. Improve appearance   4. ____
____ 5. Improve manners   5. ____
____ 6. Manage time and money   6. ____
____ 7. Overcome self-consciousness 7. ____
____ 8. Prepare for marriage   8. ____
____ 9. Understand opposite sex   9. ____
____ 10. Use new equipment   10. ____
____ 11. Doesn't help them   11. ____

B. How does it help school and community
____ 1. Exchange classes   1. ____
____ 2. Give information on careers 2. ____
____ 3. Have counselor stress values 3. ____
____ 4. Help needy   4. ____
____ 5. Improve school building   5. ____
____ 6. Invite other classes   6. ____
____ 7. Participate in assembly   7. ____
____ 8. Prepare exhibits   8. ____
____ 9. Provide reading materials   9. ____
____ 10. Publicize activities   10. ____
____ 11. Sponsor club   11. ____

Indicate number in attendance
1. Parents   ____ men ____ women
2. Non-Hmkg Teachers   ____ men ____ women
3. Counselors   ____ men ____ women
____ 4. Co. Supt.
____ 5. Dist. Supt.
____ 6. Hmkg Teacher
____ 7. Principal
____ 8. Vice-Prin.
____ 9. Other (list)

Name of school _____

Filled out by _____

III. HOW COULD PROGRAM BE STRENGTHENED?

A. What has limited advancement?
____ 1. Attitudes of counselors
____ 2. Courses not practical
____ 3. Difficulties of scheduling
____ 4. Inadequate budget
____ 5. Inadequate in-service training
____ 6. Inadequate supervision
____ 7. Lack of community understanding
____ 8. Poorly equipped department
____ 9. Rapid turnover of teachers
____ 10. Teacher shortage
____ 11. University requirements

B. What understandings should pupils, parents, and teachers have?
____ 1. Areas included in homemaking
____ 2. Careers related to homemaking
____ 3. Correlating with other subjects
____ 4. Course content
____ 5. Goals or objectives of homemaking
____ 6. How homemaking helps later
____ 7. Purposes of FHA

C. How can courses be made more appealing to students?
____ 1. All right as they are
____ 2. Attractive and convenient rooms
____ 3. Broad program
____ 4. Equipment suited to community
____ 5. Mixed classes
____ 6. New learnings
____ 7. Planned class time
____ 8. Practical projects
____ 9. Program geared to individuals
____ 10. Teacher-pupil problem-solving
____ 11. Understanding, impartial teachers

A Co-operative Study Sponsored by the Bureau of Homemaking Education, California State Department of Education, and the Department of Home Economics at the University of California, Los Angeles.

Figure 2. Conference Guide Sheet (Form CGS)

An interviewer should not be disturbed by periods of silence on the respondent's part. Neither should he expect an interviewee to wait for the next question while he records a previous response. When a person hesitates or says he does not know, the interviewer must decide whether to probe and, if so, how much he should press for an answer. Parten has listed several reasons why people say they do not know and what an interviewer might do under these circumstances:[31]

(1) They may be thinking aloud--they may not have thought about the question before, but will reach a decision if given time....

(2) Lack of information on the subject.

(3) Lack of understanding of words or phrasing of the question. Sometimes if the question is repeated, an answer will be forthcoming.

(4) No conception of what the issue is, or what type of answer is expected....

(5) Inability to decide between alternatives. Such cases may merely require time.

(6) Fear of possible consequences should the respondent's opinions come to the attention of persons in power over him. A guarantee of confidential treatment of responses may help in such cases.

(7) Belief that his facts are inadequate for him to make a decision.

(8) Belief that it is not his province to hold an opinion on the subject--that it is up to those "in the know" or "in authority" to handle the issue. Such people should be encouraged to express their own views.

(9) Hesitance at expressing an unpopular or minority view. The "Everybody has a right to his own opinion" line may be useful for such cases.

(10) Fear of being wrong. The interviewer may obtain an explicit answer by remarks such as "There aren't any right or wrong answers; we just want to give people a chance to say what they think.

Probing is difficult, as Kahn and Cannell pointed out, because you are trying to stimulate an interviewee to amplify and expand his remarks, and yet you do not want to bias his responses. They suggest three approaches: *(1) showing understanding and interest through such remarks as "I see" or "Um-hm"; (2) using the simple and often effective technique of pausing; and (3) making a direct bid for more information through neutral phrases such as: "I'd like to know more about your thinking on that," "Why do you think this is so?" or "Do you have any other reasons for feeling as you do?"*[32]

A good way for closing an interview is for the interviewer to mention when he reaches the last question. He should express appreciation for the interviewee's cooperation and helpful responses. The respondent should be left with a feeling that his participation was worthwhile and enjoyable.

RECORDING RESPONSES. --Errors in recording might result from recording something that the interviewee did not say or failing to record something he did say. Responses

---

[31]*Ibid.*, page 362.

[32]Robert L. Kahn and Charles F. Cannell, The Dynamics of Interviewing. Third printing. New York: John Wiley & Sons, Inc., 1957. Page 207.

should be recorded accurately, either at the time they are being given or immediately following the interview. It takes a highly skilled interviewer to be able to write intelligible notes while he is carrying on the interview. Oldfield pointed out that note-taking possesses certain incidental advantages. It enables the interviewer to take his eyes occasionally off the respondent, who may find constant regard to be disconcerting. If the interviewer perceives what the interviewee considers to be important, and makes notes accordingly, the respondent's confidence in the interviewer is built up.[33]

A checklist enables the interviewer to indicate essential ideas immediately. However, a checklist forces the interviewer to make "on-the-spot" decisions even when the respondent's answers have been ambiguous. Space should be provided for explanatory information and for responses other than those on the checklist.

Verbatim and rather complete replies may be recorded in several ways, such as using abbreviations, taking shorthand, or writing key words at the time and completing the details later. Asking for examples or using minor questions are ways in which the interviewer can have time for recording the full responses to major questions without long pauses. Using a tape recorder permits a complete and unbiased transcription of the responses later.

Group interviews present difficult problems of recording. In the California attitude study, these problems were resolved by having two regional supervisors attend each group conference for parents and teachers. One supervisor served as the conference leader and the other as recorder. The recorder had an opportunity to take notes during the conference. Immediately following the discussion, both persons filled out a checklist independently. Then they discussed their interpretations of various parts of the conference and recorded the results of their combined judgments.[34]

Two or more interviewers, using the same interview schedule with the same respondents, can check on the validity of individual interviews. Other ways of estimating the dependability of interviews is to have a respondent discuss the same subject matter in a questionnaire and in an interview. Also, you might include certain questions to check the truthfulness of the interviewee's answers (such as whether or not he reads a given magazine--which does not really exist).

SELECTED REFERENCES

Bingham, Walter V.; Bruce V. Moore; John W. Gustad. *How to Interview*. Fourth revised edition. New York: Harper & Row Publishers, Inc., 1959. Pages 62-78.

Burchinal, Lee G. and Glenn R. Hawkes. "Home Interviews with Families." *Journal of Home Economics* 49: 167-172; March, 1957.

Cannell, Charles F. and Robert L. Kahn. "The Collection of Data by Interviewing." in Festinger, Leon and Daniel Katz, *Research Methods in the Behavioral Sciences*. New York: Holt, Rinehart and Winston, Inc., 1953. Pages 327-361.

Good, Carter V. *Essentials of Educational Research*. New York: Appleton-Century-Crofts, Inc., 1966. Pages 227-242.

Hillway, Tyrus. *Introduction to Research*. Second edition. Boston: Houghton Mifflin Co., 1964. Pages 199-201.

Parten, Mildred B. *Surveys, Polls, and Samples*. New York: Harper & Row Publishers, Inc., 1950. Pages 79-82.

Rummel, J. Francis. *An Introduction to Research Procedures in Education*. Second edition. New York: Harper & Row Publishers, Inc., 1964. Pages 99-110.

Selltiz, Claire et al. *Research Methods in Social Relations*. Revised edition. New York: Holt, Rinehart and Winston, 1959. Pages 574-587.

---

[33]R. C. Oldfield, The Psychology of the Interview. Fourth edition. London, Methuen, 1951. Pages 58-60.

[34]Olive A. Hall, What's the Next Move in Homemaking Education? Bulletin 24, Number 2. Sacramento: California State Department of Education, 1955. Page 5.

OBSERVATION

Direct, systematic observation often bridges the gap between what people say or believe they would do in a specific situation and what they actually do. Overt behavior may be observed in its natural setting or in situations that are created especially for the study of certain factors. The observer may be inconspicuous, his presence may be obvious to the group though drawing as little attention as possible, or he may be an active participant in the group he is observing. The latter situation, where a person is a participant-observer, enables him to be accepted as a member of the group, and the group behavior is least likely to be affected by his presence.

When Observation is Appropriate

Observation probably has had its widest application in the study of young children. This is to be expected because of their limited ability to express their feelings in words. Their behavior is genuine and not so likely to be influenced by the presence of an observer. Observation is particularly useful also in studies of intercultural understanding, mentally ill persons, or other groups who lack facility in verbal communication.

The following summary indicates, in general terms, other kinds of situations for which direct observation might be a useful technique in home economics research:

1. Observing behavior under conditions of normal functioning

2. Studying behavior of someone who would have difficulty in communicating verbally

3. Obtaining an accurate description of a specific event

4. Observing the communication, problem-solving, or other aspects of interaction in small groups

5. Determining the critical incidents, or requirements, that are essential for accomplishing a specific task. As the name implies, the critical-incident technique refers to a study of significant aspects of some observable human activity. For example, it could be used to determine factors that lead to unusual success or failure on a job, such as teaching. A home economics teacher could apply the same principles in identifying and reporting facts about behavior in any classroom situation of limited complexity. The technique is designed to distinguish between behaviors that are critical and those that are not critical, but it does not discriminate between behaviors with regard to degrees of criticalness. Once the significant behaviors are determined, they can be used as the basis for forming categories in an evaluation instrument. Among its applications are the following:

    (a) Measures of typical performance (criteria)
    (b) Measures of proficiency (standard samples)
    (c) Training
    (d) Selection and classification
    (e) Job design and purification
    (f) Operating procedures
    (g) Equipment design
    (h) Motivation and leadership (attitudes)
    (i) Counseling and psychotherapy[35]

[35]John C. Flanagan, "The Critical Incident Technique." Psychological Bulletin 51: 327-358; July, 1954.

6. Self-reporting of an individual who keeps track of what he does for a certain period of time with respect to a specific behavior or who looks back on situations in which he manifested certain behavior

As is true of any research technique, observation has certain limitations. Since observers tend to see only what they are trained to look for, careful advance planning, including a description of the characteristics to be observed, is necessary in order to obtain meaningful data. On the other hand, a person may become so obsessed with his hypothesis that he is looking for facts to support it and he ignores facts that are in disagreement. In some instances, people may be willing to give self-reports on events or behavior of a highly personal nature that could not be observed by an outsider. The presence of an observer may cause individuals or groups to change their usual behavior and try to create a good impression. The cost of observation is likely to be high, including the salaries of highly trained observers who may be required to devote several hours to each observation, and the expenses of recording, analyzing, and interpreting the data. Still another limitation is the difficulty in knowing exactly when a desired event might occur spontaneously so as to have an observer present on such occasions. Usually, observations are focused upon small aspects of behavior and we may fail to see this behavior in its true contect. Although it is easier to observe overt acts, we must not neglect important qualitative aspects that can help us know how to interpret the behavior which is observed.

Four studies have been chosen to illustrate some of the home economics research in which the observational method was used:

TEACHING FOODS. --Shaw was concerned with management problems associated with meal preparation in a 55-minute period. Following a survey of literature related to her problem, she observed three classes with varying levels of experience as they prepared and served meals. She observed their "planning, time management, energy expenditure, condition of kitchen, table service, hospitality, food preparation, and table setting." From her analysis of these observations, she was able to determine some of the weaknesses and to plan laboratory lessons on methods of work simplification.[36]

DECISION MAKING. --Paolucci asked 24 beginning teachers to keep a log for two weeks indicating their decisions regarding management. This part of her study involved a planned self-report where the teachers were asked to keep their own records on a specific topic for a given length of time. She supplemented the teachers' self-reports by visiting each teacher to see her at work and interview her after the logs had been completed.[37]

TEACHER EDUCATION. --Wylie combined interviews and observation in her study of the functions of the college teacher of home economics education. She visited student teaching centers with teacher educators and attended conferences that the teacher educators had with student teachers and cooperating teachers. She observed college classes and committee meetings of the teacher educators.[38]

---

[36] Dorothy Maxine Shaw, "Interests and Problems Related to Meal Management in the Fifty-five Minute Period." Unpublished Master's thesis, University of Wisconsin, Madison, 1957. (As reviewed in Studies of Home Economics in High School and in Adult Education Programs 1955-58. Vocational Division Bulletin Number 286, Home Economics Education Series Number 32. Washington, D. C.: U. S. Department of Health, Education, and Welfare, 1960. Pages 32-33).

[37] Beatrice Paolucci. "Decision-Making in Relation to Management in Classes of Home Economics by Beginning Teachers." Unpublished Doctor's dissertation, Michigan State University, 1956. (As reviewed in Studies on the Teaching of Home Economics in Colleges and Universities 1955-56. Vocational Division Bulletin No. 276, Home Economics Series No. 31. Washington, D. C.: U. S. Department of Health, Education, and Welfare, 1959. Page 12-13).

[38] Mary M. Wylie, "The Functions of the College Teacher of Home Economics Education." Unpublished Doctor's dissertation, Teachers College, Columbia University. (As abstracted in Journal of Home Economics 48: 210; March, 1956).

COOPERATION. --Healthy and unhealthy competition and cooperative ways of working toward goals were defined by Halstead. She obtained her data by direct observation of high school home economics teachers in their relations with students. She described 42 learning situations and analyzed them according to the patterns of working toward goals.[39]

Procedures for Observing Behavior

In a complex situation, no one can expect to observe everything that takes place. Observations must be selective and specific. The most relevant aspects should be chosen and defined in advance. Specific activities or behavior should be identified with the qualities to be observed. Since most observational studies involve social interactions or personality development, you might benefit from the list of significant elements of every social situation as given by Selltiz. However, you should select only the most relevant items from the following list if you are planning an observational study:[40]

1. The participants--including who they are, how they are related to one another, and how many there are.

2. The setting--its appearance; the kinds of behavior it encourages, permits, discourages, or prevents; the kinds of behavior likely to be perceived as expected or unexpected, approved or disapproved, conforming or deviant.

3. The purpose--the official purpose and reactions to it, other goals that seem to be pursued and whether these goals are compatible or antagonistic.

4. The social behavior--what the participants do, how, and with whom; what was the stimulus for behavior, toward whom or what is the behavior directed, what form does the behavior take, what are its qualities (intensity, appropriateness, duration), what are its effects?

5. Frequency and duration--when did the situation occur, how long did it last, does it recur?

Observation must be systematic. Careful planning and control should be exercised over such factors as the number of observations, replications to see whether the same results will be obtained on other occasions, length of the observation periods, and the interval between them.

Recording Observations

Observations should be recorded objectively, indicating what actually happened rather than what the observer thought the behavior represented. Immediate recording in precise, concrete, and quantitative terms helps to increase accuracy. Shorthand records, still or motion pictures, and sound records are helpful in obtaining complete records which can be studied and analyzed thoroughly following the observation period.

Good and Scates emphasized that: *"The results of systematic observation of behavior can be checked and often verified, by comparing the results of different observers*

---

[39]Georgia Halstead, "Some of the Ways Teachers and Students Work Together Toward Goals." Unpublished Doctor's dissertation, Pennsylvania State University. (As abstracted in Journal of Home Economics 47: 205; March, 1955).
[40]Selltiz, op. cit., pages 209-210.

or by repeating the study. [41] Before gathering data for the major part of a study, observations of the same behavior should be made by two or more persons to see how well they agree on the frequency of certain occurrences. If a high reliability of observation is found, one observer's results can be accepted for the remainder of the study. If the observers are not satisfied with the reliability of their observations, they should work on ways of improving the validity and reliability of their method. A simple formula for finding the per cent of agreement between two observers is:

$$\frac{2 \text{ X number of agreements}}{\text{total of observer A + total of observer B}}$$

In a case where more than two observers were used (N represents the number of observers), the general formula would be:

$$\frac{N \text{ X number of agreements}}{\text{total A + total B + total C ... total N}}$$

In carrying out the formula for two observers who agreed on ten ratings, and each observer had made 25 independent ratings, the per cent of agreement would be:

$$\frac{2 \text{ X } 10}{25 + 25} = 40\%$$

SELECTED REFERENCES

Association for Supervision and Curriculum Development. *Research for Curriculum Improvement.* Washington, D. C.: The Association, a Department of the National Education Association, 1957. Pages 93-94.

Good, Carter V. *Essentials of Educational Research.* New York: Appleton-Century-Crofts, Inc., 1966. Pages 242-258.

Rummel, J. Francis. *An Introduction to Research Procedures in Education.* Second edition. New York: Harper & Row Publishers, Inc., 1964. Pages 84-98.

Selltiz, Claire et al. *Research Methods in Social Relations.* Revised edition. New York: Holt, Rinehart and Winston, Inc., 1959. Pages 200-234.

Thorndike, Robert L. and Elizabeth Hagen. *Measurement and Evaluation in Psychology and Education.* Second edition. New York: John Wiley & Sons, Inc., 1961. Pages 399-420.

Van Dalen, Deobold B. and William J. Meyer. *Understanding Educational Research.* New York: McGraw-Hill Book Co., Inc., 1962. Pages 46-57.

SCALING METHODS

Scaling techniques enable us to obtain appraisals which can be translated into quantitative facts and analyzed statistically. In education, scales are used in a variety of ways, such as for measuring attitudes, rating food products or constructed garments, evaluating personal characteristics or behavior, and identifying interests. They vary from those which are quick to answer without much thought to the more complex ones where the rater is forced to discriminate between degrees of behavior.

This portion of the chapter presents some of the factors which influence the dependability of ratings, some of the kinds of scales which are appropriate in research studies, and some specific illustrations of the use of various techniques in home economic education.

---

[41] Carter V. Good and Douglas E. Scates, <u>Methods of Research</u>. New York: Appleton-Century-Crofts, Inc., 1954. Page 648.

Dependability of Ratings

Many problems arise when you try to obtain ratings on the extent to which a person possesses certain traits. Thorndike and Hagen discussed the following problems:[42]

> *Factors affecting the rater's willingness to rate conscientiously*
>   *Unwillingness to take the necessary pains*
>   *Identification with the persons being rated*
>
> *Factors affecting the rater's ability to rate accurately*
>   *Opportunity to observe the person rated*
>   *Covertness of trait being rated*
>   *Ambiguity of meaning of dimension to be rated*
>   *Uniform standard of reference*
>   *Specific rater idiosyncrasies*

Among the errors that enter into ratings are: a tendency to rate everyone too high, neglecting to use the "below average" side of the scale; rating everyone too low (because of the judge's personal bias), rating everyone in the middle position (especially in a three-point scale), using similar ratings for several attributes possessed by one individual (allowing your general impression of the person to influence your rating of his specific traits), and misinterpreting the meaning of various statements.

As a means of overcoming the tendency to be too generous or too lenient in rating, you can instruct a rater to compare a person with certain percentages of his group. For example, is he in the highest 10 per cent of his class, but not in the top 2 per cent?

Variations of Scales

Rank-order scales involve a serial arrangement of items in relation to others in a specific group. Rating scales enable you to determine the extent to which an attribute exists without relation to any specific group. An individual may place himself somewhere on a scale, as in a self-administered questionnaire, or another person may rate his behavior and assign it to a scale position.

The remainder of this section presents a number of variations in rating scales, with examples of how they have been or might be used in home economics education.

RANKING--One of the simplest types of scales involves the placing of individuals or items in order, according to their excellence. If the rater is competent and he is judging a specific characteristic, the results can be highly reliable. Usually we can rank more easily if we pick out first the highest and the next one or two, then the poorest and next to the poorest, and finally fit the middle ones into position. The resulting scale is an ordinal scale, giving merely the rank order of stimuli on a given characteristic but no information on the size of difference that separates the ranks.

Ranking becomes very difficult when a group is large. Thorndike and Hagen have summarized its advantages as follows:

> *It forces the person doing the evaluation to make discriminations among those being evaluated. The ranker cannot place all or most of the persons being judged in a single category, as may happen with other reporting systems. Secondly, it*

---

[42]Robert L. Thorndike and Elizabeth Hagen, <u>Measurement and Evaluation in Psychology and Education</u>. Second edition. New York: John Wiley & Sons, Inc., 1961. Pages 355-361.

washes out individual differences among raters in generosity or leniency. No matter how kindly the ranker may feel, he must put somebody last, and no matter how hard-boiled he is, someone must come first. Individual differences in standards of judgment are eliminated from the final score.[43]

Cutler used a ranking scale in her instrument on values in choosing a home.[44] The respondent was instructed as follows:

What kind of home would you be happiest to live in? Would you like to know the answer to this question? Then read the directions carefully in the following pages and do exactly what you are asked to do and when you get to page 14 you will have the answer.

First, look through the list of homes below and decide which home you would like best to live in and put a 1 beside that place. Look through the list again and write 2 by the place you like next best. Then look for your third choice and write 3, and keep going until you number every place. There should be 10 numbers.

	Your choice		*Your choice*
A very beautiful home	_____	*A home where hobbies or other interests can be followed*	_____
A very comfortable home	_____	*A home which gives you privacy*	_____
A home with everything convenient	_____	*A home that will be safe*	_____
A home in a very good location	_____	*A home where you can do things together and bring your friends*	_____
A home planned for good health	_____	*A home that isn't expensive*	_____

PAIRED COMPARISONS.-- With the method of paired comparisons, every person or item is compared with each of the others and judged to be better or worse than the other. Two items (one pair) are responded to at a time. Paired comparisons can be used for scaling values, attitudes, or products. This approach is useful only with a small number of items. When ten items are used, 45 pairs must be compared. Fifteen items would necessitate 105 comparisons. You can determine how many pairs would be necessary by applying the following formula, where n stands for the number of items:

$$n (n - 1) / 2$$

In her instrument on values in choosing a home, Cutler had the respondents rank the ten values according to their *"first thought"* or verbalized pattern of values. Then she asked them to read descriptions of each value, such as:

This is a beautiful home. It has nice colors and good design. It is good to look at both inside and outside, and fits in with the surroundings. You may not have much chance to carry on your hobbies and may not have much privacy but it is very beautiful.[45]

---

[43]Thorndike and Hagen, op. cit. , pages 371.

[44]Virginia F. Cutler, Personal and Family Values in the Choice of a Home. Cornell University Agricultural Experiment Station Bulletin 840, November, 1947. Page 8.

[45]Cutler, loc. cit.

Following this, each word was paired with each other word, and the individual was asked to indicate his preference in each of the 45 pairs.

For example:

> *1--is the <u>beautiful</u> home. It has nice colors and good design. It is good to look at both inside and outside.*

> *10--is the <u>inexpensive</u> home. It won't cost much to operate and will suit the family income.*[46]

When this part of the test was completed, a score was obtained for each of the values in comparison with the other choices, thereby indicating the individual's "functional pattern of values."

GRAPHIC SCALE. --The rank order and paired comparison scales involve making a relative judgment as to how one item compares with another. In other forms of scaling, absolute judgments are made in which the respondent makes a judgment on one item at a time until he has completed the series of items.

The graphic rating scale is suitable to use with young students or with adults who have not been privileged to complete high school or college. Behaviors to be rated can be stated very concisely; response categories can be very simple; and the respondent merely places a check at any point along a continuum. A neutral or average position usually is at the center of the scale.

For example, students in a foods laboratory might rate their performance on a scale such as this:

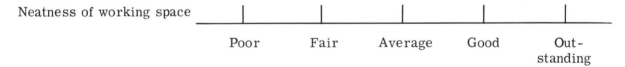

Neatness of working space

Poor   Fair   Average   Good   Out-standing

BEHAVIORAL DESCRIPTION. --Although a graphic scale has few words and appears to be easy to answer, it has the disadvantage of being ambiguous. How neat must the working space be to be rated "good"? Does average refer to the typical performance in this one group or to the performance that should be expected of most individuals at this level? Vivid and meaningful descriptions at two or more levels are helpful. Notice the reduction of ambiguity as the behavior on the graphic rating scale is described to indicate what is meant by poor performance, average performance, and outstanding performance. This item is only one of a series included in the <u>Minnesota Check List for Food Preparation and Serving</u>:[47]

	1	2	3	4	5	Score
NEATNESS OF WORKING SPACE	No space to work; food spilled; table cluttered with dishes and utensils which are not put to soak or washed		Not very orderly but working space made available when needed; dishes and utensils fairly well cared for as used.		Working space always available; clean and orderly; minimum number of dishes used; dishes and utensils properly cared for.	1)____

[46]Cutler, <u>loc. cit.</u>

[47]Clara M. Brown, <u>Minnesota Check List for Food Preparation and Serving</u>. Minneapolis: University of Minnesota Press, 1945.

When using a scale that contains behavioral statements, the rater is instructed to read each description and decide whether the person's behavior is described by one of the statements, or whether he should be rated in between two of the categories. The corresponding number is then written on a blank at the right side of the page. The total score is obtained by adding the ratings on each of the items.

EQUAL APPEARING INTERVALS. --Thurstone originated a technique for measuring attitudes that is called "equal appearing" intervals. This method was used by Herrington in preparing her scales on attitudes toward family living. Home economics teachers who were participating in a Curriculum Workshop wrote several hundred statements expressing various beliefs regarding personal, family, and community relations. After eliminating duplicate ideas and editing the items, she presented the statements to a group of 45 judges who worked independently in classifying the items. Each item was placed in one of 11 piles, ranging from the highest appreciation of family living in the first pile to the least favorable attitudes toward family and community living. The median of the judges' ratings became the scale value of an item. An item was discarded as ambiguous if the judges' ratings varied beyond what she considered an acceptable semi-interquartile range (Q).

The following items have been selected from the scale, Choosing a Life Partner. They illustrate the kinds of attitudes that represent various points on the continuum from the least favorable to the most favorable attitudes:[48]

1.0	25.	*Boys and girls should know something about managing finances before they marry.*
2.0	44.	*Marriages are happiest when both partners are of the same social status.*
4.6	33.	*A boy should have the consent of the girl's family before marrying her.*
5.6	34.	*It is difficult for a girl to get into circulation again after going "steady."*
6.6	17.	*Inter-faith marriages should be avoided.*
8.4	10.	*Although a boy has bad habits, he will reform if he loves a girl enough.*
10.2	14.	*Divorces should be easier to get in case one makes a mistake in choosing a life partner.*

When selecting the items to appear in the attitude scale, you should try to have approximately an equal number from the various points along the continuum, from one extreme to the other. The number of items may be reduced to as few as 20 if the scale is a reliable measure of a single attitude.

An individual responds to this type of scale by checking only the items with which he agrees, and his score is the average of the scale values for these items. Normally, his responses will represent items of similar scale values if his beliefs are consistent and the scale is valid. An individual whose responses are scattered over several scale positions probably does not have well-crystallized attitudes on that subject, or the attitude scale is not functioning well in measuring his attitudes.

---

[48] Evelyn Herrington, Choosing a Life Partner. Syracuse: Syracuse University Press, 1948. (See also Carolyn R. Wickes, "A Study of the Attitudes of Three Groups of Married Couples," Unpublished Master's thesis, Syracuse University, 1956.)

Selltiz discussed the following objections to the Thurstone-type of scale:

> *First, many have objected to the amount of work involved in constructing it. . . .*
> *A second criticism has been that, since an individual's score is the mean or median*
> *of the scale values of the several items he checks, essentially different attitudinal*
> *patterns may be expressed in the same score. . . . A still more serious question has*
> *to do with the extent to which the scale values assigned to the items are influenced*
> *by the attitudes of the judges themselves.*[49]

LIKERT-TYPE SCALES. --The Likert technique overcomes some of the objections to the Thurstone methods, particularly in eliminating the judges. In responding to each item, a person indicates how strongly he approves or disapproves, usually on a five-point scale. Responses that are most favorable are given the highest ratings (or lowest, as long as the same plan is followed throughout the scale). An individual's score is the sum of his ratings on each item. The statements are selected on the basis of the scale's internal consistency--that is, each item discriminates well between people who obtain high scores and those who receive low scores on the scale. Items which fail to correlate with the total score are eliminated as not contributing to the internal consistency of the scale.

Pace and Wallace included six items on the Household in their survey of the opinions of Syracuse University graduates. Respondents indicated the degree to which they agreed with each statement, according to the following scale: *SA--strongly agree; A--agree; ?--no opinion at all; D--disagree; SD--strongly disagree.* The first item of the scale was:[50]

> *SA   A   ?   D   SD*
> *1   2   3   4   5   Keeping a family or personal budget is*
> *   more trouble than it is worth.*

The advantages and disadvantages of the Likert-type scale were summarized by Selltiz as follows:

> *First, it permits the use of items that are not manifestly related to the attitude*
> *being studied. . . . Second, a Likert-type scale is generally considered simpler to*
> *construct. Third, it is likely to be more reliable than a Thurstone scale of the*
> *same number of items. . . . Fourth, the range of responses permitted to an item*
> *given in a Likert-type scale provides, in effect, more precise information about*
> *the individual's opinion on the issue referred to by the given item.*[51]

SCALOGRAM ANALYSIS. --Guttman developed a technique of measuring attitudes that could be helpful in home economics studies, although the method is beyond the scope of this book. Briefly, the scalogram hypothesis is *"that the items have an order such that, ideally, persons who answer a given question favorably all have higher ranks on the scale than persons who answer the same question unfavorably."*[52]

Items used in a scalogram have a cumulative property so that an individual who checks a given response would also have checked the responses below that level. A hypothetical illustration of such a scale is this:

1. Do you have one or more siblings?   _____ Yes _____ No
2. Do you have three or more siblings?   _____ Yes _____ No
3. Do you have five or more siblings?   _____ Yes _____ No

---

[49] Selltiz, op. cit., pages 362-363.

[50] C. Robert Pace and Donald G. Wallace, A Questionnaire on the Activities, Opinions, and Experiences of College Graduates. Syracuse University, 1948.

[51] Selltiz, op. cit., page 368.

[52] Samuel A. Stouffer, Measurement and Prediction. Vol. IV. Studies in Social Psychology in World War II. Princeton, N. J.: Princeton University Press, 1950. Page 9.

Unless a person misunderstood the question or was careless, he could not check "Yes" for item 3 without also checking "Yes" for items 1 and 2. For this type of question, the order is implicit.

If you use subjective kinds of questions, you need to have judges determine the rank of the items in advance. Only those items on which judges have close agreement should be included in the scale analysis.

Selltiz gave the following illustration of an item using the Guttman technique of scale analysis:[53]

> *1. A young child is likely to face serious emotional problems if his parents get divorced.*
>
> *2. Even if a husband or wife are unhappy in their marriage, they should remain together as long as they have any young children.*
>
> *3. Divorce laws in this state should be changed to make it more difficult to get a divorce.*

In responding to this item, an individual indicates whether he agrees or disagrees. If his score is two, and the items form a perfect cumulative scale, you can tell immediately that he agreed with items 1 and 2.

MAN-TO-MAN COMPARATIVE SCALES. --In this technique, a rater is asked to compare an individual with people whose characteristics are known to him. He may be directed to compare with given individuals whose names are on the rating sheet. He may be instructed to think of someone he knows well who is very high on the trait to be rated, and then think of someone who fits each of the other categories. The person to be rated is compared with those whom the rater has placed at the various positions.

Reliability of ratings can be enhanced by focusing the rater's attention on one aspect at a time. Good and Scates raised a question about the isolation of elements from complex situations but concluded that this was not a serious problem because: *"Improvements in practice or in objects such as school buildings are usually made in terms of details, which is in keeping with the nature and use of appraisal instruments."*[54]

FORCED CHOICE. --Thorndike and Hagen discussed a pattern in which *"the rater considers a set of attributes at one time and decides which one (or ones) most accurately represents the person being rated."*[55] Theoretically, each choice is equally attractive, as in the following example for evaluating Air Force technical-school instructors:[56]

> a. *Patient with slow learners.*
> b. *Lectures with confidence.*
> c. *Keeps interest and attention of class.*
> d. *Acquaints classes with objective for each lesson.*

In reality, the choices are not equal. One has been found to distinguish between good and poor instructors, and it is given a rating of 2 (part a in this illustration). The least discriminating item, on the basis of the preliminary investigation, is given a score of 0 (part b). The other two items, have a score of 1.

---

[53] Selltiz, op. cit., page 374.

[54] Good and Scates, op. cit., page 683.

[55] Thorndike and Hagen, op. cit., page 372.

[56] R. W. Highland and J. R. Berkshire, A Methodological Study of Forced Choice Performance Rating. San Antonio, Texas: Human Resources Research Center, Lackland Air Force Base, May, 1951. Research Bulletin 51-9.

By forcing raters to make choices without knowing how these choices will contribute to a total score, it is possible to eliminate some rater bias. Although the technique shows considerable promise, it may antagonize the persons who have to do the rating, because they must decide between items which all seem to be equally descriptive of the candidate or none of the items seems to fit the candidate.

SCORE CARDS. --In distinguishing between rating scales and score cards, Good and Scates said that rating scales usually have fewer characteristics and may include descriptions of various degrees or characteristics. On the other hand, score cards usually include more aspects or characteristics of the object and call for an evaluation of each aspect, not merely its presence or absence. A score card assigns a definite number of points to each item and may set general standards, describing only a satisfactory level.[57]

Tinsley developed a score sheet for rating three-day food records. On the basis of the total scores, she classified diets as poor, fair, or good. Her score sheet was set up as illustrated in the first part which follows:[58]

FOOD GROUPS	NO. OF SERVINGS	RATING				DIET SCORE
		0	1	2	3	
1. Green and yellow vegetables (some raw, some cooked or canned). Average serving: 2/3 cup cooked or 1 cup raw.		none	one	two	three	1._____

Q SORT. --Although a large part of research is based upon the testing of groups, Stephenson thought it should be possible to make a scientific study and reach valid conclusions based upon the measurement of one individual. The technique which he developed is called the "Q Sort." Basically it is a type of correlation. Each person performs the same task, such as scoring a set of statements or ranking a series of paintings. The resulting pairs of scores for each description can be correlated.

The first step is to prepare a list of statements (or other stimuli) toward which the individual is to react. Validity of the set of statements is a prime factor in determining the usefulness of the responses an individual makes. You will need to define your subject and obtain expert opinion as to whether or not the statements measure what you wish to measure.

About 100 statements are usually included in the set. However, as few as 50 or as many as 150 might be included. Each statement is written on a separate card and numbered at random. The cards are given to an individual with the instructions that he is to sort them into piles, placing a specified number of statements in each pile (a "forced-choice" technique). The following example shows typical distributions that might be used with a series consisting of 100 items and another series of 50 items:

	Prefer least								Prefer most		
Pile	1	2	3	4	5	6	7	8	9	10	11
Number of cards											
(100 items)	2	4	8	12	14	20	14	12	8	4	2
(50 items)	1	2	4	7	7	8	7	7	4	2	1

[57]Good and Scates, op. cit., page 682.

[58]Clara B. Arny, Evaluation in Home Economics. New York: Appleton-Century-Crofts, Inc., 1953. Page 219.

When 50 - 80 items are used, the number of piles might be reduced to nine. When more than 100 items are included, the number of piles might be increased to 13.

Although the number of piles and the number of statements to be placed in each pile might vary, the distribution is approximately a bell-shaped or normal curve. The advantages of a forced choice is that the distribution is the same for all raters. The disadvantage is that an individual cannot be scored. His responses are compared with those of other individuals or with his own responses (self-sort) on other occasions.

The respondent is instructed to pick out the items for the four best-liked categories first (or those that are most descriptive of him). Then he chooses the four-least-liked categories and, finally, he fills in the middle categories. This procedure is used because it is usually easier to declare what you like or dislike intensely than what you feel neutral about. Moreover, the extreme positions are more important than the middle ones in determining the size of correlations and so it is important that they be as reliable as possible.

The Q Sort forces a normal distribution of responses. No matter how many statements an individual might wish to endorse, he is forced to limit his choices to the number specified on each card. He is free to consider each statement in the light of all other statements and to weigh the relative value he feels should be assigned to any statement. This approach may have an advantage over the usual attitude scales where an individual responds that he agrees, disagrees, or doesn't know how he feels about a single item, without viewing it in relation to the entire picture.

The Q Sort lends itself to both individual and group analysis. For example, an individual's responses might be analyzed for relative dominance of various values or attitudes being measured, the correlation between Q Sort responses made by the individual at the beginning and end of a course (or on other occasions), a comparison of the individual's self-concept on various occasions, the correlation between an individual's rating of himself and his ideal self, the correlation between a student's self-rating and a rating by one of his professors, or a comparison between the responses of a husband and wife. Group responses might be analyzed to determine the mean for each value or attitude measured by the Q Sort, the extent of variation within a group of statements, correlations between ratings of various groups, and the significance of the differences between groups of students who have had different levels of experience.

The Q Sort is versatile. It can be used with a sample of photographs, drawings, art objects, descriptions of behavior, or personality traits as well as with a set of statements. Stephenson reported using a sample composed of 60 colored papers, including brilliant colors and delicate hues. Individuals were asked to select those they liked the most and those they liked the least. Correlations were factored to see if their choices might be a basis for classifying persons.[59] He also studied the esthetic values of art students by using 120 cards containing various arrangements of colored rectangles, some of which were overlapping while others were not overlapping, some were of regular design while others were irregular. He was testing the hypothesis that experienced artists would prefer irregular and overlapping designs.[60]

SEMANTIC DIFFERENTIAL. --How an individual reacts to a situation is determined by what the situation means to him rather than by the intrinsic properties of the event. Osgood developed a way of measuring "meaning," of determining how an object, person, or idea affects an individual.[61] The Semantic Differential is the result of an attempt to subject meaning to systematic quantitative measurement.

[59] William Stephenson, The Study of Behavior. Chicago: The University of Chicago Press, 1953. Page 9.
[60] Ibid., pages 128-144.
[61] Charles Osgood et al., The Measurement of Meaning. Urbana: The University of Illinois Press, 1957. 342 pages.

The Semantic Differential measures connotative rather than denotative meaning. Underlying the Semantic Differential is the hypothesis that the connotative, or affective, components of meaning can be measured by rating objects or ideas with respect to bi-polar adjectives. It is assumed that pairs of bipolar adjectives (such as strong versus weak) are continua along which connotative meanings are expressed. Each pair of adjectives is called a scale. An individual is asked to respond to a number of these scales and he may be asked to rate one or more objects or ideas on the scales. Seven-step scales are used and the individual makes one check mark on each scale to indicate how closely he associates the concepts with the end points of that scale. If the bipolar adjectives seem to him to be unrelated to the concept, he would presumably place a mark toward the middle of the scale. Here is the way the concept "Home Economics" might be rated on a number of scales:

Home Economics

Good	:	:	:	:	:	:	*Bad*
Valuable	:	:	:	:	:	:	*Worthless*
Foolish	:	:	:	:	:	:	*Wise*
Powerful	:	:	:	:	:	:	*Weak*
Hard	:	:	:	:	:	:	*Soft*
Heavy	:	:	:	:	:	:	*Light*
Active	:	:	:	:	:	:	*Passive*
Slow	:	:	:	:	:	:	*Fast*
Dull	:	:	:	:	:	:	*Sharp*

Factor analysis has shown that it is not necessary to think in terms of many small dimensions. Three "super" dimensions are sufficient to treat most of the meaning in the concepts. The individual scales are not really independent--things that are rated as good as generally rated as valuable, beautiful, sweet, nice, honest, pleasant, wise, positive, and reputable. Therefore, only a few scales need be used to sample the important super dimensions, or factors: Evaluation, Potency, and Activity. Evaluation is the most important factor and this is illustrated by the first three scales above. The next three scales illustrate the Potency factor and the last three are from the Activity factor. Usually three or four scales are used to measure each of the three super dimensions and the score for the concept on each factor is determined by averaging the scores for the scales used to measure that factor.

Among the ways in which the Semantic Differential has been used are the following:

1. A comparison of attitudes of certain groups toward education. These groups might include liberal arts professors, education professors, and students working for credentials.

2. An investigation of the meaning structure in American culture and in other cultures.

3. Choosing a brand name for a new product. The manufacturer or the advertiser considers the group of consumers who might buy the product and decides what

image would be most attractive to them. Some prospective names are administered to a sample of the consumers to determine what the images of these names are. Then the brand name is selected which most closely approximates the chosen image.

4. Studies of public reactions to social issues, minority groups, commercial products, or various social and family roles.

SELECTED REFERENCES

Ahmann, J. Stanley and Marvin D. Glock. *Evaluating Pupil Growth.* Boston: Allyn and Bacon, Inc., 1958. Pages 73-74, 323-326, 337-338, 437-442.

Hall, Olive A. and Beatrice Paolucci. *Teaching Home Economics.* New York: John Wiley & Sons, Inc., 1961. Pages 91-96, 325-328.

Nunnally, Jum C. *Tests and Measurements.* New York: McGraw-Hill Book Co., 1959. Pages 377-389.

Parten, Mildred B. *Surveys, Polls, and Samples.* New York: Harper & Row Publishers, Inc., 1950. Pages 190-198.

Rummel, J. Francis. *An Introduction to Research Procedures in Education.* Second edition. New York: Harper & Row Publishers, Inc., 1964. Pages 198-226.

Selltiz, Claire et al. *Research Methods in Social Relations.* Revised edition. New York: Holt, Rinehart and Winston, Inc., 1959. Pages 344-384.

Thorndike, Robert L. and Elizabeth Hagen. *Measurement and Evaluation in Psychology and Education.* Second edition. New York: John Wiley & Sons, Inc., 1961. Pages 353-384.

Underwood, Benton J. *Experimental Psychology.* Second edition. New York: Appleton-Century-Crofts, Inc., 1966. Pages 191-214.

Chapter 9
STATISTICAL TREATMENT AND SIGNIFICANCE OF DATA

STATISTICIAN: a person who carefully assembles facts and figures for others who carefully misinterpret them.
-- Comic Dictionary

Statistics is a term that refers to methods of collecting and interpreting facts. As a home economist, you need to have an understanding of the many types of statistics that are applicable to educational studies. You should be familiar with the assumptions underlying their use, as well as with the procedures and interpretation of the statistics used. Since the kind of a sample you select influences what kinds of statistical procedures can be applied, sampling is discussed in the first part of this chapter.

SELECTION OF A SAMPLE

The word, population, refers to a specified group of individuals or objects having a common, measurable characteristic. These could include events, test items, objects, attributes, or fabrics, as well as human beings. Often a population is too extensive to be enumerated. Even if it were possible to identify each of its elements, to study a whole population might be very costly and time-consuming. Therefore, most studies are based on a sample, or a portion of the population. When a sample is a good one, we are able to predict certain things about the population from which it was drawn. This is known as statistical inference.

Benefits of Sampling

Parten discussed the following advantages of sampling:

1. An estimate of the characteristics of the total population can be secured in a much shorter time. In certain types of studies the time-saving is particularly helpful in making possible the analysis of data before they become out of date.

2. Properly designed samples may reduce the cost of a study by requiring fewer persons to gather and process the data and by reducing the necessary space and equipment.

3. The money saved by sampling can be used to study the same cases more intensively, extend the study to other groups, or repeat the study in the same area at a later time.

4. More attention can be given to each return, thus increasing the accuracy of analysis and trustworthiness of the results. [1]

---
[1] Mildred B. Parten, Surveys, Polls, and Samples. New York: Harper & Row Publishers, Inc., 1950. Pages 109-110.

Principles in Designing a Sample

Sample design is concerned with determining which elements of the population to observe. This includes decisions on how many cases and how to select them. In developing a sampling plan, you should strive for the following:

1. Accuracy of the sampling estimate so that it approximates the true figure.

2. Reasonable precision for the purpose of the study. The degree of precision can be stated in advance. Precision refers to the degree to which the sample estimate approximates the results that would be obtained if a complete enumeration were made of the population by the same methods used in the sample. The necessary size of sample can be predetermined by means of probability sampling.

3. Adequacy of sampling procedure so that the probability of selecting each unit of the population is known. When techniques of stratification are used, there must be careful definition as to the individuals or groups included or excluded. Specific techniques should be suggested for handling refusals or other problems in carrying out the sampling plan.

4. Limited number of subclassifications:

    (a) Number of breakdowns justifiable for size of sample.
    (b) Subclassifications based upon intimate knowledge and experience with the various interrelationships.
    (c) Plan for selection of subdivisions requiring less effort and cost than would be necessary for studying the total population.

5. Economic feasibility.

According to Parten, the first step in designing a sample is to define the population as to the *"place, time, and relevant characteristics of the group to be sampled."*[2] Actually, an investigator determines his own definition of the population. The sampling problem becomes a matter of selecting a representative group from within the total population as it has been defined for a given study.

The second step, as suggested by Parten, is to determine the *"sampling unit."* The basis for this choice might be *"geographical, social group, family or dwelling, individuals, events, behavior segment, or trait."*[3] The size of the sample should be considered in terms of the precision necessary for the study, the types of tabulations desired, and the resources available.

Several types of sampling are appropriate for home economics studies, so the third step is to decide which sampling method is best for a specific study. After deciding on the sampling procedures, you should select your sample and evaluate it before proceeding with your study.

Types of Sampling

Several common methods of drawing samples are described in the following paragraphs along with a discussion of their advantages and possible difficulties. Some procedures are suggested for drawing each type of sample. Problems relative to the matching of individuals and groups were discussed previously--in the chapter on experimentation.

---

[2] Ibid., page 116.
[3] Ibid., page 117.

RANDOM SAMPLING. -- *"Random selection is the term applied when the method of selection assures each individual or element in the universe an equal chance of being chosen.*[4]

In order to obtain a random sample, it is necessary to have a complete listing of the individuals constituting the population. Each element of the population is assigned a number. The procedure is to use a lottery method of drawing numbers or to take consecutive numbers from a table of random numbers such as those found in many statistics books.

When properly carried out, a sufficiently large random sample is likely to be representative of the population. Systematic differences between the sample and population tend to cancel each other out. Statistical procedures have been developed for estimating the required sample size and for judging the reliability of data based upon sample estimates. It is relatively easy to obtain a random sample, since you do not need to have knowledge of the characteristics of the population which might be important to your study. Many of the statistics that are widely used, such as the mean, standard deviation, and analysis of variance, are appropriate only when a random sample is used.

Among the difficulties you may encounter in selecting a random sample are:

1. A complete listing of the universe may not be available.
2. Selecting a large random sample may be a laborious task.
3. You should check the list of the population to be sure that it does not contain duplicates (as in a list of parents who might have more than one child in a school).
4. The sample may be widely scattered geographically, increasing the costs of an interview study.
5. You might obtain a poor or misleading sample. For example, the mean of a sample might differ significantly from the mean of the population. Fortunately, such deviations occur infrequently.
6. A random sample may not provide sufficient cases, if you wish to break up the total sample group and analyze data from special subgroups.

CLUSTER SAMPLING. --Sometimes groups are selected as the sampling unit because of greater ease in identifying groups rather than individuals, and less expenditure of time and/or effort. When a complete listing of the population would be impossible, as in the case of all ninth grade home economics students in a given state, cluster sampling might be used. This method may involve several stages of sampling, such as selecting certain counties, then certain schools, and finally, specific classes or individuals.

The term "cluster" is used with reference to various groups, such as schools, classes, households, departments, and geographic areas. When this approach is used to select a sample of individuals who reside in a specific area, the method is called area sampling. Parten has provided a helpful illustration of the steps in arriving at the city blocks and individual households to be sampled for a census or other types of community surveys.[5]

Selltiz pointed out that:

> *With this kind of sampling procedure it is no longer true that every combination of of the desired number of elements in the population (or in a given stratum) is equally likely to be selected as the sample of the population (or stratum).*[6]

---

[4] *Ibid.*, page 219.

[5] *Ibid.*, page 241.

[6] Claire Selltiz et al, Research Methods in Social Relations. Revised edition. New York: Holt, Rinehart and Winston, Inc., 1959. Page 534.

A possible disadvantage of cluster sampling is that "natural stratification" might exist. Persons who live or work together might tend to be homogeneous in race, background, education, income, or other factors.

SYSTEMATIC SAMPLING.--When a complete list of the elements of a population is available, it may be easier to select a sample directly from that list rather than go through the process of numbering each item and drawing random numbers. Systematic or serial sampling can provide an equal opportunity for all units to be drawn, if you select the first item at random. This can be done by deciding on what size sample you want, dividing the total number in the population by your desired sample size, and using this number as the basis for your systematic selection. For example, if you have a list of 400 schools from which you wish to draw a systematic sample of 50 schools, eight is the size of your interval. You start by drawing at random a number between one and eight, and use this as your first unit of the sample. Then you continue, taking every eighth one on the list until you have completed the sample of 50.

STRATIFIED SAMPLING.--Stratified sampling consists of subdividing the population into two or more strata or classes. A random sample is drawn from each of the subgroups. The strata chosen should be important to the subject under investigation and should be capable of accurate classification. Because of this latter requirement, we tend to use such variables as geographic location, age, sex, socio-economic status, or education as the bases for stratification. Stratified sampling is useful in community surveys or polls of adult groups.

In proportional stratification, the characteristics of the sample are drawn in the same proportion as they are represented in the universe. For example, in a statewide study of home economics education, you might start with a list, by counties, of all of the secondary school home economics teachers. If you desire to have a 10 per cent sample, you assign a number to each teacher and then proceed to draw numbers at random until you have reached the desired number from each of the strata. The counties having the largest numbers of teachers have greater representation in this type of sample than do the counties having fewer teachers.

Disproportional stratification means that an equal number of cases is drawn from each subgroup regardless of the proportions in the population. For the type of study described in the preceding paragraph, you would select at random the same number of home economics teachers from each county regardless of the total number of teachers in the county. The advantages of disproportional sampling lie primarily in the economy of gathering data from a small group and in the ease of comparing data when the subgroups are of equal size. In reality, we usually find that some of the strata have too few persons to provide even the minimum number needed for the sample, or some of those who were chosen do not respond. As a result we have inequality in numbers. The sample often *"has the combined disadvantages of unequal numbers of cases, smallness, and nonrepresentativeness."*[7]

Stratified sampling helps to insure the inclusion of each essential group in the sample. Another advantage is that it is not necessary to have a complete list of the population. When the population is homogeneous and the data for stratifying are accurate, you may achieve greater precision with fewer cases than would be possible with a random sample. A further advantage is that the statistics which are applicable to random samples may be applied when the individual cases selected for each strata have been chosen at random.

One of the possible difficulties you might encounter is in choosing the strata significant to your study. Which factors to select is important as well as their relative frequency

---

[7]Parten, op. cit., page 229.

in the population. If a sample is to be stratified on several factors, you also might have difficulty in finding enough cases to meet your specifications. Since random cases are selected within each stratum, it is possible to obtain a poor representation.

Selltiz indicated that the:

> . . . *procedure of drawing a simple random sample and then dividing it into strata is equivalent to having drawn a <u>stratified</u> random sample using, as the sampling fraction within each stratum, the proportion of that stratum that turned up in our simple random sample. Thus, even though we were not in a position to stratify in advance, we can take advantage of the increased efficiency of stratified sampling.*[8]

"JUDGMENT SAMPLES."--Cornell classified several techniques under the heading of "judgment samples" because they have an unknown possibility of error. If you choose to use a nonrandom method of sampling, you should remember that the usual procedures of statistical analysis are not applicable because the sample cannot be considered representative of any known population. Nevertheless, if good judgment is used in drawing a sample, you can obtain useful information about a group which may suggest significant problems and hypothesis for study with a more extended population from which you can generalize. "Judgment samples" include:[9]

1. Sample of convenience, such as using a class that is handy.
2. Canvas of experts, such as mailing a questionnaire to carefully chosen, <u>informed</u> persons.
3. Sample based on an absolute list not adequately covering the population, such as a telephone directory for use in sampling the adult population of a city.
4. Sample with a high degree of nonresponse, which might be the result when a questionnaire is mailed to individuals.
5. Pinpoint or representative-area sampling, such as the purposive selection of a <u>typical</u> school, classroom, or community.
6. Quota sample, in which a system of selection is worked out, but the interviewers are free to select their own individuals to fill their subsample quotas. For example, an interviewer might go to heavily populated places, such as an airport, where the quota could be filled easily but the respondents would probably not be typical of the population. [9]

Evaluating a Sample

Ideally, a sample represents the population from which it was drawn. For example, if 25 per cent of the home economics teachers in a state have taught for five years or less, a sample of that population should have approximately 25 per cent of its teachers with five years of teaching experience or less. Data on the important characteristics of the universe are not always available, so other methods must be used for judging the adequacy of a sample.

Peatman has suggested that the character of a sample depends upon the methods used in sampling the universe. The precision of a sample refers to *"the extent to which any measure derived from it agrees with the value of that measure for the universe sampled."*[10]

---

[8]Selltiz, <u>op. cit.</u>, page 533.

[9]Francis G. Cornell, "Sampling Methods" <u>in</u> Chester W. Harris, <u>Encyclopedia of Educational Research</u>. New York: Macmillan Company and the American Educationsl Research Association, 1960. Pages 1181-1183.

[10]John G. Peatman, <u>Descriptive and Sampling Statistics</u>. New York: Harper & Row Publishers, Inc., 1947. Page 313.

The following guides are helpful in determining the precision of a sample:

1. Precision is a function of the size of a sample
2. Sampling statistics are based upon the assumption that only chance errors affect the result.
3. Larger samples are required for smaller differences to be significant.
4. A larger sample is necessary when the population is heterogeneous than when it is homogeneous.[11]

Slonin summarized the factors that determine the sample size required: *degree of precision desired, variability of the data being sampled, sampling method used, and estimating procedure employed.*[12]

Parten showed ways of computing necessary sample size and permissible errors of tolerance in sampling.[13]   Usually it is desirable to determine the size of sample necessary and then draw a slightly larger one to allow a margin of safety.   Riley cautioned that *"bias is not affected by the sample size. Large samples are no more successful than small samples in (1) overcoming distortion in the designation of the frame..., (2) offsetting the tendency of interviewers (if left to their own devices) to select only certain types of respondents, or (3) counteracting the greater readiness of certain respondents to reply (if respondents are allowed to select themselves)."*[14]

SELECTED REFERENCES

Parten, Mildred B. *Surveys, Polls, and Samples.* New York: Harper & Row Publishers, Inc., 1950. Pages 219-244.

Rummel, J. Francis. *An Introduction to Research Procedures in Education.* Second edition. New York: Harper & Row Publishers, Inc., 1964. Pages 66-83.

Selltiz, Claire et al. *Research Methods in Social Relations.* Revised edition. New York: Holt, Rinehart and Winston, Inc., 1959. Pages 509-545.

PURPOSES AND APPLICATION OF STATISTICS

Such a broad topic as statistics cannot be covered thoroughly in only a portion of one chapter in this book. This chapter presupposes that you have a basic knowledge of statistics and that you will refer to a book on the subject for a thorough understanding before you attempt to apply statistics in any home economics study. For these reasons statistical formulas are not included here. The discussion centers around what statistical procedures might be useful, rather than how to apply them. You should plan your analysis of data before starting to gather the data in order to be sure that you can interpret and make generalizations from your study.

Statistical analysis and interpretation of data reveal the true significance of facts. The proper use of statistics will enable you to describe and interpret data, to estimate the amount of confidence you can have that your sample represents the total population, and to determine whether two samples appear to have been drawn by chance from the same population. You can also tell whether or not you would be justified in generalizing from your sample to a larger group.

---

[11]Ibid., pages 313-315.
[12]Morris J. Slonin, Sampling in a Nutshell. New York: Simon and Schuster, Inc., 1960. Page 72.
[13]Parten, op. cit., pages 304-309.
[14]Matilda W. Riley, Sociological Research: A Case Approach. New York: Harcourt, Brace & World, Inc., 1963. Page 291.

Statistics may be used to describe or as the basis for making inferences. Descriptive statistics tell about the central tendency of the data, their variability, relationship between different factors, and differences between two or more groups. Inferential statistics help to establish the reliability of generalizations that might be drawn from a study. Nonparametric statistics are useful when certain assumptions regarding the normality of the population variance are not met.

Central Tendency

Among the most widely-used statistics are the measures of central tendency--indications of what is average or typical in a series of scores. The mode, median, and arithmetic mean are easy to understand and to compute, but any measure of central tendency by itself does not give an adequate picture of a group. As you will see later, the variability of a group usually needs to be reported as well.

MODE. --The mode is the value or item that occurs most frequently in a statistical series. When scores are arranged in order of their size, as in a frequency table, the mode can be determined readily by inspection. It is not as reliable as the median or mean, especially in small samples, and it may fluctuate from one sample to another. The mode of one sample cannot be combined with the mode of another distribution. The mode is easy to determine and to understand. It is not necessary to know the values of the highest and lowest scores in the series since these extreme scores do not affect the mode. The mode fluctuates widely from one sample to another.

When you are interested primarily in a quick, rough estimate of the most typical item, trait, or score in a group, the mode is useful. For example, you might report the mode in answering such questions as the following:

1. What is the average state minimum salary for beginning teachers throughout the United States?

2. What make of electric range is used in the average high school home economics department?

3. How many minutes in length is the typical class period for a seventh grade home economics class?

4. What is the most typical major curriculum of high school students who are enrolled in home economics courses?

MEDIAN. --A median is a point on a measurement scale below which half of the scores lie and above which the other half of the scores lie. When an odd number of scores is involved, this point is identical with the value of the middle score. If an even number of scores is used, the median is midway between the two middle scores. The median is useful when you plan to report percentile scores, since the median is the same as the 50th percentile. It is more appropriate than the mean when there are a few extremely high or low scores that cause a marked skewness in a distribution. One disadvantage is that the medians of two or more distributions cannot be combined to find the median of the combined distribution.

The median is appropriate when answering such questions as:

1. What is the average age of women at the time of their marriage?

2. What is the average salary of home economics teacher educators in a state?

3. What is the median scale value assigned by a group of judges to an item on s Thurstone-type attitude scale?

4. Is Mary Jones' score in the upper or lower half of the scores made by entering home economics freshmen at a given college on the <u>Cooperative Reading Test</u>?

ARITHMETIC MEAN. --The mean is an average obtained by adding all the scores in a series and dividing by the number of scores. It is the most widely-used measure of central tendency because of its accuracy and stability from one sample to another. Tate explained that *"the means of random samples drawn from a normal population differ less among themselves and less from the actual point of central tendency of the population than do other averages."* [15] The means of two or more subgroups may be combined, making possible further statistical manipulation of the data. Since each value affects the size of the mean, an extremely high or low score may exert undue influence on the mean.

The mean is appropriate for most sets of data in which consistency from sample to sample is desired and where the distribution is symmetrical.

Group Variability

A measure of the central tendency of a group gives a picture of what is the typical or average case, but it does not indicate whether the cases tend to cluster near the average or how much they spread out. The extent and manner of variation are the distinctive properties of a frequency distribution. Three measures of variability are common--the range, quartile deviation, and standard deviation.

RANGE. --The crudest measure of variability may be obtained simply by noting the difference between the lowest and the highest scores in a series. Since only two scores are used in determining the range, it is not as reliable as other measures of variability. The range is easily determined and understood. It is a useful estimate of population variability when the sample is drawn from a normal population. Usually it is more meaningful when combined with other measures, as in Arny's summary of the undergraduate programs of teachers participating in the Minnesota study of the effectiveness of the home economics program. She listed eight subject areas, such as physical science, and showed the average number of credits, the per cent of credits, and the range of credits the participating teachers earned in these subject areas.[16]

When comparing two distributions, the range should be used only when the units of measurement are the same and the sizes of the two groups are similar.

QUARTILE DEVIATION. --A quartile deviation is most likely to be used in situations where the median and percentiles are applicable, since it is obtained by locating the 75th percentile (Q_3) and the 25th percentile (Q_1). The distance between Q_3 and Q_1 is divided in half to obtain the value of Q (called the semi-interquartile range). In a symmetrical distribution, the quartile deviation is useful in showing the range of the middle 50 per cent of the cases. It is independent of the effects of extreme cases.

STANDARD DEVIATION. --Just as the quartile deviation is linked with the median, the standard deviation is a measure of the spread of a distribution from the arithmetic mean. Since it is affected by the deviation of each score, it should not be used when there are a few extreme values in a series. In a normal distribution, approximately

---

[15]Merle W. Tate, Statistics in Education and Psychology. New York: Macmillan Co., 1965. Page 56.

[16]Clara B. Arny, The Effectiveness of the High School Program in Home Economics. Minneapolis: University of Minnesota Press, 1952. Page 50.

two-thirds of the cases fall in the distance between one standard deviation below the mean and one standard deviation above the mean. When the sample is quite large, most of the cases fall within the range of six standard deviations, three below and three above the mean. The standard deviation is the most commonly-used measure of variability because of its reliability and its usefulness in further statistical analyses. It is the square root of the variance.

Relationship between Variables

Correlation refers to the relationships between variables that can be quantified and for which pairs of scores are available for the same individuals in a given group. (e.g., whether test intelligence is related to academic success. Several methods of finding correlation are in use, but only the two most common ones are discussed here.

A correlation may range anywhere from -1.00 through zero and up to +1.00. A positive correlation, between zero and +1.00, indicates the degree to which a high score on one trait means a correspondingly high score on the other trait. A negative correlation, from -1.00 to zero, refers to the degree to which high scores on one trait are accompanied by low scores on the other trait. Perfect correlations are rare, but the closer a correlation approaches either -1.00 or +1.00, the greater is the likelihood that the two sets of variables are related. You are confronted, then, with the problem of determining how significant any correlation is. Guilford discussed the complications of this problem.

The question regarding size of r cannot be fully answered without making reference to particular uses of r. One common use is to indicate the agreement of scores on an aptitude test with measures of academic or of vocational success. Such a correlation is known as a validity coefficient.... Common experience shows that the validity coefficient for a single test may be expected within the range from .00 to .60, with most indices in the lower part of that range....

It is well recognized that a reliability coefficient, which could be found by correlating two forms of the same test, is usually a much higher figure than a validity coefficient.... in practice we expect reliability coefficients to be in the upper brackets of r values, usually .70 to .98, and validity coefficients to be lower, usually .00 to .80.

...a correlation is always relative to the situation under which it is obtained, and its size does not represent any absolute natural fact.[17]

Arny cautioned against three common errors in the interpretation of correlation coefficients:

1. Assuming that if two variables are highly correlated, one causes the other. Both may be influenced by another factor or factors.

2. Generalizing from the sample for which the computation was made to groups of which it was not representative.

3. Assuming that a correlation coefficient of a given size always has equal significance. We can place more faith in a correlation coefficient which was computed for a large number of cases than when only a few were involved; when the distributions were "normally" distributed than when they were not; and when each group was relatively homogeneous than when it was very heterogeneous.[18]

[17]J. P. Guilford, Fundamental Statistics in Psychology and Education. Fourth edition. New York: McGraw-Hill Book Co., Inc., Pages 103-105.

[18]Clara B. Arny, Evaluation in Home Economics. New York: Appleton-Century-Crofts, Inc., 1953. Pages 301-302.

One way in which we use correlation is to determine the reliability of test scores. Three common ways of finding the reliability of tests are the split-half technique, test-retest, and the use of comparable forms. The <u>split-half</u> method consists of dividing the test in two parts. This is done usually by computing separate scores for the odd-and-even-numbered items and finding the correlation between the scores on the halves of the test. Since a longer test is usually more reliable than a shorter test, the Spearman-Brown formula is used to estimate the reliability of a test that would be twice as long as the half-tests and composed of items similar in difficulty and discrimination to those on the half-tests.

The <u>test-retest</u> method consists of administering the same test on two separate occasions and correlating the scores obtained by each individual. The use of <u>comparable forms</u> means that two different forms, considered to be equivalent, are given on two occasions and the results for each individual are correlated.

PRODUCT-MOMENT CORRELATION. --The most common method of computing correlation is the Pearson's product-moment method, which involves the use of a scatter diagram unless a calculator is available. With a calculator, the computation requires just one step in addition to those necessary for finding the means and standard deviations of two sets of data. The additional step, which can be taken simultaneously with finding the sums of the raw scores and sums of the squares of the raw scores, is to obtain the sum of the XY products for each pair of scores.

RANK ORDER CORRELATION. --The Spearman rank order correlation method is adaptable particularly to small groups, in which the number of paired scores is 30 or less. Since it depends upon placing scores in their order, from highest to lowest, it may be used when exact scores are not available and only the rankings are available. Rank order correlation assumes that the measures are independent of each other.

The first step in computing this type of correlation is to place each set of scores in rank order, usually with the highest score having a rank of 1. The lowest score has a rank identical with the number of paired scores being ranked. When two scores are tied, they are temporarily assigned to two rank positions, then the distance between these two positions is divided equally, and both scores are assigned that rank. For example, if two scores of 12 would occupy the positions of 5 and 6 when being placed in rank order, both of the scores are ranked as 5.5. If three scores are tied, all three receive the rank of the middle score (for example, if there were three scores of 12 that would occupy the positions 5, 6, and 7, each of the scores would be ranked as 6).

Item Analysis

One method of estimating the validity of an instrument is to measure the extent to which each item correlates with the total test scores. A question is considered to be discriminating if it differentiates between people who obtain high total scores and those who receive low total scores. Since discrimination is influenced by the difficulty of an item, a thorough item analysis consists of finding both the discrimination value and the level of difficulty of each item.

According to the method developed by Flanagan, the maximum discrimination is obtained by using the papers of the highest 27 per cent and the lowest 27 per cent on the basis of their total scores. This method, which was described by Thorndike is particularly useful when 100 or more papers are available for the analysis.[19]

---

[19]Robert L. Thorndike, <u>Personnel Selection: Test and Measurement Techniques</u>. New York: John Wiley & Sons, Inc., 1949. Pages 227-256.

Hall and Paolucci described a way of analyzing items for groups with fewer than 100 papers.[20]

Differences between Groups

The chi square technique, which may be used when each category has a frequency of 10 or more, is a means of comparing a set of obtained proportions with what might be expected of theoretical proportions. Although any number of categories may be used, usually we test the significance of differences between two groups on two responses.

When small groups are being compared, the t test is more precise than chi square. It is used to determine the significance of differences in the means of two groups. McMillan used both chi square and the t test in comparing the differences in reaction to the proposed program of family life education for elementary schools as evaluated by teachers, parents, and students.[21]

When more than two groups are to be compared, the F test (analysis of variance) indicates whether there is more variability between the groups than within the groups. If F is significant, then it is worthwhile to compare each set of two groups to determine which ones are significantly different. Webber compared home economics teacher education majors at the University of California, Los Angeles, with other women teacher education majors in the College of Applied Arts. She applied the F test first to see if there were significant differences on the quantitative, linguistic, and total scores these students obtained on the Psychological Examination for College Freshmen of the American Council on Education. When the F test indicated significant differences between the groups, she applied the t test to each two groups to determine where the differences were.[22]

A more complicated technique is the analysis of covariance, in which differences between groups are compared while one factor is held constant. In studies where it is impossible to match groups before applying an experimental variable, the analysis of covariance technique makes it possible to eliminate the effects of some important factor such as intelligence.

Statistical Inference

One of the most remarkable things about using statistics is that you can take the information obtained from a rather small group, and from it estimate what a larger group would be like. You can even estimate the accuracy of your prediction. However, if you are to be able to generalize from a sample, you must remember that statistical theory is based on the idea of random sampling.

In order to understand statistical inference, you need to know the characteristics of the normal distribution curve. You can solve quite a variety of problems by applying facts about the area and the per cent frequency under the normal curve. You know that 34.13 per cent of the cases lie between the mean and one standard deviation above it; 68.36 per cent of the cases fall in the area that extends from one standard deviation below the mean

---

[20]Olive A. Hall and Beatrice Paolucci, Teaching Home Economics. New York: John Wiley & Sons, Inc., 1961. Pages 334-335.

[21]Marian McMillan, "An Experimental Program of Family Life Education for Elementary Schools." Unpublished Doctor's dissertation, Pennsylvania State University. (As abstracted in Journal of Home Economics 49: 224; March, 1957).

[22]Vivienne L. Webber, "The Performance of Home Economics and Non-Home Economics Teacher Education Majors at the University of California, Los Angeles, on the American Council on Education Psychological Examination for College Freshmen." Unpublished Master's thesis, University of California, Los Angeles, 1957. 93 pages.

to one standard deviation above it. By referring to the normal curve table you can find answers to such questions as these:

1. How many girls in your home economics classes can be expected to maintain the necessary average to graduate from high school?

2. What proportion of home economics graduates from University A cannot be expected to make a score of 700 or higher on the Graduate Record Examination?

3. What is the lowest test score that a graduate student can make on the Graduate Record Examination and still be in the highest 5 per cent of those who take the test at University A?

4. What is the probability that a student selected at random from among all of the home economics graduate students will have a score of 1200 or higher on the Graduate Record Examination?

As you can see from the kinds of questions just listed, it is possible to determine the probability level, or the odds for or against a certain situation being found. When we speak of probability, we mean the number of times out of 100 that an event will occur. This concept is tied in with "levels of confidence." When we obtain the mean of a sample, we want to know whether it is likely to correspond to the true mean of the population. Imagine that you have taken a series of samples from the population. You have several different means from these samples. From a distribution of these means, you can obtain an estimate of the true mean. Since you really have only one mean on which to base your estimate of the true mean, you compute a standard error of the mean. From it, you can determine confidence limits that indicate the per cent of cases which can be expected to fall within certain deviations from the true mean. If the chances are only 1 in 100 that a sample mean would deviate this much from the true mean, you can have a high degree of confidence that your sample mean is different from the population. We would say that this difference is established at the 1% level of confidence.

The other level of confidence that is used frequently is 5%, meaning that the chances are 5 in 100 that the obtained mean differs from the population mean. If chance alone were operating, we would expect some differences. Suppose that you have been using two methods of instruction and you want to determine whether or not differences of the size that you obtain can be expected, or whether one group really has a higher level of achievement than the other. If the means indicate a difference that is significant at the 5% level of confidence, you can have a high degree of confidence that one group does have a higher level of achievement than the other. Most investigators use either the 1% or the 5% level, but they are not willing to use a less stringent probability level. When we speak of accepting or rejecting a hypothesis at the 1% or 5% level of confidence, we are referring simply to the probability that such a statement should be accepted or rejected. We have not proved that a hypothesis is true or false.

There are four possible results when testing a hypothesis about a population:

1. A true hypothesis will be accepted.
2. A false hypothesis will be rejected.
3. A true hypothesis will be rejected
4. A false hypothesis will be accepted

When you apply a statistical test, you hope to achieve one of the first two results. "Type I error" is a term that refers to the possibility of rejecting a true hypothesis and "Type II error" refers to accepting a false hypothesis. The problem is complicated because if you take steps to reduce the risk of making a Type I error you are increasing the risk of making a Type II error. For example, you can reduce the risk of rejecting a true hypothesis by choosing the 1% level of significance (meaning that you would reject not more than one true hypothesis in 100). You could make the risk of a Type I error as small as you wish, but you must keep in mind that a hypothesis that is not rejected is considered to be acceptable and so you are actually increasing the risk of accepting a false hypothesis. If you were studying a new method of teaching home economics and this method would require drastic changes in class size and expensive equipment, you would want to be quite confident that the new method would be better than the old method. On the other hand, if the new method would be no more expensive and as practicable as the old, you could accept weaker evidence in rejecting the null hypothesis that the new method is no better than the old method. Generally, a low probability or small region of rejection would be selected when there are serious consequences of rejecting a true hypothesis.

Walker and Lev have outlined the steps in formulating and testing a statistical hypothesis:[23]

> 1. *Select the measures on which the investigation will be based.*
> 2. *Specify the general nature of the population and the parameter or parameters needed for the investigation.*
> 3. *Formulate a hypothesis about the population and decide on the alternatives.*
> 4. *Determine a statistic by which the hypothesis is to be tested.*
> 5. *Ascertain the distribution of the statistic.*
> 6. *Choose a level of significance.*
> 7. *Determine the region of rejection on the basis of the level of significance and the alternatives to the hypothesis.*
> 8. *Draw a random sample of size N from the population.*
> 9. *Compute for this sample the value of the previously specified statistic.*
> 10. *Determine whether the computed value of the statistic is in the region of rejection.*
> 11. *Reject the hypothesis if the value of the statistic is in the region of rejection; otherwise accept it.*

In our effort to achieve control and obtain significant results, we should heed Grenwood's caution: *"We must not confuse the exactness of the findings with their significance."*[24] Simple problems may yield to better control but greater validity might be maintained in more complex social settings.

Nonparametric Statistics

Many statistical tests are based on the assumption that the variance of the sample or population is normally distributed. In educational practice, this assumption may not be met. Newer statistical techniques, known as the nonparametric or "distribution-free" tests, are based upon the distributions regardless of the shape of the population variances. When the assumption of normality is valid, the parametric techniques (described previously in this chapter) should be used because they are more "efficient" and they use all of the data.

---

[23] Helen M. Walker and Joseph Lev, Elementary Statistical Methods. Revised edition. New York: Holt, Rinehart and Winston, Inc., 1958. Page 232.

[24] Ernest Greenwood, Experimental Sociology. A Study in Method. New York; Morningside Heights: King's Crown Press, 1945. Page 92.

Barnes has summarized some appropriate uses of nonparametric tests:

1.   *One sample*

Binomial Test--*is useful when a single population consists of only two classes, a "head or tails" situation.   The binomial expansion can be used "to determine how often a sample as unusual as the one observed would come from some hypothesized population wherein we are testing a deliberately introduced independent variable (say psychic powers of the coin-tosser)."*

Chi Square Test--*tests the significance of differences when a sample can be subdivided into two or more categories.   The observed frequency is compared with the frequency that could be expected if chance alone were operating.*

2.   *Two related samples*

Sign Test--*involves using matched pairs or having each individual serve as his own control.   The two sets of scores are compared by counting the number of positive and negative signs and referring these values to a probability table.*

3.   *Two independent samples*

Mann-Whitney U Test--*is used to test the difference between two distributions of scores, even though the two groups differ in size.   The procedures involve ranking the scores as a composite and obtaining the sum of the ranks for the two groups separately.*

Median Test--*tests whether or not two independent groups have been drawn from populations with the same median.   The two groups need not be the same size.*

Chi Square Test--*is useful when frequencies can be expressed in separate, discrete categories which are subgroups of the total sample and which account for all of the cases.*

4.   *More than two related samples*

Friedman Two-Way Analysis of Variance by Ranks--*tests the null hypothesis that three or more samples have been drawn from the same population or populations with the same median.   The groups must consist of individuals who have been matched on relevant characteristics and then assigned at random to one of the experimental situations.*

5.   *More than two independent samples*

Kruskal-Wallis One-Way Analysis of Variance by Ranks--*can be used with groups that have not been matched and are not of the same size.   It indicates whether three or more samples are from the same population or from populations with similar averages.*

Extension of the Median Test--*tests the null hypothesis that no difference exists in the medians of the populations from which the samples were drawn.*

Chi-Square Test for More than Two Independent Samples--*is an extension of the chi square test for two independent samples.*

6.   *Measure of correlation*

Spearman Rank Correlation Coefficient--consists of ranking each individual on variable X and on variable Y, then obtaining the difference between his two ranks. When the correlation coefficient is obtained, it ranges between +1, 0, and -1.[25]

SELECTED REFERENCES

Arny, Clara B. *Evaluation in Home Economics*. New York: Appleton-Century-Crofts, Inc., 1953. Pages 275-334.

Guilford, J. P. *Fundamental Statistics in Psychology and Education*. Fourth edition. New York: McGraw-Hill Book Co., Inc., 1965. Pages 43-112, 136-226.

Lindquist, E. F. *Statistical Analysis in Educational Research*. Boston: Houghton Mifflin Co., 1940. Pages 48-104.

Selltiz, Claire et al. *Research Methods in Social Relations*. Revised edition. New York: Holt, Rinehart and Winston, Inc., 1959. Pages 409-422.

Siegel, Sidney. *Nonparametric Statistics for the Behavioral Sciences*. New York: McGraw-Hill Book Co., Inc., 1956. 312 pages.

Tate, Merle W. and Richard Clelland. *Nonparametric and Shortcut Statistics*. Danville, Illinois: Interstate Printers and Publishers, Inc., 1957. 171 pages.

Tate, Merle W. *Statistics in Education and Psychology*. New York: Macmillan Co., 1965. Pages 42-90, 181-234.

Thorndike, Robert L. *Personnel Selection: Test and Measurement Techniques*. New York: John Wiley & Sons, Inc., 1949. Pages 227-256.

Underwood, Benton J., et al. *Elementary Statistics*. New York: Appleton-Century-Crofts, Inc., 1954. Pages 44-214.

Walker, Helen M. and Joseph Lev. *Elementary Statistical Methods*. Revised edition. New York: Holt, Rinehart and Winston, Inc., 1958. Pages 65-105, 141-243.

---

[25]Fred P. Barnes, Research for the Practitioner in Education. Washington, D.C.: National Education Association, Department of Elementary School Principals, 1964. Pages 86-107.

Chapter 10
PRESENTATION AND INTERPRETATION OF DATA

Every man has a right to his opinion, but no man has a right to be wrong in his facts.
-- B. M. Baruch

Among the most interesting stages of a research study are those involving analysis of the findings, selection of the most important results, determination of interesting and effective ways to present the significant data, and interpretation of the findings to others. An important decision in many kinds of studies centers around when and how to use tables or graphs in presenting your findings. You should not attempt to present all of your data in tables or graphs--to do so would make a monotonous report. On the other hand, the true significance of data can be presented to a better advantage sometimes in a table or graph rather than just appearing in the regular text of a manuscript.

This chapter is intended to assist you in understanding technical data and to stimulate your interest in studying educational literature. A further purpose of this chapter is to suggest appropriate techniques and standards for persons who want to present data effectively to other educators or lay people. The first part of the chapter presents general guides which apply to the use of either tables or graphs. Then a special section is devoted to the construction of tables, and another section to graphs and other types of illustrations. Finally, the interpretation of tabular and graphic data is discussed.

GENERAL GUIDES FOR PRESENTING DATA

As a general guide in determining when to use tables and graphs, Campbell suggested: *"When a straightforward statement will suffice, illustrative materials need not be used."*[1] He mentioned, furthermore, that a long string of numbers detracts from the smoothness of one's writing and may hinder a reader from understanding the data.

No matter how accurate the data, a table or graph will be effective only if people look at it. An inviting appearance is an important characteristic of any illustrative material, especially in these days when the general public is accustomed to a professional presentation of materials on many television programs. When planning a table or graph, you should strive to create a meaningful "picture" with adequate margins, pleasing proportions, proper balance, and a feeling of unity. A table or graph does not need to fill an entire page; rather, it should be drawn together to tell a unified story in a pleasing manner, and it should be able to stand alone whenever possible without being dependent upon the text for explanation. Careful planning and concise legends are essential to make the table or graph independent.

---

[1]William G. Campbell, A Form Book for Thesis Writing. Boston: Houghton Mifflin Co., 1954. Page 45.

A short table, with fewer than four or five items, or a small graph, may be placed on the same page with the text immediately following the paragraph in which it is first mentioned, or on the next page, if necessary, so that it can be presented in full. Triple-spacing separates the text, both above and below from the table or graph.

Generally, each table or graph is placed on a separate page immediately following the first reference to it. Each page is numbered consecutively as a part of the manuscript, and the number is in its regular position even though a table is placed broadside (with its top on the bindery side of the manuscript). A table or graph is referred to by number rather than by an expression such as "The following table."

Each table is numbered consecutively; this also applies to any which are included in the appendix. Formerly Roman numerals were recommended for tables and Arabic numbers for graphs, but the trend now is for Arabic numbers for all types of illustrative materials. Graphs, diagrams, photographs, and other types of illustrative materials may all be numbered consecutively in a series called "List of Figures." However, if you have a large number of any one type of Figure, such as photographs, you may list them separately. The "List of Tables" and "List of Figures" follow the Table of Contents.

Usually the number and title are placed above a table but below a graph or other type of illustration. However, recent recommendations suggest that the title of a graph may be placed above it, especially if that location presents a more unified picture. The title should be concise and clear, omitting such superfluous phrases as "A table showing" or "A graph comparing." A title should indicate such facts as what is being shown in the table or graph, from whom the data were obtained, how many participants were included, and possibly when and where the data were gathered.

If a report contains a number of long titles, a block style may be used in which the title runs the width of the table or graph. Various authorities differ slightly in their recommendations on this point. In any case, when you decide on a style, follow it consistently. The following are examples of block styles:

TABLE 1.--Extent of teacher turnover in the participating
schools and in the other schools during the period of the
project.

Table 1.   Extent of teacher turnover in the participating schools and in the other schools during the period
of the project.

Table 1.   Extent of teacher turnover in the participating
schools and in the other schools during the period
of the project.

An inverted pyramid style is widely used for titles. In this style the number of the table, or figure, is centered above the title. The first line of the title is the longest, with each succeeding line decreasing in length. Each line is centered, each letter is capitalized, and no terminal punctuation is used.

TABLE 1

EXTENT OF TEACHER TURNOVER IN THE PARTICIPATING

SCHOOLS AND IN THE OTHER SCHOOLS DURING THE

PERIOD OF THE PROJECT

TABLES

When specific figures are necessary for clarity, and when a series of numbers is manageable in size, a table may be an effective means of presenting data. When long series of raw data must be presented, the tables may be placed in the appendix so that they do not detract from the continuity of a report.

The goals in setting up a table are to make it accurate, neat in appearance, and easy to interpret. A table achieves these goals when it is kept simple, presenting only one kind of information and only a few aspects related to it. A table should stand alone; that is, it should not be dependent upon the text for its meaning to be clear.

A table consisting of only two columns is completely open--it has neither vertical nor horizontal rulings. Tables of three or more columns are ruled usually, although vertical rulings are optional in a typewritten report. When columns are close together, vertical rulings help to separate various sections of a table. If done carefully, vertical rulings may be made by placing tables in a long-carriage typewriter. Black India ink may be used in doing them by hand.

Stub

The first column heading is called the "stub." If the line titles cannot be summarized briefly, the heading "Item" may be used, but a more descriptive heading is usually possible and preferable. The heading should be centered, both vertically and horizontally, in the space allotted to it.

The line titles should be arranged in a logical order such as alphabetically, chronologically with the most recent date at the top, or numerically with the largest frequency at the top. They are aligned at the left when words are used and at the decimal point when numbers are involved. Only the first word and proper nouns or adjectives are capitalized.

If a line title extends beyond one line, each continuing line is indented to the third space. The data in such cases are on the same line as the last line of the item. A series of subitems is indented in the same manner. Period leaders are often useful to guide to a reader's eye across the open space to the right word or number in the first column. When fewer than ten line titles are used and each title is short, they may be double-spaced. If the titles occupy more than one line, double-spacing may be used but it is probably not necessary. With more than ten line titles, single-spacing is used except between groups of approximately every five items.

Headings

Each column has a box heading to clarify the data being shown in that column. When a heading applies to two or more columns, it is called a spanner heading. A heading should be related only to the material in the column or columns under its span. However, two or three levels of subheadings may be used for clarity. If you wish to refer to columns by number, you can place the number in parentheses below each heading, starting with number (1) under the stub and continuing consecutively in the columns at its right.

All headings are separated from the body of a table by a single line the full width of the table. A double horizontal line separates the headings from the table title. Each box heading is centered, with a blank space above and below it, and space at both ends. Single-spacing is used with a heading.

Long box headings may be placed vertically (broadside), reading up from the bottom of the table. When broadside tables are placed in a report, the title is on the bindery side. Consistency in capitalization is important--usually the first word and proper nouns are capitalized, although it is acceptable to capitalize each important word in a heading.

Cut-in headings may be used to combine materials which would otherwise have to be placed in two or more small tables. The University of Chicago Manual suggested that cut-in heads should not extend through the stub area.[2] However, they are sometimes extended the entire width of a table. Table 2 illustrates the use of cut-in headings.

TABLE 3*

RELATIONSHIP OF EMPLOYMENT OF ALUMNAE

TO COLLEGE MAJOR

Relationship	Home Economics Graduates		Non-Home Economics Graduates	
	N	%	N	%
First Employment:				
Same field as College Major	21	36	26	55
Related Field	2	3	2	4
Different Field	19	33	12	26
Never Employed	16	28	7	15
Total	58	100	47	100
Present Employment:				
Same Field as College Major	10	17	9	19
Related Field	2	3	7	15
Different Field	4	7	5	11
Not Now Employed	26	45	19	40
Never Employed	16	28	7	15
Total	58	100	47	100

* Quoted from Sister Marie Stephen Chapla, C.S.J. "A Study of the Personal, Social and Professional Development of the Graduates from the Department of Home Economics and Other Departments of Mount St. Mary's College." Unpublished Master's thesis, University of California, Los Angeles, 1960. Page 53.

---

[2] The University of Chicago Press, A Manual of Style. Chicago: The University of Chicago Press, 1949. Page 161.

Double vertical lines may be used to separate two sections of a table when the same box headings apply to both sections and the sections are placed side-by-side.

Tables that are too wide to fit broadside may be typed on a wider page which can be folded inconspicuously and neatly into place. However, a photostatic copy can be used to reduce the size sufficiently so that a table is readable and yet fits into the normal size.

When a long table must be continued on another page, the box headings are repeated on every page and the same dimensions are used on each page. The table number and the word "continued" are given on the following pages, but not the title. No horizontal line is used at the bottom of a page until the end of the table is reached.

If the numbers in a column would all be preceded by 0, it needs to be indicated only before the first and last numbers of the series or after a break in the series. Plus or minus signs, degrees, and dollar signs need to be indicated only beside the top number. All numbers in a series should be aligned with the decimal point. An omission may be indicated by a blank space, although period leaders or dashes are preferable to guide the reader's eye to the right positions and to indicate that the omission was caused by a lack of data rather than an oversight in preparing the table.

When totals are presented for each row, the total column is placed at the extreme right. Totals for each column are indicated in a space at the bottom, separated by a horizontal line from the body of the table. The sides of a table are left open, with no vertical lines at either side.

Footnotes

Abbreviations are sometimes used in the box headings or body of a table. Whenever possible, these should be standard forms. Footnotes are used to explain abbreviations, to point out significant differences between parts of the data, or to explain how a difficult table should be read.

Lower-case letters or symbols, instead of numbers, are used in referring to footnotes. If most tables have only one footnote, a single asterisk may be used. Lower-case letters are preferable to double or triple asterisks when several footnotes are necessary. Within a report, either symbols or letters should be used consistently and exclusively.

A footnote is placed one single space below a table, is indented as a paragraph, and is extended the width of a table. If more than one line is necessary, single-spacing is used between each line of a footnote. Double-spacing separates one footnote from another. When a footnote is used with a long table, it is placed on the first page and is separated from the body of the table by the horizontal line which normally precedes a footnote in the text.

SELECTED REFERENCES

Arny, Clara B. *Evaluation in Home Economics*. New York: Appleton-Century-Crofts, Inc., 1953. Pages 259-263.

Campbell, William G. *A Form Book for Thesis Writing*. Boston: Houghton Mifflin Co., 1954. Pages 45-49.

Dugdale, Kathleen. *A Manual of Form for Theses and Term Reports*. Revised edition. Bloomington, Indiana: The Indiana University Bookstore, 1962.

A Manual of Style. Chicago: The University of Chicago Press, 1949. Pages 158-172.

Walker, Helen M. and Joseph Lev. *Elementary Statistical Methods*. Revised edition. New York: Holt, Rinehart and Winston, Inc., 1958. Pages 20-34.

Whitney, Frederick L. *The Elements of Research*. Third edition. Englewood Cliffs, N.J.: Prentice-Hall, Inc., 1950. Pages 409-415.

GRAPHS AND ILLUSTRATIONS

Visual presentation is widely used and is often more effective than tabular or verbal description. Its benefits have been summarized by Modley:

> *Visualized information is faster, more direct, more dramatic and easier to remember. For the large part, also, visual communication conveys a personal feeling which arouses the interest of the average reader.*[3]

Because of these advantages, Campbell found it necessary to caution that: *"As a general rule, Figures are not both easily and inexpensively reproduced."*[4] You must be selective, and then only use them where they are most effective and set a high standard. In general, graphs should be used to clarify numerical data, in presenting relationships among variables, revealing trends or changes over a period of time, or to show how a total is made up of its component parts.

Criteria for Effective Graphic Presentation

This portion of the chapter is devoted to general guides that are applicable in the preparation of various types of graphs and other illustrative materials. Following this, specific suggestions are given for the use of line graphs, bar graphs, pictographs, pie charts, flow charts, sociograms, maps, photographs, and photostats. All of these types of visual materials may be classified as figures. For a more complete understanding of the use of graphic materials, refer to the first part of this chapter, which contains guides for placement, numbering and labeling of tables and graphs. Also, refer to the last part of this chapter for information about discussing and interpreting tables and figures.

As you prepare graphic materials, you should strive to fulfill the following criteria:

1. Accuracy

    All of the data must be correct to start with. The points must be plotted accurately. Intervals should be appropriate in size to show the data clearly and without distortion. Numerical figures shown as part of a graph must be checked for accuracy. They should be placed in a position where they will not distort the data--either on the bars or to the left of each bar so they do not appear to add length to the bars. All scale values should be indicated from zero on to avoid giving a misleading picture.

2. Clarity

    Graphic data may be clarified by including numerical data as part of the graph or in a separate table. However, for a written research report, you should ordinarily choose the most appropriate technique for each type of data rather than present the same data in two different forms.

    Independent variables (such as dates) are placed on the horizontal axis with the low values at the left and high values at the right. The dependent variable, or measured trait, is on the vertical axis with low values at the bottom and high values at the top. A key or legend should be given when necessary. The title

---

[3]Rudolf Modley and Dyno Lowenstein, Pictographs and Grpahs. New York: Harper & Row Publishers, Inc., 1952. Pages 3-4.
[4]Campbell, op. cit., page 50.

should be clear and complete, yet concise. When curve lines are used, they must be distinguished sharply from each other and from the background rulings.

3. Simplicity

Relatively large intervals and as few words as possible contribute to the ease of interpreting a graph. Only the co-ordinate lines that are necessary to guide the reader's eye to the proper position should be shown. As Spear stated, *"The purpose of a chart is to display facts--not to disquise them."*[5]

4. Ease of reading

A careful selection of the best method for showing data is important for readability. All numbers and lettering should be large enough to be read easily. Whenever possible, they should be placed in the proper direction for easy reading. Different colors or various types of lines are efficient ways of differentiating between parts of a line graph.

5. Orderliness and neatness of arrangement

The quality of workmanship is an important factor in the effectiveness of visual material. All pencil lines should be erased. Black India ink or clear, dark colors may be used for drawing graphs. Gummed tape (such as Zip-a-tone or Contak sheets) is available in an assortment of lines. When two or more designs are needed on one chart, they should be distinctive in pattern and shading. The gummed sheets can be cut easily to any desired size or shape. If an error is made, the tape can be removed and relocated easily without leaving a trace. Since this tape has a tendency to loosen in time, its use is recommended for photostatic work rather than for original copies to be placed in a thesis.

Arkin gave a concise summary of the criteria to keep in mind when preparing graphic materials:

An effectively prepared graph should accomplish much the same functions as an advertisement:
  1. It should attract the attention of the reader.
  2. It should deliver its message quickly and simply.
  3. It should be completely self-explanatory and readily understood.
  4. It should inspire confidence in the reader by its workmanlike construction.[6]

Types of Illustrative Material

Each of the following types of illustrative material has a place in home economics educational research. Brief suggestions and possible uses are discussed.

BAR GRAPHS. --Sometimes we refer to vertical bars as forming a column graph, which is similar to a bar graph (normally composed of horizontal bars). Bar graphs may be used to show relationships of two variables for which information is given for one or more groups (usually not more than three groups). Bar graphs are widely used, quick to prepare, and easy to understand. Bars may extend horizontally with the zero position at the left, vertically with the base line at the bottom, or in both directions from a position in the middle of a base line (as in a profile chart).

[5]Mary E. Spear, Charting Statistics. New York: McGraw-Hill Book Co., Inc., 1952. Page 37
[6]Herbert Arkin, Graphs, How to Make and Use Them. New York: Harper & Row Publishers, Inc., 1940. Page 20.

All of the bars within a single chart should be of the same width. The space between bars is usually not more than half the width of a bar. When two or more groups are being compared, the bars for any one item touch each other and a space separates those bars from the ones pertaining to the items on either side of it. The number of cases may be indicated on each bar.

When we wish to compare pairs of items, they may be placed opposite each other with the item being listed between the two parts of each pair. These are called paired bars. The right side of the chart is used for the most important category, and it determines the order in which the items are listed. (See Figure 3).

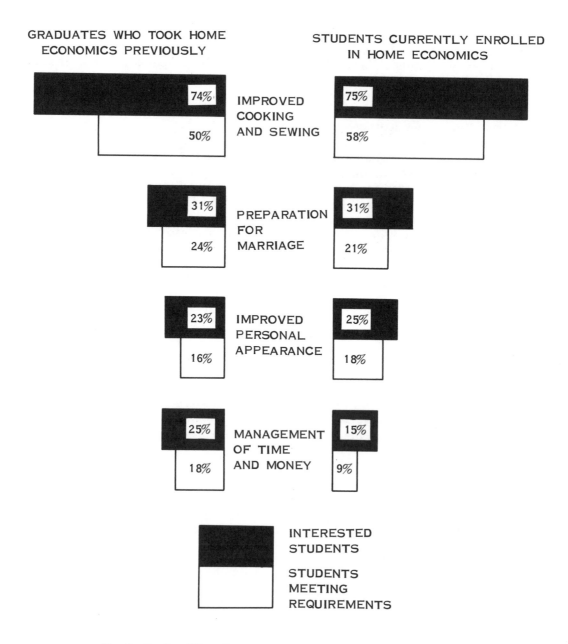

Fig. 3. Benefits of Home Economics to Interested Students as Compared with Those Merely Fulfilling Requirements

When all of the bars are of equal length, representing 100 per cent for each group, they are referred to as <u>100 per cent bars</u>. Shaded areas within each bar, showing the size of its components, should be indicated in the same order on each bar. The heaviest stippling is sometimes placed at the left or bottom, with each section being progressively lighter. (See Figure 4).

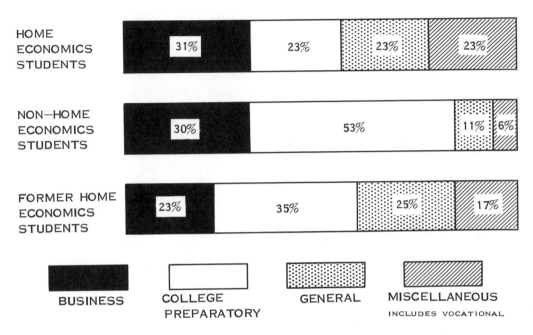

Fig. 4. High School Curriculums of Home Economics and
Non-Home Economics Students

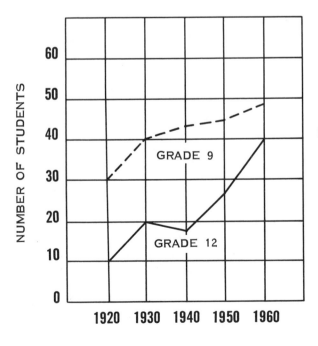

Fig. 5. Students Enrolled in Home
Economics in Grades 9 and
12 of Martin Senior High
School for the Years 1920 - 1960

LINE GRAPHS. --Line or curve charts are used to show the relationship between two variables such as time, age, or test scores. Several series of data may be compared over a period of time. The positions are indicated with a circle or X, and a rounded line connects them. Not more than four or five lines can be shown clearly in one figure. To differentiate between groups, you may use a variety of lines such as solid, hollow, dash, dotted, and a combination of line and dot. (See Figure 5.)

Color is satisfactory when each copy of a report is to contain an original copy. However, color cannot be reproduced in microfilm, which is used commonly to make doctoral dissertations available for interlibrary use. The expense of color reproduction in printing may make its use prohibitive, especially where more than one color is necessary.

Several types of simple line graphs are useful in presenting home economics data:

1. Frequency chart--to show the distribution of a group
2. Percentile chart--to make comparisons between groups
3. Profile chart--to give the relative rank of an individual on a series of measures
4. Surface chart--to emphasize the movement or the magnitude of a trend.

PICTOGRAPHS. --A pictograph often starts with a bar graph. An appropriate symbol is selected to fill in the bar and add interest to the chart. Whenever possible, a symbol should be small enough so that one whole symbol stands on the shortest bar. Each symbol represents 10, 100, or some other unit of children, food, or whatever is being shown. Increasing numbers are shown by adding more symbols of equal size rather than by increasing the size of the symbol (doubling the size of a figure actually increases its area four times).

According to Modley, a good symbol is one which is *"correct, artistically acceptable, sufficiently stylized to be reduced in size without losing its essential characteristics."* [7] He further defined the characteristics of a pictorial symbol as follows:

1. *It follows the principles of good design.*
2. *It is usable in either large or small size.*
3. *It represents a general concept rather than an individual of the species.*
4. *Each symbol is clearly distinguishable from every other symbol.*
5. *It is interesting.*
6. *It is clear as a counting unit.*
7. *It is usable in outline as well as in silhouette form.* [8]

Walker and Lev pointed out that pictographs probably are more interesting to persons unfamiliar with graphic techniques, but there is a trend now to use color and background pictures to create interest rather than to use pictographs:

> *The pictograph has several disadvantages over other types of graphs: (1) Drawing little symbols takes some inventiveness; they must be very simple and must depend more on outline than on detail; different symbols used in the same chart must be easily distinguished. (2) The construction of a bar graph or a line graph is easier except for large agencies which can have a symbol reproduced by a rubber stamp. (3) The pictograph is inflexible and suitable only for very simple data.* [9]

---

[7] Modley and Lowenstein, op. cit., page 22.

[8] Ibid., page 47.

[9] Helen M. Walker and Joseph Lev, Elementary Statistical Methods. Revised edition. New York: Holt, Rinehart and Winston, Inc., 1958. Page 48.

PIE CHARTS. --A pie chart (or area or volume chart) shows how an entire area or volume is divided. This is often used in the form of a three-dimensional silver dollar to show a family or national budget, or the way in which money has been spent. (See Figure 6.)

For materials having not more than five or six parts, a pie chart may make an attractive, simple presentation. The pie chart is of greater interest when its sections are of uneven size than when each one is equal.

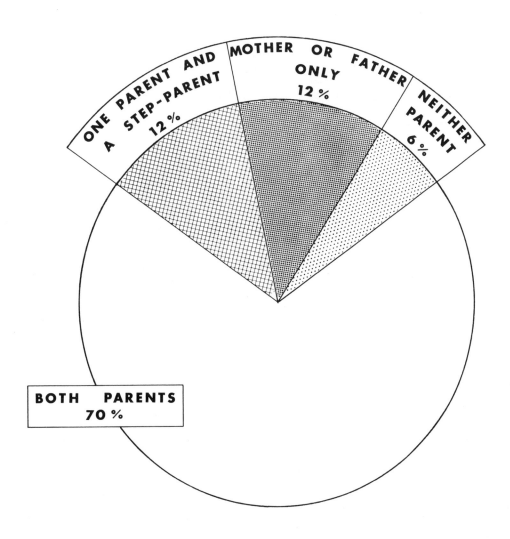

Fig. 6. Home Economics Students Who Are Living with Both Parents and
Those Living in Broken Homes

The largest segment is usually the lightest and is often placed at the top. Other sections follow in a clockwise direction, according to their size, and each is progressively darker. A picture or symbol may be used in each segment along with the printed name of the category and the numerical size. If space within the circle is too small, the labels or pictures may be placed outside. Emphasis may be given to one portion by cutting it and withdrawing it slightly from its normal position in the circle.

The areas for each segment must be of correct size. The proper number of degrees on the circumference of the circle should be measured with a protractor.

FLOW CHARTS. --A flow chart (or organization chart) is a diagram showing the relationship of various parts of an organization. It is used to illustrate such matters as the relative positions of authority, the flow of work in an organization, or the number of persons being admitted to or dropping out at various stages of a process.

Each name or office is centered in a rectangle with the highest position at the top. Lines connect each office to the others with which it is related.

SOCIOGRAMS. --A sociogram indicates the name of each person in a group and shows how he interacts with the other members of the group. Connecting lines with an arrow in one direction reveal a preference of one individual for another. Arrows in both directions indicate mutual choices.

MAPS. --A circle or other symbol may be used to spot locations on a printed outline map. If larger areas are to be shown, gummed tape or coloring are helpful.

PHOTOGRAPHS. --Color photographs may be effective, but the precautions that were mentioned under line graphs must be kept in mind when photographs are to be used in a dissertation or in printed matter. Photographs should be mounted with dry mounting tissue or stationer's rubber cement. Excess rubber cement can be rubbed off, leaving no trace.

PHOTOSTATS. --Photostatic copies are useful in reducing tables or figures to normal page size. Dugdale gave directions for keeping the proportions of a typewritten page and for obtaining a good copy. [10] A new black typewriter ribbon is important to insure clean clear copy. Pale blue lines on graph paper are eliminated in the photostatic process. Each photostated page is given a regular page number in a research report.

Visual materials can be very effective methods of presenting research findings when they are planned carefully, executed with high standards, and interpreted with caution. You must be careful not to distort the true picture by using improper proportions in a graph. Numerical values placed outside bars or segments of a pie chart may change the apparent proportions being represented.

SELECTED REFERENCES

Arny, Clara B. *Evaluation in Home Economics.* New York: Appleton-Century-Crofts, Inc., 1953. Pages 263-274.
Campbell, William G. *A Form Book for Thesis Writing.* Boston: Houghton Mifflin Co., 1954. Pages 50-54.
Dugdale, Kathleen. *A Manual of Form for Theses and Term Reports.* Revised edition. Bloomington, Indiana: The Indiana University Bookstore, 1962.
Modley, Rudolf and Dyno Lowenstein. *Pictographs and Graphs.* New York: Harper & Row Publishers, Inc., 1952. Pages 24-58, 68-79.
Spear, Mary E. *Charting Statistics.* New York: McGraw-Hill Book Co., Inc., 1952. 253 pages.
Walker, Helen M. and Joseph Lev. *Elementary Statistical Methods.* Revised edition. New York: Holt, Rinehart and Winston, Inc., 1958. Pages 35-49.

---

[10] Kathleen Dugdale, A Manual of Form for Theses and Term Reports. Revised edition. Bloomington, Indiana: The Indiana University Bookstore, 1962. Pages 44 and 46.

INTERPRETATION OF TABLES AND GRAPHS

Whitney pointed out that there are two distinct steps in reporting research data--discussion and interpretation. He emphasized that discussion alone is not sufficient; a research worker must be able to present an *"illuminating interpretation of his data."*[11]

Discussion of Data

A previous chapter recommended the use of small sheets of paper for the analysis of data, with each segment of the data on a separate page. A flexible system such as this enables you to arrange the data in logical sequence for discussion.

At the beginning of the discussion, you might explain your plan of procedure for discussion and interpretation. Just as tables and graphs should stand alone, the text in which findings are discussed should be complete and understandable by itself. The goal for discussion is to clarify the data and present significant aspects more forcefully. It is neither necessary nor desirable to refer to all parts of a table or graph, or to restate each item. One helpful procedure is to select the items to be discussed, and then present them in the order of their appearance--working from left to right and from the top to the bottom.

In your discussion, you should call attention to such facts as the following:

1. Outstanding or significant points
2. Common elements in various parts of the data
3. Prevailing tendencies or averages
4. Trends in the data
5. Inconsistencies within the data
6. Differences between parts of the data
7. Deviations from normal expectancy
8. Relationships of two or more items

Interpretation of Data

Whitney explained the difficulties involved in adequate interpretation:

... interpretation means something so intimately related to the content of each separate study that it is almost impossible to discuss it in general.... In general, interpretation means an adequate exposition of the true meaning of the material presented.[12]

Illuminating interpretation is in terms of answering such questions as the following:

1. What are the basic principles applicable to the data and how do they apply?

2. How reliable is the information? When you interpret your research data, you must be honest in evaluating possible weaknesses that could affect your results. Your interpretation might reveal extraneous factors such as ambiguity of questions or a nonrepresentative group of respondents. You might compare how closely you could expect your results to be duplicated on another occasion with how stable a comparison is necessary for this type of data. Inconsistencies within the data should be explained on such bases as inadequate sampling or improper controls.

---

[11] Frederick L. Whitney, The Elements of Research. Third edition. New York: Prentice-Hall, Inc., 1950. Page 410.
[12] Ibid., pages 411-412.

3. To what extent are the measures true and dependable? One way of indicating validity is by comparing results with related data already in existence.

4. What other information is necessary before you can be sure of your interpretation of the data? Statistical measures of significance are helpful, but you must be alert also to the social and educational significance of your findings.

5. What are the implications of the data? Although you must refrain from making judgments as to cause-effect relationships, your interpretation might include an analysis of possible causes for the conditions described, a prediction of their probable effects, or a recommended course of action suggested by the data.

SELECTED REFERENCE

Smith, Eugene R. and Ralph W. Tyler. *Appraising and Recording Student Progress.* New York: Harper & Row Publishers, Inc., 1942. Pages 38-76.

Chapter 11
CONCLUSIONS AND RECOMMEN-
DATIONS BASED UPON RESEARCH

I honestly beleave it is better tew know
nothing than tew know what ain't so.
-- Josh Billings

Perhaps the most frequently-read portion of a research report is the section which summarizes the whole study and highlights those conclusions that the author considers to be justified on the basis of the data. Busy people, who must plan efficient use of a limited amount of time, can read a wider variety of materials by concentrating on their most significant parts. The summary chapter, then, must be very stimulating and sound if such readers are to be attracted sufficiently to read the entire report.

SUMMARY TECHNIQUES

An overview of the purposes and findings of a study not only gives the reader an effective, concise presentation, but it also paves the way for a clear understanding of the author's conclusions and recommendations. A summary is simply a miniature picture of the study. If a famous oil painting of museum size were photographed and reduced to the size of a small snapshot, the same general features would be recognizable even though specific details would no longer be evident. In the same manner, when a detailed research report is reduced to a summary, the essential framework must be retained. The summary should contain a statement of the problem, the method of attack, a review of the findings, and their meaning or application. A summary should not attempt to present details of the data or to introduce findings that have not been discussed elsewhere in the report.

The length and content of a summary are dependent upon the purpose for which it is intended. Several types of summaries are in general use.

Introductory Summary

A technique which is applicable, especially for reporting research results to lay people, is that of beginning the report with a striking conclusion or some of the most interesting findings. The interest of the reader may thus be captured, and he will want to read the rest of the report. The <u>Time Magazine</u> survey of college graduates used this approach in introducing many of its chapters. One example is quoted here:

They come from all kinds of places and all kinds of homes; they go to many different types of campuses, meet many breeds of professors, and study everything from Aristotle to zoology, including, as we have noted, bait casting and tearoom service. Yet in life after the campus, the college graduates have one trait very much in common. Viewed strictly from a materialistic point of view, they are conspicuously successful. They hold the best jobs, the positions of greatest prestige. They make a great deal more money than their non-college contemporaries. By all conventional standards of worldly attainment they have made good almost to the man.[1]

The introductory type of summary is sometimes used in reporting research for professional journals. For example, Dalrymple used this technique in introducing a research report in the Journal of Home Economics:

> *A study dealing with the experiential background of student teachers in home economics showed that richness or sparsity of their experience with homes and children was associated with their teaching proficiency.*[2]

Chapter Summary

A summary at the end of each chapter helps the reader to understand and remember the most important points that were presented. Several paragraphs may be used to present a chapter summary, or the main points may be listed briefly with very little comment, as in the following illustration from the California co-operative study of attitudes:

> *Those who have participated in this study want the homemaking program to be of practical application in the homes of students who are enrolled in homemaking courses; to allow for only the minimum of duplication of what has been learned previously at home or in the school; and to place an emphasis upon the training of both girls and boys for responsibilities in the home.*
>
> *To achieve this type of program, the participants in the study felt that there was a need to increase the attractiveness of homemaking departments and to select and support homemaking teachers who could maintain helpful and understanding relationships with the students in their classes.*[3]

Chapter summaries may go beyond a review of findings. For example, the American Vocational Association study of teacher satisfaction used rather extensive chapter summaries to present the findings, interpret them, and suggest courses of action:

> *Living conditions which these teachers said they found satisfactory were those where they had satisfactory food and well-balanced meals together with some privacy combined with an opportunity to feel at home and entertain their friends. At the same time they wanted some facilities for storage and laundering and pressing. These satisfactions were more frequently realized when they lived with their families or lived alone....*
>
> *The differences in satisfaction with living conditions among regions and among individuals indicated that there were many teachers whose living conditions needed to be improved.... In situations where teachers find many elements of dissatisfaction with living, action is called for in order that individuals will be less likely to leave teaching because of this dissatisfaction.... Supervisors and school administrators might take the initiative in interesting communities in investigating such questions as:*
>
> *Are salaries adequate to enable teachers to live comfortably?*

[1] Ernest Havemann and Patricia S. West, They Went to College. New York: Harcourt, Brace and World, Inc., 1952. Page 25.
[2] Julia Dalrymple, "Relation of Experiential Background to Proficiency in Student Teaching in the Field of Home Economics." Journal of Home Economics 46: 161; March, 1954.
[3] Olive A. Hall, What's the Next Move in Homemaking Education? Volume 24, Number 2. Sacramento: California State Department of Education, 1955. Pages 89-90.

Do living arrangements need improving so that teachers are able to maintain desired privacy? So that they have freedom to entertain friends? [4]

Final-chapter Summary

The final chapter of a thesis usually contains conclusions and recommendations based upon the findings. As an orientation for the reader, the chapter begins with a summary of the purpose, method of procedure, and results. This summary helps the reader to keep the general plan in mind and guides him in thinking about the meaning of the study.

Abstract

Many graduate schools ask each candidate who submits a thesis to write an abstract of a few hundred or thousand words to accompany the thesis. Sometimes an abstract is used as an introduction to a bulletin, such as the research reports published by the Agricultural Experiment Stations.

The Journal of Home Economics rendered an invaluable service by publishing annually, in the March issue, abstracts of doctoral dissertations related to home economics completed during the preceding year. One of these abstracts is quoted as a means of showing how an overview of a study can be given in a few paragraphs:[5]

The purposes of the present exploratory study were: (1) to identify some of the factors (real or latent) which may have a bearing upon the reasons why students do or do not choose home economics as a major field of study in college and (2) to identify personality characteristics of individuals which tend to be dominant in a selected group who have chosen home economics as an area of specialization in college.

It was hypothesized that there would be no significant difference in the personality structure of students who select home economics as an area of specialization in college and those who select other areas of specialization.

The study was limited to 48 white female students enrolled in the University of Tennessee, 1959-60. Four areas of specialization were chosen--home economics, liberal arts, business administration, and nursing. Sophomores and seniors (eight groups in all) participated in the study. Selection of students was limited to those who rated in the upper 10 per cent of their class scholastically. Only single students between the ages of 17 and 24 were included.

Two diagnostic instruments were used for obtaining the data. The major instrument was comprised of a series of five cartoons from the Blacky Pictures, a projective test designed to get at the underlying factors of personality structure. The second instrument was the Traditional Family Ideology Scale. This scale was designed to identify one's ideological orientations regarding family structure and functioning.

An analysis of the data from the Blacky Pictures revealed that the home economics subjects showed less disturbance on the personality dimensions as measured by the Blacky Pictures than did those subjects from the other three areas who participated in the study. Furthermore, the difference between the neutral responses of the home economics subjects and the nursing subjects on the total number of neutral responses indicated that the two groups differ.

---

[4] American Vocational Association, Factors Affecting the Satisfactions of Home Economics Teachers. Research Bulletin Number 3. Washington, D.C.: American Vocational Association, 1948. Page 77.

[5] Nell P. Logan, "Personality Correlates of Undergraduates Selecting Home Economics As an Area of Specialization in College." Unpublished Doctor's dissertation, University of Tennessee. (As abstracted in Journal of Home Economics 53: 232-233; March, 1961.)

An analysis of the data from the Traditional Family Ideology Scale also revealed a number of statistically significant differences between the means of the obtained scores.

The major significance of this study lies in the attempt to identify personality characteristics which tend to be dominant in a selected group who have chosen home economics as an area of specialization in college. The following conclusions suggested by the data of this exploratory investigation seemed justified:

Home economics subjects tended:

1. To be less dependent upon other people
2. To give evidence of creative potentialities
3. To be less conventional in their approach to life
4. To hold a positive self-concept
5. To place emphasis on self-discipline
6. To reveal evidence of positive parental identification

The preceding conclusions delineated from the analysis of the data of this exploratory study support the rejection of the hypothesis as tested by the two diagnostic instruments used in this study.

SELECTED REFERENCE

Rummel, J. Francis. *An Introduction to Research Procedures in Education.* Second edition. New York: Harper & Row Publishers, Inc., 1964. Pages 262-265.

CONCLUSIONS

Occasionally you will find a research report in which a description of the method used, the purpose of the study, or a detailed repetition of the findings is called "conclusions." In such instances, the writer has failed to fulfill the real function of conclusions. Worthwhile and sound conclusions may consist of general factual summaries, critical analyses of the shortcomings or limitations of the study, or advisory hints on the application of results, but their essential function must not be overlooked--they should be generalizations that are warranted by the evidence obtained in the study.

Conclusions are the building-blocks which help your reader synthesize the knowledge he has gained from your study so that he can move toward increased understanding and wissom in applying this knowledge to his daily living. Davis has stressed that synthesis is basic to understanding and it requires the ability to see relationships:

In unifying experiences, ideas and the like, the joining together is possible when the individual SEES where one experience may "hook into" another, where one concept may "hook into" another. This process is continued until a cluster is formed.... The old saying that there is nothing more useless than an unattached fact is balanced by, "There is nothing more dangerous than an unconnected idea." [6]

Each of your conclusions should be analyzed critically since it is possible for you to reach a wrong conclusion. Davis has given the following guide that may help you examine your conclusions:[7]

[6] Elwood C. Davis, The Philosophic Process in Physical Education. Philadelphia: Lea and Febiger, 1961. Page 122.
[7] Ibid., page 117.

In the critical analysis of a statement, we analyze, examine, investigate, and scrutinize:

1. *The statement itself (its meaning, clarity, coherence, et cetera)*
2. *Purpose(s) implied (by the statement)*
3. *Quality and quantity of supporting evidence*
4. *Weakness(es) and strength(s)*
5. *Values implied or obvious*
6. *Validity*
7. *Scope (echelon, hierarchy)*
8. *Applicability and feasibility*
9. *Reliability*
10. *Utility (usefulness)*
11. *Controversiality*
12. *Relationships*
13. *Consequences implied*
14. *Prognosis*

Bebell gave three guides that might assist you in drawing conclusions and making generalizations:

1. *The first thing to do with evidence gathered in a study is to use it to answer certain questions about the specific situation under investigation. . . .*

2. *Generalizations should be made cautiously and tentatively. . . . Needless to say, the wider the gap between the specific and the general the greater is the chance to make errors and lose meaning. . . .*

3. *Conclusions or generalizations should be compared with existing professional consensus. This can be done by finding out the extent to which the findings of a study agree with those of similar studies reported in the literature. It can also be attempted by asking colleagues for their reactions, or by using the jury-of-experts approach.*[8]

The principles involved in drawing conclusions are very much like those necessary for logical thinking:

1. Ability to see the point.

Mander said that the ability to recognize what is the point in question, and to stick to it until it has been dealt with, is the first essential to clear thinking.[9] Merely restating the hypotheses in different words is not a satisfactory way of drawing conclusions; nevertheless, conclusions should have a definite relationship to the purposes of the study.

In answering the question, *"To what extent has home economics education become a part of the rehabilitation program in penal institutions for women and girls in the United States?,"* Marshall studied the extent of the program in relation to course content, available facilities, teaching methods, qualifications of the home economics teacher, and satisfactions experienced by the teacher. She referred to each of these factors in her brief concluding section:[10]

---

[8]Clifford S. Bebell, "Getting Meaning from Research." in Association for Supervision and Curriculum Development, Research for Curriculum Improvement. 1957 Yearbook. Washington, D. C.: The Association, a Department of the National Education Association, 1957. Pages 136-137.

[9]A. E. Mander, Logic for the Millions. New York: Philosophical Library, Inc., 1947. Page 3.

[10]Olive Hall and Elva Marshall, "Homemaking Education as Rehabilitation." American Vocational Journal 31: 17-18; March, 1956.

1.   Home economics is assuming an important role in the educational program of penal institutions for women and girls.

2.   The majority of institutional programs are emphasizing foods, clothing, and related areas.

3.   In the majority of institutions, separate laboratories are provided for the home economics program.   In other institutions, home economics is being integrated with the cottage programs.

4.   Demonstrations, class discussions, and the laboratory method are the most common methods employed in the teaching of home economics.

5.   Administrators want teachers who meet requirements for a teaching credential in their state and who have a well-rounded, mature personality.

6.   Those who work with the girls in these institutions attain great satisfaction from observing changes in behavior that contribute to satisfactory adjustment in home and community after leaving the institution.

2.   <u>Ability to restrict generalizations</u>.

Conclusions should be kept within the boundaries established by the purposes and limitations of the study.   Replication of the findings through the use of other samples is one basis for being able to generalize.   A frequent criticism of research workers is that they try to make sweeping conclusions from limited data.   This criticism can be avoided by introducing conclusions with a statement defining the limits within which the findings from the study might be generalized to a larger population.   For example, Thompson pointed out the necessity for caution in applying his generalization about the effects of two types of educational programs on the social and emotional development of preschool children:

The experimental findings demonstrate (within the errors of measurement) that, with other variables being equal between two groups of children and with a sufficiently large difference between the relative amounts of teacher guidance directed at meeting the children's social and emotional needs in two groups, the highly-guided group will show a significantly different development in ascendance, social participation, leadership, and constructiveness (when faced with possible failure) than a group with little teacher guidance.

It follows from the findings of this study that those experimenters wishing to discover environmental factors related to intellectual growth or reduction of nervous habits must look to other sources than the personal guidance program as defined and set up in this experiment.[11]

3.   <u>Ability to base conclusions on sound facts</u>.

Conclusions should be based only on facts or findings that have been subjected to analysis.   Evidence must be clear and give strong support to the conclusions drawn.   You can take several steps to avoid conclusions that are inaccurate or unsound.   First, you should take precautions throughout your study to prevent

---

[11] George G. Thompson, "The Social and Emotional Development of Preschool Children Under Two Types of Educational Program." <u>Psychological Monographs</u> 56: 27; 1944.

errors of observation, arithmetic, or personal bias. Second, you should be sure to fulfill the assumptions required for whatever statistical procedures you use--for example, random selection of subjects is a basic assumption underlying the use of a number of statistical formulas. Application of these formulas under other conditions is meaningless and the results cannot lead to sound conclusions. When you use statistics, be sure to choose appropriate ones and to exercise care in the interpretation of your results. And finally, make a clear separation between facts and opinions throughout your report.

The California co-operative study of attitudes pointed out the care used to select a representative sample of sufficient size that the results might have general application throughout the state:

> *To the extent that the 49 schools that participated in the study represent schools in California that offer a homemaking program, the conclusions that follow may be generally applied. The participating schools have been selected at random and are representative of the schools that did not participate in the study in the following respects: the size of the community in which the school is located; the student enrollment; and whether or not the homemaking program receives State and Federal reimbursement from the Vocational Education Fund. The conclusions have been presented as a summary of the attitudes that have been given expression by those who participated in the study and represent the bases of the strengthened homemaking programs that those who participated in the study recommend.* [12]

4.   <u>Ability to analyze the limitations of the study</u>.

An investigation does not always yield the kind of data the research worker hopes to find. In your disappointment over not obtaining results that enable you to accept your hypothesis, do not overlook the benefits of negative findings. If you can recognize and report the shortcomings of your own study, you may help another investigator to conduct a similar study with better controls. By eliminating false hypotheses, you are narrowing the field in which the answer must lie. Velat and others, for example, did a careful analysis of the factors that influenced the findings of their study of school lunches and nutritional status: [13]

> *It is recognized that at best the school lunch can make only a relatively small contribution to the child's diet over a period of a year. Only 5 meals out of 21 can come from the school lunch in any one week. Since the schools studied were in session only 185 days of the 365 days of the year, a maximum of 17 per cent of the child's meals for the year might be obtained at school.... Except under unusual circumstances most children will receive a meal of some sort at noon. Whether it is obtained at restaurant, at home, or is brought to school by the child, the meal will make some contribution to the day's intake of various nutrients. This will tend to reduce the possible differential attributable to the school lunch.*

> *In addition to the relatively small contribution of school lunches, a number of other factors affect interpretation of the data in this study and may help to explain why the differences between the children with and without the school lunch were not more marked.*

---

[12] Olive A. Hall, <u>What's the Next Move in Homemaking Education</u>? Bulletin 24, Number 2. Sacramento: California State Department of Education, 1955. Page 105.

[13] Clarence Velat et al., <u>Evaluating School Lunches and Nutritional Status of Children</u>. Circular Number 859. Washington, D.C.: U. S. Department of Agriculture, 1951. Pages 67-68.

HEALTH AND NUTRITIONAL STATUS.--The initial health status of the children from both schools was found to be good.... Under such conditions, an improvement in general health would be rather difficult to demonstrate.

PARTICIPATION IN THE SCHOOL LUNCH PROGRAM.--The extent of participation of the children in the school lunch varied from week to week.... Incomplete records make it difficult to determine the degree to which the child's participation during the experimental period was representative of the entire year.

HOME DIETS OF CHILDREN.--The home diets of the families and their children in the subsample studied in both schools were fairly good for most nutrients. Thus the dietary improvement that might result from a good school lunch becomes less significant....

SOCIOECONOMIC STATUS OF FAMILIES.--The findings may have been influenced by the fact that the families of children in the groups with and without school lunches were not exactly comparable.... The lunch group contained the 10 per cent of the children who were deemed in need of lunches but unable to pay for them. In the Lunch School the lunch group was weighted by a heavy proportion of children from a rural section whose families used appreciable amounts of home-produced foods. A large number of the homemakers in the Control School were employed outside of the home.

An analysis of the limitations of a study need not be confined to a study in which results were negative or inconclusive. The California study of school drop-outs devoted a chapter to evaluation, entitled, "Are Follow-Up Studies Worth Their Salt?"[14]

The potentialities of follow-up studies as a means of evaluating and improving educational programs have been pointed out in the publication and numerous others.... But a practical question remains: Are these potentialities being realized?... Do they (school officials) use the results to improve curriculum, instruction, and guidance services?...

In order to answer these questions, an appraisal was made of the effectiveness of each of the studies that made up the California Co-operative Study of School Drop-outs and Graduates. Information was gathered to determine how the results of the local studies had been used and what the people concerned thought of the follow-up study technique....

Following are the major findings.

How Results Were Used

Distribution of reports.-- ... It appears, then, that the distribution of the reports fell short of the desired goal.

Curriculum revision.--Officials were asked, "How have the results of the follow-up study been used in revision of the curriculum?" Only one school administrator out of the nine who reported believed that the study had made a direct contribution to curriculum revision....

[14] William H. McCreary and Donald E. Kitch, Now Hear Youth. Volume 22, Number 9. Sacremento: California State Department of Education, 1953. Pages 49-52.

Guidance services.--"How have the results of the follow-up study been used in revising the guidance program or facilities?" In answering this question, about half of the respondents (15 out of 28) felt that the studies had made little or no contribution in this area. . . .

Extracurricular activities.--Still another question asked was, "How have the follow-up study results been used in the evaluation of school practices such as the extracurricular activities?" Most of the respondents (20 out of 28) said that no contribution had been made in this area. . . .

Post-school services.--Another inquiry was, "How have the results of the follow-up study been used in setting up additional services to former students, e.g., placement, counseling, adult classes, etc.?" No evidence of any action along this line was reported. . . .

In-service education.--A further question which had implications for in-service education was, "How have the results of the follow-up study been used in gaining a better understanding of the activities of former students?" Again the majority of respondents indicated that no use had been made of the data in this phase of the school program. . . .

Public relations.-- . . . Of 27 respondents, 10 indicated that the results had been used for this purpose only at the time the final report was released. This was generally in the form of newspaper articles or editorials. . . .

Evaluation of the Follow-Up Study Technique

. . . When they were asked, "What has prevented greater use being made of the data collected by the study?" they cited three major obstacles:

1. The staff lacked time to follow through on the recommendations.
2. The sampling of former students was inadequate.
3. Not enough members of the school staff participated in the studies.

The amount of confidence that you can place in a generalization depends upon several factors, such as the number of cases studied, how they were selected, the variety of circumstances under which they were observed, skill of the observer, reliability and validity of the instruments, and the appropriateness and accuracy of the statistical analyses. After stating a conclusion and establishing that it is dependable, you may want to point out its connection with other facts. In doing so, however, you should exercise caution in claiming cause-and-effect relationships.

SELECTED REFERENCES

Association for Supervision and Curriculum Development. *Research for Curriculum Improvement.* 1957 Yearbook. Washington, D.C.: The Association, a Department of the National Education Association, 1957. Pages 135-137.

Davis, Elwood C. *The Philosophic Process in Physical Education.* Philadelphia: Lea & Febiger, 1961. Pages 119-129.

Hillway, Tyrus. *Introduction to Research.* Second edition. Boston: Houghton Mifflin Co., 1964. Pages 77-83.

RECOMMENDATIONS

A single research study may seem to you, as the investigator, to be very small and insignificant. Its value may depend, to some extent, upon how much you are able to do to help put the findings into action. Some research workers feel that their obligation ends when they have reported their findings, whereas others feel that their work is incomplete until they have done something about implementing the findings.

Experience that you have gained through careful and devoted attention to a specific problem over an extended period of time places you, as a research person, in a position where you should have much to offer other people who are interested in similar problems. An evaluation of the procedures and techniques which you used may help another person to plan a similar study in a different setting and thereby clarify some of the findings or verify certain conclusions.

After discussing the factors that influenced the results of the school lunch study, Velat made suggestions for future studies. His suggestions covered two aspects: (1) the selection of a sample--nutritional condition of the children, nutritional quality of the school lunch, and variables on which the school lunch and control groups should be comparable; and (2) the experimental design of the study--the timing and administration of the physical, dietary, biochemical, and other tests.[15]

McCreary and Kitch made the following recommendations on the basis of the data obtained in the California study of school drop-outs:[16]

1. Follow-up studies should be carried to their logical conclusion. They have three phases: (1) the systematic gathering of information from former students, (2) the presentation and interpretation of that information to all persons concerned, and (3) the planned development of modifications in the educational program which the findings justify....

2. Follow-up studies should be made at regular intervals.... A systematic schedule would not only provide a regular source of data on changing educational needs in the community, but also increase staff skill in conducting studies, and make it possible to instruct students concerning their future participation in the studies....

3. Follow-up studies should be school projects, not one-man projects....

4. Follow-up study results must be handled effectively. Serious attention should be given to the process of interpreting and publicizing the data....

5. Technical aspects of conducting follow-up studies deserve greater attention. Next to "wider participation of staff members," respondents cited most often the need to plan follow-up studies more carefully and to improve the questionnaires used.

Recommendations may be given with the supporting data rather than in a separate section. In her summary of the opinions expressed by graduates of the home economics education curriculum at the University of Minnesota, Rose presented a fact and recommendation together as illustrated in the following sentence:

---

[15] Velat, op. cit., pages 68-72.
[16] McCreary and Kitch, op. cit., pages 53-54.

The fact that transfer students generally had to take 2- quarter credits of work, equivalent to one quarter and a summer session of study, more than the average regular student necessitates some study of transfer student problems. [17]

Arny used another approach in stating a major generalization, followed by a series of minor generalizations, in which she gave the supporting evidence based upon the study of the effectiveness of the Minnesota home economics program. An example of her method follows:

Learning is fostered when the curriculum and instructional methods are based upon knowledge of the physiological and psychological development of adolescents at different levels of maturity.

Certain modifications would be likely to improve instruction in foods classes.

1. More emphasis should be placed upon the preparation of meals rather than individual foods.... Students without school instruction in home economics tended to make much lower scores on management in the meal preparation test than did those enrolled in homemaking classes..., whereas the differences in the quality of the products cooked and the scores on the pencil-and-paper tests were much less marked. [18]

Recommendations may be grouped according to the type of action needed to carry them out. For example, Hatfield studied the dietary practices of junior and senior high school students in one school district and made five recommendations by which the school district could help to improve the students' food habits: [19]

(a) Offer a nutrition education program in the district, making nutrition education an integral part of the educational program, and/or offer specific classes in nutrition education at some or all grade levels;

(b) Offer an adult education class in nutrition for homemakers;

(c) Increase the school cafeteria's contribution to improving food habits by offering more of the essential foods;

(d) Improve the types of food available in the schools' snack bars; and

(e) Initiate a snack or nutrition period in both the junior and senior high schools.

Hatfield also recommended that further food studies might be done in the district to substantiate the results of her study:

(a) Follow-up studies using a random sample composed of the same age groups and given at a different time of the year. This type of study would be valuable to administer at intervening periods, to see if there was any improvement or change in the students' food habits as a result of any or all of the five active recommendations being put into practice by the school district;

---

[17] Ella J. Rose, A Study of Graduates of the University of Minnesota Home Economics Education Curriculum. Minneapolis: University of Minnesota, Bureau of Educational Research, 1951. Page 34.

[18] Clara B. Arny, The Effectiveness of the High School Program in Home Economics. Minneapolis: University of Minnesota Press, 1952. Pages 251-255.

[19] Sally Jo Laue Hatfield, "The Dietary Practices of Students in Grades Seven Through Twelve in the Inglewood Unified School District." Unpublished Master's thesis, University of California, Los Angeles, 1962. Page 124.

(b)   Food studies using the grade school children in the district which would en-able the school administrators to see any changes in dietary habits that take place as students grow older.   This would permit the school district to see if there is a critical age at which dietary patterns worsen, and therefore, at this age be able to offer an intensified nutrition education program aimed at the students and perhaps at their parents;

(c)   Food studies using more refined techniques, if time, money, personnel and resources needed were available.   This type of study would give the district the ac-tual nutritional status of its students.

(d)   Studies which would give other interesting and perhaps valuable information in regard to such factors as the relationship, if any, between scholastic attainment and food habits, actual socio-economic levels and food habits, the amount of nutri-tional knowledge that homemakers possess, and the size of the family and its effects on food habits.   To know the relationship, if any, between amount of training, or number of classes in homemaking and food habits might yield meaningful results as to the value of the entire homemaking program in the district.[20]

As an individual, you should be careful to restrict your recommendations to those which you are in a position to make and help carry out. You should be cautious in making recommendations about matters of policy that are not amenable to change without action from higher authorities.

Recommendations probably should not be highly specific as to the exact means of carrying them out. Specific suggestions as to the frequency of repeating a study, details of selecting a sample, or procedures to be followed may discourage another person from beginning a study or taking the necessary action to carry out recommendations.

Davis has presented a series of suggested aids to help one change a belief and some criteria for the acceptance of beliefs. These might well be given serious thought if you wish to make recommendations for changes in practices or policies as outgrowths of a research study:

Some suggested criteria to consider in accepting a belief are: compatibility with other presently-held beliefs; desirability; supportability (based on sound founda-tion); reliability; validity; attainability; understandability; feasibility; applicability.[21]

SELECTED REFERENCES

Davis, Elwood C. *The Philosophic Process in Physical Education.* Philadelphia: Lea & Febiger,
    1961.   Pages 129-137.
Hillway, Tyrus. *Introduction to Research.* Second edition. Boston: Houghton Mifflin Co. , 1964.
    Pages 262-264.

[20] Ibid. , pages 132-133.
[21] Davis, op. cit. , page 131.

Chapter 12
INDIVIDUAL AND PROFESSIONAL RESPONSIBILITIES FOR RESEARCH

Stand upright! speak thy thoughts! declare
The truth thou hast, that all may share!
Be bold! proclaim it everywhere!
They only live who dare.

-- Lewis Morris

Research, in itself, is a challenging experience for the investigator. However, its greatest value is lost unless you are willing to share your methods and results with others. To communicate effectively, you must have not only the ability to write and explain clearly what you mean but also to attract attention and stimulate interest. Furthermore, you should not overlook the responsibility, implicit in research, for following through and helping to bring about desirable modifications or changes based upon the results of your investigations.

This chapter presents guides for an individual research worker, and for groups who are concerned with effective planning and communication of research findings, in the field of home economics education. Two aspects of the problem are discussed--the preparation of a written research report and the role of the home economics profession in planning and supporting research.

PREPARATION OF A WRITTEN RESEARCH REPORT

To guide you in writing a report, this chapter offers some criteria for evaluating a research paper. Then your attention is directed to the organization of a research report, and finally, specific suggestions are included for writing clearly and concisely. As you read this chapter, remember what Good has said: *"In the technical report the soundness of the data and insight in interpretation are the important considerations rather than form and style as such, although commonly there is a relationship between careful organization of materials, sound interpretation of data, and effective style."*[1]

Characteristics of a Research Report

Effective research writing has the following characteristics:

1. Objectivity

   The entire report is written in the third person, with no personal pronouns used. If the investigator wishes to refer to himself, he uses some appropriate term

---

[1]Carter V. Good, Essentials of Educational Research. New York: Appleton-Century-Crofts, Inc., 1966. Pages 389-390.

such as "the investigator," "the author," or "this writer." If he refers to a group of which he is a member, he may use such terms as "the committee" or "the association members."

2. Logical organization

A suitable title for the report is selected. Usually a research report is organized in sections--each division is essential to developing an understanding of the main ideas and each has its own appropriate subheading. A smooth transition is made between the various divisions by using an introductory paragraph to present the general plan of organization and to prevent one subheading from following immediately after another one.

3. Accuracy

Chapter 3 advised you to be certain that you take adequate notes on the sources and content of similar studies that might be included in a review of literature. You must document accurately any materials that you paraphrase or quote directly. Furthermore, all statistical data used in your study must be gathered, reported, and interpreted with accuracy.

4. Conciseness

Woodrow Wilson realized the art of achieving brevity without sacrificing impact when he said that it would take him two weeks to prepare a 10-minute speech, one week for an hour's speech, and he was "ready right now" for a two-hour speech. Some people approach a subject as if they would surely hit an important point if they just write or speak long enough. The real art of writing is to be able to present clearly and concisely sufficient information for the reader's complete understanding of the problem.

5. Readability

The characteristics of a research report that contribute to its readability are: its content and focus, its organization, its format, and an effective choice of words. A report that is both readable and challenging takes into consideration what the reader already knows and at the same time stimulates his interest in learning more about areas which are unknown to him. Although a research report is written in an objective manner, you can personalize it in such ways as relating other studies to the interests of your readers, giving illustrative cases, and pointing out unusual findings.

Organization

The title of a research report should be stated as briefly as possible; yet, it should contain the essential descriptive elements. Phrases which do not contribute to a better understanding of the title should be omitted (for example: "A study of...," "An investigation of...," and "An analysis of..."). The title should contain the essence of what was studied, and include when possible, the method used and the sample (e.g., "Food Practices of Families with Adolescent Children in Three Indiana Communities.")

MAJOR DIVISIONS.--Prior to gathering data for a study, you will find it helpful to plan your study thoroughly. As a part of this planning, you should develop a tentative outline, or Table of Contents, for your report. Usually you can think of descriptive titles for the various chapters and subheadings which are in keeping with the content of your study. These help to make your report interesting. Although you may devote more than one chapter to some parts of a report, a research report generally contains four major divisions:

1. Introduction

    Your introductory chapter should aim to capture the reader's attention with the first sentence and the first paragraph. The report of the California drop-out study used this unique, concise beginning:

    One way to find out whether a product is good or not is to ask the consumer. He need not be an expert to tell what he likes or doesn't like about a certain kind of automobile, television set, or canned soup. Big business makes such consumer surveys to learn how to improve a product, a package, or a service.

    Educators make consumer surveys, too, only they're known as follow-up studies. The consumers are former students, the product is the education they received, and the purpose is to obtain information which will aid in improving the quality of the educational program.[2]

    The function of an introduction is to present the following types of information:

    (a) Nature of the study -- the subject area, the specific problem that was studied, the purpose and scope of the study

    (b) Background for the study -- historical background to aid your reader in understanding the problem area, reasons for your investigation, your point of view in dealing with the subject, and the contributions your study can be expected to make to the development of home economics education

    (c) Plan to be followed -- basic assumptions fundamental to the study, hypotheses, definitions, delimitation of the study, and its possible limitations

    (d) Relation to previous studies -- a review of related literature may be incorporated into the introductory chapter or it may constitute a separate chapter

2. Methods of procedure

    A chapter, or more than one chapter, should present enough details of the research design to enable the reader to evaluate the study, or to repeat it under similar circumstances if he should desire to do so. Methods of selecting the sample, controlling extraneous variables, gathering and recording data, and analyzing and synthesizing data should be included. Materials or instruments that were used should be described and, whenever possible, illustrations or duplicate copies should be contained in the report.

3. Analysis and interpretation of data

    Your presentation of evidence is a bridge between your introductory chapter and your conclusions. The evidence should be stated clearly and consistently. Separate chapters may be devoted to the analysis of each part of the problem. Sometimes the presentation of findings is separated from the discussion or in-

---

[2] William H. McCreary and Donald E. Kitch, <u>Now Hear Youth</u>. Volume 22, Number 9. Sacramento: California State Department of Education, 1953. Page 1.

terpretation of their meaning in order to maintain an objective view of the results. In any event, a clear distinction must be made between fact and judgment. Information the reader must have to evaluate the data should be included (e.g., the validity and reliability of the instruments).

4.   Summary, conclusions, and recommendations

From your close contact with an investigation, you, as a research worker, are best qualified to select the essential parts of your study and to summarize them concisely. In stating the conclusions of your study, be sure that they are based upon your hypotheses and that they are justified by your data. Recommendations for further research, or for specific action to bring about changes in keeping with your research results, are means of sharing your thoughts with others and assisting them in seeing how these new truths might have direct implications for strengthening programs of home economics education.

SUBHEADINGS. --In addition to determining what should be the major chapters of your report, you should plan a detailed outline to show the sequence and content of each subdivision. Various persons and groups differ in their preferences with regard to the style of subheadings. The American Psychological Association's recommendations are clear and easy to follow. When three orders of subordination are required, their order is as follows:[3]

Order I.   Main headings

Centered. Typed in capital and small letters, with the first letter of each major word capitalized. No period after the heading.

Order II.   Side headings

Typed flush to the left margin. Typed in capital and small letters, with the first letter of each major word capitalized. Underlined. The text following a side heading starts on the next double-spaced line and receives paragraph indentation. No concluding period.

Order III.   Paragraph headings

Also known as "run-in sideheads." Typed with paragraph indentation. May capitalize only the initial letter of the first word or the first letter of all main words. Underline. End with a period and dash. Text follows on the same line without extra spacing.

Subheadings are not necessary in a brief, homogeneous research report, such as a journal article. When you do use subheadings, you should determine how many types are necessary. The three orders described above are in relative order of importance. If you choose to use only one order, the center headings should be selected. If two types are needed, you should use the center headings and either the side or paragraph headings.

Capitalization of each letter in a heading should be reserved for chapter titles in order to avoid confusion between chapter titles and headings of less importance. Headings do not need to be numbered or lettered, since the organization of the paper is revealed through the style and placement of headings. For a smooth transition from one section to another, a brief introduction should be given prior to the first main heading of a chapter and preceding each second and third order heading. In other words, you should avoid

---

[3]Publication Manual of the American Psychological Association. 1957 Revision. Washington, D.C.: American Psychological Association, 1957. Page 20.

placing two headings of a different order directly together without giving the reader a guide as to the plan or outline for the section that is to follow.

Style of Writing

Research writing need not be heavy, monotonous, or dull. By giving careful thought to your choice of words and by following basic principles of writing for understanding, you can develop an individualistic and interesting style.

WRITING FOR UNDERSTANDING. --Richardson and Callahan have given home economists a key to successful writing in the *"R/C recipe for effective Communications."* Although these steps were suggested as a means of reaching homemakers through popular writing, they also have applications in research style. The "R/C recipe" contains five fundamental steps:[4]

1. Visualize your audience

   Research reports generally reach a more restricted and homogeneous group than would be visualized by a writer of a popular article. Nevertheless, defining the audience is still a basic step. Normally, we expect home economics graduate students and faculty members to be consumers of technical research reports. If you are writing a research article for a professional journal, your readers are likely to include persons from related professional fields who have not had the technical background in home economics. Should you endeavor to bring research findings to lay people through newspaper or popular magazine articles you will need to be highly selective in your content and present the results in an interesting manner.

2. Analyze your problems

   In writing, as well as in speaking, you can verbalize extensively and never actually define the point. To prevent this, define your subject and your purpose exactly and clearly in your own mind. Then, very early in your report, explain your purpose and plan of organization to your reader.

3. Organize your thinking

   Organization of a report has been discussed briefly in an earlier part of this chapter. To achieve logical organization, you should try to divide the content of your report into a few main parts, each of which covers only one phase of the topic and includes only those ideas that are closely related and adequately developed. Within each section, the points must be arranged in proper sequence to give a clear and complete picture. Summarizing at appropriate spots, such as the end of each chapter, helps the reader to understand your organization of the report and to remember the major points which have been emphasized. In brief, you should: "... tell the reader where he is going, take him there, and then tell him where he has been."[5]

4. Dramatize your presentation

   Dramatizing, or bringing life to a piece of copy, is highly important when you are writing for the general public. You may find this hard to achieve as you

---

[4]Lou Richardson and Genevieve Callahan, The New How to Write for Homemakers. Ames: The Iowa State College Press, 1962. Page 8.

[5]Carter V. Good, Essentials of Educational Research. New York: Appleton-Century-Crofts, Inc., 1966. Page 398.

strive to be objective and impersonal. Nevertheless, you can personalize your research writing by showing your reader how your report can tie in with his needs and problems or with those of his professional peers.

5.   Synchronize all of these

Then synchronize your ideas with the ideas of others.[6]

CHOICE OF WORDS:--Sentence structure and choice of words influence the effectiveness with which ideas are communicated. Although the following suggestions could lead to highly stilted writing if followed mechanically, their intelligent use should help you to develop clarity and conciseness in writing research reports.

1.   Use one exact word rather than a longer phrase.[7]

Unnecessary wordiness	More exact word
accordingly	so
for the purpose of	for
inasmuch as	since, or because
in order to	to
in the event that	if
in the neighborhood of	about
on the basis of	by
with reference to	about

2.   Omit words that contribute nothing to the meaning of a sentence.

"The following table (serves to) show ..."
"It is known that ...."
"It is evident that ...."
"The investigator has (tried to) compare ...."

3.   Avoid using words that are redundant.

Examples: refer back, repeat again, same identical

4.   Clarify the subject of a sentence.

Avoid "it," "they," "experts," unless the reference is very clear.

5.   Use connectives when necessary for clarity.

Use words like: "however," "furthermore," "likewise," "nevertheless."

6.   Be reserved and avoid the use of intensives.

Avoid: "obviously," "certainly," "extremely," "much," "very."

7.   Be cautious about using words that infer cause or relationship.

Avoid: "due to," "prove," "cause," "effect," "determine," " influence."

---

[6]Richardson and Callahan, loc. cit.
[7]Rudolph Flesch, How to Write Better. Chicago: Science Research Associates, Inc., 1951. Page 26.

8.   Be familiar with the exact meaning and possible implications of abstract ideas or technical terms used.

9.   Use intellectual and vitalized expressions rather than cliches, "big-sounding," or emotional words.

The following examples show types of cliches that you should avoid:[8]

(a) figurative description	*soft as silk, sweet as honey*
(b) descriptive of type	*talented artist, brilliant thinker, distinguished colleague*
(c) dependent on professional phraseology	*deep insight, remarkable technique, in the light of recent developments, after carefully weighing the evidence*
(d) proverbial expression substituted for precise thought.	*Virtue is its own reward.*

10.   Use strong, active verbs.

"The table shows that..." rather than "It is shown that..."

11.   Use concrete words rather than "slippery" or vague words.

Avoid: "equal," "bright," "comparable," "fast."

12.   Finish comparisons so your reader will not have to ask, "For what?" or "To whom?"

Examples of unfinished terms are: "unfit," "desirable," "good," "progressive," "dangerous," "valuable."

13.   Change the pace or emphasis to avoid monotony.

Vary the length of words, clauses, sentences, and paragraphs. Develop a natural, individualized style of expression. Find a variety of ways to express similar ideas.

14.   Simplify your sentence structure, avoiding complicated qualifications.

15.   Be consistent in your point of view.

The past tense is used in most parts of a research report, such as in stating facts reported by others and the findings and conclusions from your study. The present tense is used when stating a well-established principle (assumption) and when referring to data that are shown in a table, graph, or appendix of your report.

---

[8]William J. Grace and John C. Grace, The Art of Communicating Ideas. New York: The Devin-Adair Company, 1952. Page 93.

The following examples have been selected from actual year-end reports of projects sponsored by federal funds. Fortunately, home economists were not responsible for writing these reports, but you could probably find similar, unusual wording in their reports. Can you decipher the real meaning behind these words? Can you understand why clarity, conciseness, and accuracy are so important in a research report?

Purpose of the project

To stimulate interests of students in attaining appropriate educational and career girls.

Counsel the parents of the special problem child to avoid dropouts in their later high school years.

Activities carried on

Vocational opportunities were held with all interested students and parents alike interested.

Group counseling sessions with behavior problems were held with students.

Results of the project

All parents have been seen and collected, data interpreted with a view to mutual goals.

... three hundred fourteen families responded to the invitation for a private conference and it is anticipated that even more families will be taken advantage of this year.

Evaluation of project

From student, parent and faculty comments concerning this project have been of favorable and active acceptance.

It is extremely difficult to discourage early marriage and impossible for us to prevent pregnancies.

When writing the first draft of a manuscript, you should strive for a logical organization of ideas. You can polish the specific wording and grammar as you revise the manuscript. Most writing has to be rewritten and edited before it is really effective. In revising a report, you can give attention to such aspects as the logic of its organization, accuracy of facts, choice of words, grammar, paragraphing, and spelling.

SELECTED REFERENCES

Good, Carter V. *Essentials of Educational Research.* New York: Appleton-Century-Crofts, Inc. , 1966. Pages 394-413.
Hillway, Tyrus. *Introduction to Research.* Second edition. Boston: Houghton Mifflin Co. , 1964. Pages 253-262, 274-275.
"Information for Prospective Authors." *Journal of Home Economics* 58: 54-56; January, 1966.
McCann, Lloyd E. "Presenting That Idea in the Professional Journal." *Phi Delta Kappan* 39: 173-176; January, 1958.
Whitney, Frederick L. *The Elements of Research.* Third edition. Englewood Cliffs, N.J.: Prentice-Hall, Inc., 1950. Pages 404-409, 424-432.

ROLE OF THE HOME ECONOMICS PROFESSION

Home economics, like other major professional groups, has shown increased interest in research in recent years. Each year the American Home Economics Association devotes the March issue of the Journal of Home Economics to research, including several reports of research studies and lists of doctoral dissertations that were accepted by colleges and universities during the preceding year.

The Office of Education in the United States Department of Health, Education, and Welfare has made an important contribution to research through the publication of two bulletins, integrating many of the unpublished research studies in home economics education and related fields. These are listed at the end of this chapter.

These and other steps that have been taken are significant ones, but much still remains to be done if research is to play an important part in strengthening our profession. We might well ask ourselves a question that was raised in a publication on research in educational administration: If all of the research that has been done in the last three years were to be wiped out, would our lives be materially changed? Lamke stated that we would really notice differences in those areas of our lives that are touched by advances in medicine, agriculture, physics, and chemistry. However, he felt that educators would continue about the same as usual, because few of our studies affect educational practice. He asked whether research shouldn't be of as much worth to educators as agricultural research has been to farmers.[9]

What can we, as individuals and as members of professional associations, do to make research in home economics education more significant? Hopefully, the remainder of this book offers some suggestions that you may be able to apply in your own field of service. Certainly, it raises many questions that should challenge each of us to think about our role in fulfilling the important functions of research as means of strengthening home economics education.

McGrath summarized some trends in educational research: *using more subjective data; taking human variability into account; attacking problems on a statewide or regional basis under the direction of a responsible agency; establishing bureaus of research and service to stimulate and improve research among teachers; and studying sociological problems that have an impact on our culture.*[10]

Developing Personnel for Research

If research is to be significant in home economics education, we must place emphasis in our professional preparation on how to conduct research studies as well as on how to use research results. Actually, we must begin to develop a research attitude in the very earliest grades where home economics courses are offered. The fun of discovery and an experimental approach to problem-solving can enrich home economics programs in junior and senior high schools.

College courses for undergraduates can encourage young people to become interested in home economics careers where part or all of their duties will be related to research. For example, many courses require a term paper which can be a creative experience involving a simple research approach. In a seminar for seniors, some institutions acquaint their students with professional problems and require each student to carry out a small research project.

---

[9]Daniel E. Griffiths, Research in Educational Administration. New York: Bureau of Publications, Teachers College, Columbia University, 1959. Page 6.

[10]G. D. McGrath et al., Educational Research Methods. New York: The Ronald Press Co., 1963. Page 9.

Graduate study leading to master's and doctor's degrees is becoming increasingly important for home economics teachers, supervisors, and administrators. For a number of years, master's degrees have been granted following a program of study culminating with a comprehensive examination. This type of program can be effective only if each graduate student has considerable contact with research findings and some opportunity to carry out a study which she plans independently. When we confer a master's degree, we must be sure that the candidate is capable of understanding and applying research results and of contributing to the solution of professional problems through the use of sound research methods.

We are living in a period of rapid change and educators realize that it is utterly impossible for a person to learn in high school or in college all of the knowledge he will need in adjusting to the world about him throughout his lifetime. Recent developments in research should be given considerable emphasis in programs of in-service education. Since many teachers feel insecure about attempting to do research, guidance might be helpful on the selection of research problems and procedures for carrying out investigations.

Facilitating Research Projects

Perhaps the best way of stimulating interest in research is through your own enthusiasm. An attitude of trying to improve some phase of your work through research communicates to your co-workers that you consider research to be worthwhile in helping to solve practical problems. Inertia is one of the biggest obstacles to research. It is easier to continue doing things as we have been doing them than to put forth the extra effort to bring about change.

A wholesome attitude toward research on the part of supervisors, administrators, college teachers, and supervising teachers is vital if the average classroom teacher is to become interested as well as having the opportunity to use a research approach in solving classroom problems. Corey summarized some of the conditions that are favorable for action research. Home Economics educators might benefit from trying to create an atmosphere favorable to research in such ways as these: (1) providing an atmosphere in which teachers feel free to admit limitations of their teaching; (2) providing many opportunities for teachers to develop creative ideas about new or promising practices or materials; (3) encouraging teachers to try out promising ideas; (4) improving methods of group work; (5) striving to obtain better evidence than is presently available rather than seeking a _final_ answer; and (6) providing time and other resources (such as instructional materials, mimeographing, and clerical assistance) for persons who are participating in research studies.[11]

In addition to a receptive attitude toward research, home economics teachers usually need specific help in developing plans for research studies. From his wide experience as a teacher and consultant on action research, Shumsky has prepared a checklist for those who work with groups planning research:[12]

    1. Do I overpower my consultees by acting as an answer man and quiz master or do I encourage a climate of cooperative work?

    2. Do I rush forward prematurely with suggestions, or do I try to understand the consultee's perspective?

---

[11] Stephen M. Corey, _Action Research to Improve School Practices._ New York: Teachers College, Columbia University Press, 1953. Page 86.

[12] Abraham Shumsky, _The Action Research Way of Learning._ New York: Bureau of Publications, Teachers College, Columbia University, 1958. Page 197.

3. Do I know how to listen or do I put on a front or go off on a tangent?

4. Am I involved in the consultee's problem from the standpoint of content and process?

5. Do I make progress on my own and plan my next conference or am I dependent on my consultees?

6. Is my consultation based primarily on repetition of ideas read in books or on my own experience and thinking?

7. Am I open to experiences and ideas or do I tend to overplan and manipulate?

8. Am I accessible to my consultees as a human being or only as a scholar?

9. Do I encourage rigorous thinking, criticism, and investment of much work or is my ego satisfied with oratory, oiled relationship, participation for participation's sake?

10. Is my criticism constructive, dealing with the basic issue and suggesting needed improvement?

11. Is criticism only my prerogative or is it a two-way street?

12. Do I feel defensive or angry in criticizing or am I able to do it objectively?

13. Am I overexcited about the bright students and irritated with the slow one or am I able to judge in terms of the realness of their work to them?

14. Do I help them improve the quality of their teaching or only to write a paper?

15. Do I only teach or do I also learn?

Taba was successful in using county staff meetings to stimulate interest in research. Administrators were asked to select persons to attend the county meetings on the basis of the following criteria: (1) the teacher has something to work on and wants to work on it; (2) the teacher can spend more than a year with the project; (3) the project seems significant to other school personnel; and (4) the teacher exercises leadership with other teachers. An effort was made to have a wide distribution of grade levels and subject areas in the total group of research participants.[13]

Financing Research Projects

Some school systems have found it possible to encourage research by providing a free period of time for teachers who are serving on a research team or by providing a part-time clerical assistant and teacher-aide. In the past, much helpful research has been done in spite of inadequate time, facilities, and financial support. Only the future can reveal the accomplishments which are possible when we give proper recognition to the worth of research.

Among the major sources for financial support are the scholarships and fellowships offered by such professional associations as the American Home Economics Association,

---

[13] Hilda Taba and Elizabeth Noel. <u>Action Research</u>: A Case Study. Washington, D. C.: Association for Supervision and Curriculum Development, a Department of the National Education Association, 1957. Page 9.

Pi Lambda Theta, and Delta Kappa Gamma. If you are considering graduate study, you might find it beneficial to look in the index of the December issues of the Journal of Home Economics for information about the scholarship opportunities available for home econo- mists and how to apply for one of them. Information may be obtained directly from the national office of a home economics or education association. In some instances, a re- search proposal must be submitted as a basis for receiving an award.

Many colleges and universities offer teaching or research assistantships for gradu- ate students who wish to combine study toward an advanced degree with valuable part- time professional experiences. The Journal of Home Economics publishes a list of these opportunities biennially. Information may also be obtained directly from any institution that offers a graduate program in home economics education.

The U. S. Office of Education and a number of Foundations have research funds available to support projects of major importance, with clearly formulated hypotheses and with a competent principal investigator.

Improving the Quality of Research Projects

Informing the public of the purposes of a research study can be an excellent means of gaining confidence and trust. On the other hand, you defeat your research program if you carry out poorly-planned experiments or try to apply methods that are untried and perhaps unsound.

Improving the quality of research projects cannot be separated from the other topics which have been discussed in this chapter. For example, one way of improving research is to work cooperatively with home economists from other geographic areas so we can pool ideas and engage in larger, more worthwhile projects. Another approach is to cooperate with specialists from other disciplines in attacking problems of mutual concern. A third need is for home economists to become more sophisticated in planning research designs, using sound statistical procedures, and interpreting as well as analyz- ing data. These suggestions all relate to the first topic that was presented--developing research personnel. What we really need to do is to make it possible for more home economists to devote a major part of their professional work to research planning and guidance. As it is, most of our research is carried on by graduate students or profes- sional workers who must limit their studies to those that fit somewhat conveniently into their heavy schedules.

If we can assume that many people who engage in research have had little previous experience along this line, we are expecting a great deal from beginners. Identification of some of the major problems in the field of home economics education, on the part of the leaders who are in a position to know the problems, could be of real assistance to graduate students and others who want to select worthwhile problems for research. The two Office of Education bulletins that are listed at the end of this chapter are most helpful in pointing out many areas in which research is necessary in home economics education.

If we would take time to compare the research that we are doing in home economics education with the research being done in other subject areas, we could see many ways in which we could apply some of their approaches. Nevertheless, we must not allow ourselves always to be followers--we should take the lead in initiating studies which will be benefi- cial to home economics education and possibly stimulate the interest of people in other areas to apply some of our methods and techniques. One way to get started on a research project is simply to think of several questions that you would like to answer--questions that are really important. These kinds of questions are subject to change so any list that is given today will soon need to be revised. However, here is a start on some of the questions that you may be able to help us answer:

1. Counseling and Guidance

How can longitudinal studies on the development of skills be related to individual developmental patterns in home economics programs?

What are the home responsibilities of home economics students at different levels?

What is the nature of family life in the homes of home economics students and of other students?

What factors cause teenagers and adults to drop out of home economics courses?

What is the origin of an interest in home economics education?

In what leisure and summer activities do home economics students engage?

What changes have taken place in the freshman class of students majoring in home economics over the past ten years?

For what reasons do students and other members of the community fail to participate in school-sponsored events related to home economics?

How can we predict the success of prospective home economics teachers?

What attracts an individual into teaching?

What satisfactions does an individual derive from teaching home economics? from doing research in home economics education?

2. Curriculum

What are the implications of research studies in child development for the home economics curriculum?

In terms of the difficulty of activities and student readiness, at what grade level should various home economics activities be placed?

What are the roles of students and lay people in curriculum development?

Are the goals of home economics education consistent with current social and economic conditions?

Is there a relationship between the hobbies of students and the instruction they receive in home economics courses?

What kinds of home economics behaviors can be learned best in school and what kinds can be learned best through the home or other community agencies?

How extensively and for what purposes is the library used by home economics students?

What kinds of training and experiences are most helpful in the preservice education of home economics teachers?

3. <u>Evaluation</u>

If nutrition education is introduced in a high school program, what effect will it have on the food habits of teenagers?

How permanent is the learning that takes place in home economics courses?

Does the teaching of clothing, textiles, and related arts develop creativity in the students?

What influence does home economics education have on personality growth?

What influence does home economics education have on good physical and mental health?

How does home economics education influence the development of character and citizenship?

Does home economics education stimulate democratic family living?

Does home economics education have any effect on crime and delinquency?

Does home economics education encourage self-improvement?

What can longitudinal studies tell us about how interests in home economics develop and change?

How well are the goals of home economics education understood by faculty, administrators, students, and parents?

What are the successes and failures experienced by graduates of home economics programs?

4. <u>Methods</u>

How will student learning be affected by differences in the distribution and allotment of time for various home economics activities?

What leadership techniques can a teacher use successfully in various aspects of home economics education?

How do different types of teaching methods affect the learning of students?

5. <u>Supervision and Administration</u>

How can the home economics staff be organized most effectively to achieve the goals of the department?

How could the employment of sub-professional persons help home economists to achieve their goals?

This is just a beginning! If you are alert to the problems of teachers and the kinds of research being developed in other areas of the school curriculum, you can add other worthwhile questions to this list. The really important thing, however, is for you to start taking the necessary steps to find a sound answer to a problem which is important to you and to your profession.

To travel hopefully is better than to arrive.
-- *Sir James Jean*

SELECTED REFERENCES

Coon, Beulah I. "Co-operative Research in Home Economics: The Process." *Journal of Home Economics* 54: 191-194; March, 1962.

Galfo, Armand J. and Earl Miller. *Interpreting Education Research.* Dubuque, Iowa: Wm. C. Brown Co., 1965. Pages 234-248.

Needs in Research for the American Family. Washington, D.C.: American Home Economics Association, 1956. 15 pages.

Studies of Home Economics in High School and in Adult Education Programs 1955-58. Vocational Division Bulletin No. 286, Home Economics Education Series No. 32. Washington, D.C.: U.S. Department of Health, Education, and Welfare, Office of Education, 1960. Pages 41-42, 74-75, 87-88, 119.

Studies on the Teaching of Home Economics in Colleges and Universities 1955-56. Vocational Division Bulletin No. 276, Home Economics Series No. 31. Washington, D.C.: U.S. Department of Health, Education, and Welfare, Office of Education, 1959. Pages 13-14, 25-26, 41-42, 63-64, 76-77.

APPENDIX A

Three models are included in the appendix with the idea of illustrating some of the preliminary planning that you should do before starting to gather data. These are not intended to be followed literally. They illustrate a general approach to three types of research studies: historical, survey, and experimental. In addition, they show various ways of stating hypotheses, including the null hypothesis. They show an emphasis on subject matter as a basis for teaching home economics education and they also illustrate studies of preservice teacher education as well as inservice teacher behaviors.

MODEL FOR HISTORICAL RESEARCH

THEORY:

If the evidence derived from a study of historical materials is put together in a logical way, facts hitherto unknown may be established and generalizations may be developed regarding past and/or present events.

ASSUMPTIONS:

Current ideas, tastes, and attitudes can be understood better in the light of their origins and growth.

HYPOTHESIS:

A person who understands the textiles and designs of another land and culture will be able to recognize the influence of these textiles and designs on contemporary interior designs in America.

PROCEDURES, TECHNIQUES, AND ANALYSIS OF DATA:

1. Collection of the data
    a. Primary sources (original sources, including those produced purposely to transmit information and remains and relics not deliberately intended as records)
        Examples: houses, furniture, equipment, costumes, textiles, paintings, photographs, art objects, official minutes.
    b. Secondary sources (those that are derived from first-hand materials)
        Examples: textbooks, journals, encyclopedias.

2. Criticism of the data
    a. External criticism (authenticity or genuineness)
        (1) Examples of questions to be answered
            (a) By whom was it made (or written)?
                Signature, handwriting, characteristic features, etc.
            (b) When was it made (or written)?
                Knowledge available at that time, typical of that period, consistency with what is known about that period, etc.
        (2) May involve physical and chemical tests of ink, paint, paper, cloth, wood, metal, etc.
    b. Internal criticism (evaluating its meaning, accuracy, and worth)
        (1) Was the originator competent, honest, unbiased, acquainted with the facts?
        (2) Did he have any motives for distorting the truth?
        (3) Was he subject to pressure, fear, or vanity?
        (4) How long after the event did he make his record? Was he able to remember accurately?
        (5) Is he in agreement with other competent witnesses?

3. Synthesis of the data
    a. Topical organization may be supplemented by a chronological listing of the most important events.
    b. Resemblances or analogies in the events may be pointed out.
    c. Relationships between any single event and other events may be noted.
    d. Trends may be pointed out by comparing facts over a period of time.
    e. Hypotheses may be formulated after a critical study of the data and then tested by re-examining the evidence.
    f. Study the data to see if generalizations or laws can be derived that will be applicable to other situations.

MODEL FOR A SURVEY

THEORY:

If an individual has an experience that is designed specifically to clarify or change his concepts, differences between his concepts at the beginning and at the end of this experience can be identified.

HYPOTHESIS: (in the form of null hypotheses)

There is no difference in the concepts of the role of a home economics teacher held by freshmen college students majoring in home economics education and the concepts held by seniors just prior to their graduation.

ASSUMPTIONS:

1. It is possible to identify different concepts of the role of a home economics teacher.
2. As they go through college, home economics education students filter out many experiences that they feel are unimportant in fulfilling their concept of the role of a home economics teacher.

PROCEDURES:

1. Preparation of the instrument
    a. Develop a conceptual framework for the role of a home economics teacher.
    b. Prepare a series of statements (in behavioral terms) that describe typical behavior of a teacher in each of the classifications you have chosen. The first step might be to have a group of teachers or students submit statements in response to sentence-completion questions.
    c. Submit these statements to qualified persons for criticism and editorial suggestions.
    d. Submit the edited statements to qualified judges to determine the extent of agreement as to the relative importance of each behavior in the role of a home economics teacher.
    e. Conduct a pilot study with a group of home economics education students to see if the statements and directions are clear and to determine estimates of validity and reliability of the instrument.
    f. Refine the instrument as needed.

2. Selection of the sample
    a. Action research--using the home economics education students in your own institution. Or, a cooperative approach might be used in which a random sample could be selected from students in several institutions.
    b. Cross-sectional approach
        (1) Students enrolling as freshmen, majoring in home economics education, might respond to this instrument near the beginning of the freshmen year.
        (2) Responses might be obtained from a group of home economics education majors who are nearing the completion of their senior year. (This group would be seniors at the time the first group enters the freshman year.)
        (3) Students at a similar level in college, who are not enrolled in home economics education and who have not taken home economics courses previously, could serve as a control group.
    c. Longitudinal approach
        (1) Students who responded to this instrument as freshmen and who are still enrolled as home economics education majors as seniors would respond to the same instrument during the senior year.
        (2) The study might be extended further by asking these same persons to complete the instrument following a year or more of teaching experience.

180

    d. Self-ratings

At any of these time periods, an individual might be asked to rate herself in the role of a home economics teacher (using the same instrument, probably the Q-Sort technique).

3. Analysis of the results
   a. Determine the correlation between the various Q Sorts obtained for each individual (at different years, or self-rating with her concept of what the role of a teacher is)
   b. Study the significance of differences in the means of students:
      (1) at different levels of experience
      (2) with different personal and family background

MODEL FOR AN EXPERIMENT

THEORY:

If a person receives praise and encouragement, he tends to develop greater motivation to achieve and succeed than if his efforts are not rewarded.

ASSUMPTION:

Teachers control, to some degree, the extent of creativity of their students.

HYPOTHESES:

Students whose clothing teachers make rewarding comments (such as, "That's good, Mary") produce:
  (1) more ideas than students whose teachers make no evaluative comments or make negative comments.
  (2) ideas of higher quality (or more creative ideas) than those whose teachers make no evaluative comments or who make negative comments.

PROCEDURES AND TECHNIQUES:

1. Sample--define the universe from which a sample will be drawn, how it will be drawn, and its size.

2. Techniques
  a. Train teachers and observers as to the meaning of "negative," "positive," and "facilitating" comments.
  b. Use an observation schedule or tape recordings of teachers' comments made in the classroom.   These comments will be analyzed:
    (1) Quantitatively -- counting the evaluative comments
    (2) Qualitatively -- determining whether each comment was "negative," "positive," or "facilitating"
  c. Record the ideas students produce in a specific situation (For example: Show a film presenting a specific family situation and then have the students write their ideas as to what the family might do in solving a problem related to the family clothing budget, selection of a dress for the senior prom, etc.)
    (1) Count the number of ideas an individual student produces in a given time
    (2) Categorize the ideas according to their:
      (a) Novelty   (c) Diversity or flexibility of ideas
      (b) Relevancy   (d) Stimulus value for being picked up and developed further

ANALYZING THE DATA:

Procedure	Experimental Group	Control Group
1. Measurement of effectiveness in performing Task A (measuring creative ideas)	Pretest: E_I	Pretest: C_I
2. Events following pretest.	Practice on Task B. (Teacher's evaluative comments)	Unrelated activity or rest.
3. Measurement of effectiveness in performing Task A. (same as pretest, or equivalent form)	Post-test: E_{II}	Post-test: C_{II}
4. Determining change between pretest and post-test.	$D_E = E_{II} - E_I$	$D_C = C_{II} - C_I$
5. Test for significance of the change.	$D = D_E - D_C$	

APPENDIX B

The two pages which follow have been included to show one acceptable style for subheadings and quotations in a typewritten research report, such as a master's thesis or doctor's dissertation. These pages illustrate the principles that were discussed in Chapter 12.

In using the style illustrated here, keep in mind that this sample contains only a small portion of the content that would normally be placed within each section of a report. Since the purpose of this sample is to illustrate style rather than content, examples of three orders of subheadings and of both a direct and indirect quotation are shown within the two sample pages.

Subheadings are used to clarify the organization of a report, but, if used excessively, they can make the material seem choppy. The order of subheadings, as illustrated here, gives greatest prominence to the major headings and decreasing importance to headings of lower rank. When fewer than three types of subheadings are desired, any of these styles may be chosen but they should be kept in this order. For example, you could use center headings and then skip to the paragraph headings.

CHAPTER II

CHANGING GOALS OF HIGH SCHOOL HOME ECONOMICS

As background for this study, the investigator reviewed literature related to three aspects of the problem: goals of home economics, social and economic changes affecting family life, and ways in which home economics education is meeting the challenge of change.

Goals of Home Economics

On the occasion of the fiftieth anniversary of the organization of the organization of the American Home Economics Association, home economists took a look at the early goals of home economics and the success with which these goals had been accomplished. At the same time, they re-evaluated the goals and methods that were being used to fulfill them.

Early Goals of Home Economics

Home economics, as conceived by the pioneers who attended the Lake Placid Conferences, was concerned both with man's physical environment and with the nature of man as a social being.[1]

---

[1] Lake Placid Conferences on Home Economics: Proceedings of the Fourth Annual Conference. September 16-20, 1902. Lake Placid; New York, 1902. Page 70.

2

New Directions in Home Economics

Well-established goals are not easily changed. However, at least two forces can be influential in bringing about gradual or drastic changes in the goals of a profession whose work affects individuals and families in American society. Leaders within the profession may take a careful look at the effectiveness of their profession in meeting present needs and in preparing for the changes that are anticipated in the future. Another way in which changes may be brought about is through pressures exerted by persons outside of the profession. Both the self-evaluation by home economists and the constructive appraisal of other persons will be reviewed briefly in this section.

Objectives as viewed by home economists.--Although the basic goals of home economics have remained throughout the past half century, home economists have been forward-looking in adapting their goals to the changes taking place in the world about them. The Philosophy and Objectives Committee of the American Home Economics Association formulated the following statement on the focus of home economics:

> Home economics is the field of knowledge and service primarily concerned with strengthening family life through:
> educating the individual for family living
> improving the services and goods used by families
> conducting research to discover the changing needs of individuals and families and the means of satisfying these needs
> furthering community, national, and world conditions favorable to family living.[2]

---

[2] Home Economics--New Directions: A Statement of Philosophy and Objectives. Washington, D.C.: American Home Economics Association, 1959. Page 4.

INDEX